G.W.R
STEAM
MY PERSONAL ENCOUNTER

Douglas A. Trigg

ISBN 0 906025 50 8

Published 1992
by
Pathfinder
Stag House, Gydynap Lane
Inchbrook, Woodchester
Gloucestershire GL5 5EZ

Produced for the Publisher by Mopok Graphics
128 Pikes Lane Glossop Derbyshire SK13 8EH

Contents

Prelude

To the middle-aged rail enthusiast, who was fortunate—privileged even—to be brought up during the demise of steam traction on our railways, there is a distinct advantage over today's diesel or electric motive power follower.

The characters the steam locomotive bred were a race apart. To be able to talk to such men was indeed a personal communication coveted among friends. A fair proportion of these steam crews are now retired. Many, in fact, have passed on.

Much has been written about the subject of railways old and new. There are literally thousands of photographs to illustrate what the steam railway world was like. Pictures of trains in stations, on famous bridges or leaving tunnel

Nationalisation of the railways in 1948 had little immediate outward effect on the Great Western Railway. One visible change, however, is the lion and wheel emblem on the tender of this 0-6-0 locomotive photographed at Grange Court, a station the author knew very well. This was the junction where the Hereford branch left the Gloucester-Newport main line. (N. E. Preedy)

edifices; locomotives, carriages, wagons, photographed from every conceivable angle.

Yes, there are many written accounts, books about railway establishments, rolling stock, etc. But what about the railway workers themselves? One or two books—not nearly enough in the writer's eye. Tales of the trials and tribulations regarding steam locomotive engines that almost 'gave up the ghost' then, after careful coaxing and nursing, have been brought back to life once again to perform near miracles.

Here now is a first rate account of life for a young man on the footplate GWR-style during those austerity years of World War II.

You will read about Douglas Trigg's childhood days, how his railway adventures began as a calling up boy, to box boy, the account of boiler washing with Tom Evans, including changing the lead gasket on a mudhole cover whilst the locomotive still had a fair head of steam! The greedy Italian PoWs, who, it would seem, were better fed than the average British family at that time. Then there are tales of the long shift, the Yanks, along with legendary 'Tuffley Races'! It's all here, a whole host of stories to keep the reader enthralled right to the last page.

As Douglas rightly says, "We were boys given men's work to do"

Yes, the steam locomotive. No other mechanical contrivance devised by man could arouse such praise one minute, derogatory curses the next. Backbreaking work, heat, extreme cold during long winter shifts. To take a walk back into the railway world of fifty years ago is indeed a return to a bygone age. There was more to life on the rail in those days than any of us will ever realise. The rail enthusiast today is the poorer for not having been part of that world. Nowadays it is talk of HSTs, DMUs, computerised signalling. Not quite so romantic as 'Castles', 'Saints' and 'Panniers'.

Douglas has written his own personal biography that is heartily recommended for either holiday reading or those long winter nights.

A final note; beware of becoming entranced whilst travelling by train or bus—you may go past your stop!

Derek Harrison
Author, Broadcaster
Birmingham, 1991

Foreword

I would like to dedicate this book to all the colourful characters mentioned in the following pages. Without them there wouldn't be much left to tell!

This is an account of some of the incidents that happened to me during my short railway career, and although I may, after 46 years, have made a few errors in my description of some signals, siding or loop, apart from these (should they exist) all the incidents are true; they all happened to me.

I make no apologies for introducing so much hunger, sleepless exhaustion, and back-aching work, together with either spinning or skidding, spark-producing locomotive wheels. Extremeties of heat and cold, elation and despair, of smoke-laden steam as it belched from the smoke stack to the accompaniment of an often near-deafening blast, because that is exactly how it was to me.

We were boys who were given men's work to do, but railwaymen had never been asked to work under circumstances such as these before, or since. Even if physically scarred, most of us managed to survive to see easier living.

Yes, my brief encounter with the Steam Locomotive was like a stimulating but exhausting love-hate affair with a very unforgiving schizophrenic mistress who sadly came to a very untimely end. Looking back over the years, I realize my thoughts have mellowed somewhat—I'm now so glad we met.

The Author

The Final Run

As I emerged from the enveloping heat of the cab the cold night air struck me through my sweat-soaked shirt like ice. 'Watch your head Jockey' called out my mate. Driver or fireman, it made no difference, it was always 'my mate'. Having clambered, pick in hand, from the footplate up on to the coal in the tender in order to 'fill in the hole', as the operation was known, in actual fact I was attempting to pull as much coal forward as possible down between the tool boxes, which were situated one on either side of the tender, ready for my relief—my last relief, to take over from me on this 2-8-0 locomotive. A few seconds later, engulfed in steam and smoke, we passed slowly under the bridge at 'Over Junction', and I ducked my head at my mate's warning. Straightening up I could see the 'distant signal' and 'outer home' of Gloucester West signal box.

Both signals were against us but neither of us uttered a word, though the driver was probably swearing under his breath. Enough trouble was experienced in pulling away from 'Over sidings' where we had stopped for a few minutes in order that a fast train might pass on the main line.

After applying a little sand, we were now laboriously climbing the steep bank towards the station, knowing full well that unless the signalman could give us the road into the station it would take quite a few shakes of the sand handle to enable us to pull away from the signal, which was situated almost at the brow of the hill. The signal remained at danger. Slowly my mate eased the regulator down until we were at a standstill. The huge engine sounded like a lamb now, rather than the lion of a few seconds previous.

The vast volume of steam and smoke cleared away leaving tiny wisps of steam as the regulator was shut off completely. We halted without the usual clatter, as many sets of buffers banged together when bringing a goods train to a halt on the level, or downhill gradient. I scrabbled down over the big lumps of coal on to the footplate, quickly winding on the handbrake. With an almighty roar, the safety valve forced open by the excess steam proceeded to 'blow off' This is the recognised railway term for this function. My mate immediately looked at me; I could read his thoughts as he sported a faint smile. Seldom in the three years I had been with him had we ever had steam to spare—I imagined he thought it ironical that this manifestation should occur in the last few minutes of my short railway career! A glance at the water gauge told me that even now there was little or no steam to spare, so, quickly turning the injector on, the noise of the steam slowly abated as the water began gently bobbing higher and higher in the gauge glass until it eventually went out of sight.

While this was happening a good spray of the footplate with the pep pipe enabled all coal dust and small pieces of coal to be swilled away, leaving a gleaming footplate. The injector was shut off. All was quiet. Glancing down to where the blacked-out street must lie, its position was just discernible, appearing like some gulley between the dark irregular shapes of the buildings on either side.

Because of the blackout not one glimmer of light was to be seen in any of the windows, or on the streets. The traffic was very scarce in view of the petrol rationing—petrol was only allowed for essential journeys. A small ration for my motor cycle was available but the exact route to and from work had to be stated when filling in the application form. A small amount of petrol was allocated to the motor cycle for use in 'Dad's Army' or Home Guard.

I joined the Westbury-on-Severn platoon two months before my sixteenth birthday. To begin with we were collected by 'Aylands' bus of Westbury-on-Severn, but later I used the motor bike for journeys to Newnham-on-Severn, where we were trying to form a Signal section. Yours truly covered more mileage on the road at that time than most people.

Accidents on the railways are fortunately relatively rare occurrences. When they do happen, as here at Over Junction, they attract a fair amount of attention. The precise details of this event are not known, but it seems to have been rather destructive. The bridge has long since gone, being by-passed by a new road layout. *(Author's collection)*

A dim light came into view down in the street; it was a cycle. I suppose a pedestrian or perhaps another cyclist would be able to see the light, but it was not much use to the cyclist himself. Lamps had, or were supposed to be, fitted with a type of shade, usually a metal disc with a slit cut into it. Not that many battery lamps needed shades, batteries were all but unobtainable unless you knew someone! There was one way to get a battery on odd occasions, you simply bought a new lamp. Many people began to dig out their old paraffin lamps, which had more or less been thrown out or left amongst rubbish of the type that accumulates in nearly every tool shed and garage, though I think anyone who boasted a garage in those days was hardly likely to be sporting a couple of cycle lamps, especially of the paraffin type.

Suddenly realising that I had just shivered involuntarily for about the third time,. I stood with my back towards the fire for a few minutes to quickly alter the situation, before pulling on a serge jacket. After crossing the footplate to the fireman's side of the cab, I flipped the small wooden hinged seat into a horizontal position to slump down on it for a short breather. A fireman had fallen down into the alley some months earlier when his train had stopped on the viaduct. On that occasion the train crew had done exactly as we had just done, the difference being that they were virtually groping their way up the incline in a very thick fog.

Whether or not the fireman was unfamiliar with the spot I cannot say. He apparently thought when he reached this signal that he was in the station. Before his mate could stop him he had stepped off the engine to have a look round. He went over the parapet and fell through the fog to the alley below. Whether he ever fully recovered isn't known.

I turned back to the job of making up the fire ready for my relief to get a good start on the uphill gradient out of Gloucester. As already stated, I had filled up the hole as usual but there was one place where this seldom happened. This was when we Gloucester men relieved Birmingham crews at Stratford-on-Avon; they usually said 'I let the fire down mate because I could not keep her quiet coming down the bank'.

As a lad of seventeen years, and not very big with it, discretion did not allow me to point out that in view of the uphill gradient we would have to face for the main part of the journey back to Cheltenham, he might at least have filled the hole in with half a ton of coal, though even that would have looked a bit sick by the time I had got the fire rebuilt ready to pull away. The only way to show my disgust with these grown men, who should have known better, was to completely ignore them and get furiously stuck into the job, which in fact I knew I had to do if we were not to stop at the next station to get up steam, where we would probably make a very unceremonious arrival.

Fortunately these people were very much in the minority. There were a lot of splendid chaps on the job, the best of these was, of course, my old mate the late Ron Carlile. What a time he'd had with me. Looking over at him as he sat writing up his sheet, I wondered who would be with him tomorrow, and what his next trip would be. He finished writing and put his pencil and paper away. Taking a packet of cigarettes from his overall pocket he carefully selected one—there was no hurry anyway, we might be there for hours. Lighting this precious weed he drew deeply on it. Not smoking at that time I deduced that if his stomach was like mine, and it must have been, then that cigarette must have meant something. I recall eating the remainder of our food, making our last can of tea before taking over this train at Severn Tunnel Junction, that was about 5.15pm; the time was now 11.45pm, having clocked-on at 09.15 that morning.

'Have you any grub left Jockey?' he asked. I gave him a look which meant something like 'Are you kidding?' then replied 'I've got six shallots and some salt.' He then put his hand in his pocket and brought out something which in the firelight looked rather like a toffee in white paper which he passed to me. It turned out to be one of the Horlicks tablets which he produced from time to time. I can't say that I felt any less hungry after having eaten it.

The climb to Gloucester's Great Western Station as seen from Over bridge. The signal on the right is for trains coming down the gradient bound for the Ledbury branch.   *(Author's Collection)*

I was tired, really tired; this was not the result of today's turn of duty, it had been getting gradually worse during the four years I had been on the job. Obviously many people are able to get their sleep in the daytime, but not I. Having been asleep for perhaps two hours, something happened to wake me up; I seldom dropped off again. My eyeballs ached as though I had been lightly punched in each eye. Finally, I visited the doctor, who deduced that I was slowly becoming a physical wreck. Partly through working long hours, with little food—everyone did that in those days—chiefly my trouble was lack of sleep. It was the end of the railway life for me.

As with many other experiences in life, this job provided some varied emotions, changing as each situation developed, with each different engine or journey. It was initially very frightening, and thereafter a constant source of stimulation, to work a locomotive on a very dark night, being somewhat dazzled by the fire, at the same time unable to see anything at all outside the confines of the cab. Whether travelling fast or slow. The faster we were moving the greater the mess, should we be unfortunate enough to hit something. The only thing there was to be seen, and we had to be sure we saw them, were the signal lights.

Referring to the signal light of those days, it was no high-powered electric beacon, but a small dim light, which was produced by the flame from a wick set in a well of paraffin, known as an oil lamp. The signal porter, or whoever cleaned, trimmed and refuelled the lamps, needed to be careful as he relit them, to get the best flame possible without getting too carried away, otherwise if the flame was too great the glass would become smoked up and the light would be difficult to see, or perhaps burn out. Of course, when it rained hard it was much worse. It was almost impossible to see through the small cab windows so we were forced to pop our heads out for a second or two, to be sure of seeing the signal.

I remember how the rain stung my face and eyes before dodging back into the cab again, only to be constantly repeated until the signal had been seen, usually by the driver and fireman at the same time. The exception being when approaching a curve, then whoever was on the inside of the curve saw it first.

Frosty nights were different, especially if there happened to be a moon. We were generally running well above the fields, roads and hedgerows, and so we had, for the main part, what was approaching a panoramic view of things. The short winter grass in the fields looked white with frost. The cows could be seen easily, but the sheep, blending with the frost, were not so visible. That is until our firelight shone on their eyes—that was a most unusual sight. There was a ray of light beginning at the firebox door, it shone at an angle out of the cab through the narrow doorway we used to clamber on to the footplate, fanning out to a wide beam which travelled across the whole scene at variable speeds. As we passed the animals, the reflection from their eyes came in a sort of tapering strip which began some way across the fields ending at the firebox again.

Bright sunny mornings were best; I saw many day breaks in various areas all the year round, likewise evenings. But whatever time of day or night we were on the job we got attached to whatever engine we were working on; it became our home for the shift, long or short. On many occasions we have waited on some windy embankment or rainswept flats, often for several hours, where, if we were facing in the wrong direction the wind and rain would drive into the cab and we would stand with our backs to the fire, or huddle, each in his respective corner by the window, where, although away from the direct firelight, we still kept comfortably warm with the heat from the boiler.

Unaffected by the weather as the steam engine was, it appeared to totally ignore whatever the elements chose to thrust upon it. Rain or sunshine, frost or snow, the engine went clattering on its way, no matter what.

It was quite strange sitting in some loop or siding with a gale blowing, to be in or on some vehicle that the wind made no discernible impression upon, though I must admit that, when drawing a long train of empty coal trucks in a high wind, they did sometimes appear to be held back as a result of it.

As for myself, sometimes when having paused for a few moments in my duties to glance at what was happening in the outside world, and seen the rain driving past in sheets, I would stand there, shoulders hunched in a warm corner and watching it all happen. At times like that one experienced a great sense of well-being and security.

Saint Edmond Hall rattles through Stroud in February 1962. For all the power that a steam locomotive had, as the Author comments the effect of a strong wind could be felt upon the train's performance.

(Author's Collection)

Early Days

Casting my mind back to the time when I first encountered steam trains, I realised that they were among the first things that I remember seeing from my pram. Quite often at Westbury-on-Severn halt, but mainly between Grange Court Junction and Broken Cross level crossing.

Of all the mechanical inventions there ever were, there can surely never have been one that captured or held the interest of so many people. Usually, boys from their early days and quite often to the end of their lives like the Steam Locomotive; townsman and countryman alike. Where people first encountered steam trains depended a lot on where they lived. Usually the town boy would see a passenger or goods train pulling hard away from the main station to some unknown destination, quite often crossing a bridge over a busy street, where the noise it made often drowned momentarily the sound of passing traffic. It seemed quite natural to see people walking along the pavement turn and look back to see this huge piece of machinery thundering away, with fantastic exhaust beats, sparks and smoke flying, occasionally wheels slipping if the rails were wet.

Perhaps a level crossing, where people and traffic waited as the gates closed for an incoming train to pass. As the signal was set up or down, depending on the railway company involved, a great air of expectancy prevailed, often in silence. Suddenly it was there in the distance, rapidly becoming a discernible shape and larger every second, approaching quite quickly with the regulator shut and the engine coasting, often with a beautiful rhythmic whistling noise coming from the cylinders. Thundering past, blowing off surplus steam, water dribbling from the injectors, one became aware of a screeching of brakes on the rear carriage wheels, as the engine itself now approached the station platform; it left a smokey acrid atmosphere and rush of air in its wake.

At times like this it must have seemed to people waiting at the crossing as though the world stood still. Everything was blotted out for a few moments, nothing else seemed to be in motion except the train. Its passing dominated everything in the surrounding area, until the crossing gate opened and comparative peace reigned once more.

The country boy would encounter trains in a very similar way, the only difference being a slightly different setting. For instance, boys walking along a country lane, perhaps blackberrying, birds nesting, or up to just plain boyish mischief, would see the smoke rising away in the distance, long before the train came into view. Often they would run to the bridge where they would stand looking over the parapet to watch this thing thunder through. It approached with a loud deafening roar, disappearing under the bridge, nothing more to be seen but a cloud of steam and smoke whirling over the parapet, enveloping them. Thereupon they would run to the opposite side of the bridge, where they had to wait a few moments until the air cleared, only to see the tail end of the carriage, now several

13

hundred yards away, receding very quickly with a swaying motion.

The farm worker in the field often didn't need a watch—he knew exactly what the time was by the local passenger, and certain goods trains, which ran regularly. He knew when to start heading for home in the afternoon, or when to tether his horse in the shade, and light a fire ready to boil a kettle for his lunch time cup of tea. If he dropped off to sleep another train would wake him; he would say to himself 'Well, that's it, five past two, I should be on the job'.

When people were travelling in the countryside, whether riding or walking or whatever their particular pursuit of the day, it wasn't long before they would see in the distance a cloud of smoke rising somewhere in the sky beyond the trees. If they were on a hill they may have seen as many as four different trains at different stages of their journey. For instance, one of the best vantage points in our area was Mayhill. Looking to the southeast, the main South Wales expresses could be seen, perhaps a train going in each direction at the same time. Then towards the northeast in the direction of Gloucester, where the Great Western and Midland railways crossed each other within Gloucester, several little puffs of smoke could be seen in the distance. Then, of course, if one looked round northwest towards Wales, there were the Hereford and Ledbury branches. Quite often up to six trains could be seen in this way at one time, the sights of these puffs of smoke and steam were an everyday occurrence taken for granted; those of us who remember, miss them.

We had to cross the main South Wales line daily at 'Broken Cross' to get to the cottage in the fields where we lived. As a young child may become used to a large dog barking loudly in the house, the noise grew on us and we were hardly aware of the trains passing.

Railways were very much part of my life in those days—my father was a railwayman, my grandfather before him. I travelled to school on a full-blown passenger train, coming home on what was known as the 'Cinderford Car' This was a little tank engine which pushed and pulled depending on the direction of travel, with one single carriage. Passengers left through a large door in the centre. Trains were part of everyday life, what with travelling on them, and continually hearing them roar up and down the South Wales main line.

Quite often at night, coming home late, we would wait for a train to pass at 'Broken Cross'. I recall father mentioning things like the 'milk train', 'fish train', 'paper train', the 'midnight mail'; the names of which sounded ominous to me. The 'Midnight Mail' had something specially forbidding about it.

Many years later, it seems difficult to believe that we used to stand in pitch darkness, apart from the red and green paraffin lamp on the crossing gate, within six or eight feet of the rails, as these towering black objects in the form of wagons, thundered and clattered past on the rail joints.

My father worked on the track. He was used to trains rushing and trundling past him all day. Even if caught between two trains passing in opposite directions at the same time,

14

he was so unaffected by them he just kept walking, although the Great Western Rule Book instructs that anyone so placed must lie down. So I suppose him standing there so unconcerned led my mother, brother and myself to act likewise, without giving it a second thought.

Whenever we travelled to Gloucester from Grange Court station, we would be looking out to wave to father. One day, whilst working above Grange Court station, there was an incident that I can never forget.

We had seen father working on the line bank just above the station and decided to wrap up an orange and two buns for his lunch, to be thrown to him through the train window. I recall father looking up as the train passed, expecting to see us. Having thrown my little parcel, it flew past his head, landing in a grass fire on the line embankment. One of those things that have remained from a very early age.

At that time a great uncle became an express driver—there were very few people in the countryside who were able to even boast of knowing an engine driver—I was naturally very proud of the fact.

Our cottage was about 300 yards away from the railway line and if we heard Uncle Tom Norton sounding his whistle we would hurry out to the garden wall to wave to him. This

The Author's father, Arthur Thomas Trigg, holding a sledgehammer, photographed with a gang of permanent way workers at Over Junction. Notice the traditional oak keys in the chairs holding the bullhead rail. *(Author's Collection)*

would sometimes happen when we were on our way home across Walmore Common, having perhaps been to fetch bread left for us at Cotshill Farm, or coming home from my grandfather's where we may have spent an autumn evening cider making, with the old stone mill. On these occasions we would hurry to a clear spot to wave a hurricane lamp.

It made no difference if we were indoors, sat round the fire on a winter's night. In those days, about 1932, we were not destined to have a wireless set, with wet batteries strewn all across the floor, for another six years, so we were able to hear Uncle Tom as he passed up or down the South Wales line. Whatever the weather, someone would rush out to wave a lamp.

In those days, people living in the heart of the country seldom travelled far. This was the case with our family—perhaps to Gloucester and back once or twice a year. Perhaps a day trip to Weston or Barry. One seldom encountered really fast trains, of course, but there were one or two considered fast at that time.

Grange Court station was an important junction at that time. The single line to Hereford branched off here. The Hereford-Gloucester and Cardiff-Gloucester passenger trains passed at about 8.45am, within about five minutes of each other. If we stood on the centre platform we could see the Cardiff train run straight through. It could be heard in the distance and as it came nearer there came one shrill blast from the main whistle, one long blast always meant train on main line, as opposed to two blasts for a train in the siding or

Broken Cross was one of the earliest places where the Author saw trains. This photograph, taken in 1987, brings back many memories. *(D. A. Trigg)*

16

loop line, asking for the road into a siding or loop.

Rivetting my eyes through one of the bridge arches, I would see a never to be forgotten picture of what usually turned out to be one of the Castle Class locomotives suddenly appearing into view, with surplus water trickling from the exhaust injector pipe, white steam and smoke from the smoke stack signifying that the train was fairly near its journey's end — the fire being worked down ready for shed. But most of all my eyes were focused on the front bogey wheels, swaying violently on the sharp curve. Actually it was the rest of the engine that swayed and the bogey that remained comparatively steady. However, through the eyes and mind of a child the engine was determined to touch the platform. On each occasion I saw this spectacle, the two appeared to come closer than the time before. At the last second everyone would automatically step quickly backwards, as what had previously been a vivid fast-moving picture, suddenly became an almost indescribable dark, roaring, clattering mass of steel and billowing steam, some of which appeared to be seeking refuge from this terrible monster which had produced it. It hurriedly climbed into the roof of the veranda above the platform, where it hung for a second or two, before being whipped away to the far end of the station by the vacuum-like turbulence that followed in the wake of the last carriage, finally fading away in its own good time.

All that would be left in my view was the drab indistinct end of the rear coach, capped by a small swirling cloud of steam, rocking and rattling into the distance. Now we were brought back to reality by yet another sound as the signal was put back to danger, followed by the signal which allowed the Hereford train to enter the station, which it did with screeching brakes and a sudden belching of steam. The safety valves opened. Had we been watching the same scene in the dark we would not only have heard the brakes, we would also have seen streams of sparks coming from the brake blocks, as though we were watching a big grinding tool in an engineering workshop. In the last seconds, some of the rear carriage wheels would shudder violently as the brake blocks ground on tighter. If ever a task needed a lot of practice and skill, stopping a long passenger train smoothly at the exact spot desired was one. A driver lacking in either could find himself having to apply the brakes hard at the last second, causing much shuddering of wheels and springs, or having to open the engine up, making a terrible din in the station as he attempted to pull a dozen or more carriages, some with wheels almost tied. It was all to do with the vacuum brakes taking effect on the wheels of the rear carriage first. It is one of those things which would have been easier to demonstrate than describe. Actually, had I remained on the job, I would not have needed to start studying the proper locomotive mechanics for some years, but I did observe some functions of these fantastic Titans.

As a child, on country stations — certainly at Grange Court junction — the Station Master and his staff, the porters, were not just faceless people in uniform, but people who lived in the neighbourhood who were on friendly speaking terms with all the passengers — even toddlers like myself.

Some snatches of those conversations heard while waiting on the station still come to mind. 'Who got drunk at the Junction Inn last Saturday night and fell off his bike, to be dragged from the roadside ditch by some lads of the village cycling home late from Barton Fair in Gloucester?'

The fox disturbed whilst engaged in killing Farmer Hoddles fowls late last Thursday night by my father and his brothers, taking a short cut home from the Junction Inn.

The latest unbelievable feat of strength performed by someone's horse. The horse that had bolted with an empty cart from the station yard, as a heavy freight train started out from the down loop line, whilst waiting for the afternoon train from Cardiff to pass by. This particular horse had taken a corner too sharply, turning one wheel up the roadside bank, tipping the cart; the horse neither large or heavy, was thrown as well. The animal skinned its knees and flank. 'Pity that, they bent never the same wunss thaya bolted'. I seldom got the complete stories because I was usually trying to get tuppence from Mum to enable me to operate the huge Nestles chocolate machine or, if unsuccessful, then perhaps just gazing at it, fascinated by the many bars of chocolate visible through the thick glass.

I can just remember the retirement of Mr Kirk, the Station Master; he was presented with a clock to mark the occasion. This was not just a railway affair, I believe many passengers and villagers contributed also. He then moved to his new house, 'Applegarth' at Chaxhill. I recall the names of some of the people who were seen on or near the vicinity of the station, names like Kirk, Draper, Tucker, Sargent, to name but a few. Later I saw more of the permanent way men as we travelled past, frequently throwing off huge lumps of coal near their huts. Most of these men are now gone. I remember some of their names—Dobbs, Wilks, Cleveland, Young, Stevens, Trigg and others.

The Junction Inn is very different now to what I remember as a child—I only saw it from the outside, of course. The first time I saw anything of the inside was when I climbed down from a horse-drawn trap in which I had been left while my father went in for 'a quick half'. I peered round the door post and wondered what the odd noise was that came from the bar on the left of the doorway.

It was the sound of many voices all talking at once, each man hoping to make himself heard. I think a passage ran right through the house from front to back. There was also a rather cheerless room on the right which was seldom used. I hardly recognise that room today, it having been altered and improved over the years.

My treat on these occasions was a packet of crisps. No choice—there was only one make of crisps that I knew at the time—plain, with a small amount of salt in a twist of blue paper. I was able to choose any drink as long as it was ginger beer; this came in a bottle with a glass marble, or pop alley, in the neck. I was able to get the crisp packet open and fish around in the bottom for the salt. However, I had to call on my father or someone else to force the pop alley down the bottle neck, to enable me to drink the pop. Try as I might,

I could never avoid the effervescent effect of this. I would anxiously await it hitting the roof of my mouth before finding its way out of my nose, making my eyes water.

A particular early memory I have, reminding me of the Junction Inn, was one of the landladies of fifty or more years ago; her name—Mrs Evans.

Mother and I met her one day going into the station drive; we have a laugh about it now. Imagine me, about four and a half years of age, holding mother's hand as I skipped and scuffed my way unwillingly along the driveway, at the prospect of what was considered a long walk, through the lanes to Broken Cross Crossing, then down the field to the cottage on Walmore Common. Suddenly, coming towards us, was this very elegantly dressed woman, the latest fashion in high heels, a dark fitting coat, a large silver fox fur round her shoulders, the head of which was so lifelike it scared me half out of my wits. Above it all was a huge hat, set at a jaunty angle, and I thought this is what I've heard my uncles call a 'fancy high stepper'. As we drew near she spoke to mother, then looked down at me and as she tripped past she said, in a high pitched effectual voice, 'Here comes Douglas with a dimple in his chin, the money'll come rolling in, you know Douglas.'

Well, so far she is only right in the reference to my chin—the money is apparently having great difficulty in rolling!

There was a rail running across the front of the Inn at the road edge. This was used for hitching the horses whose owners frequented the bar for a few pints. As far as I can recall those who were making a longer stay often took their horse and traps etc to the yard at the rear; this was comparatively small compared to the car parking area of today.

A story I heard many years ago is believed to be true, though I can't remember the names of the people involved. As they say about beer, there's no bad beer — some are better than others. So it was with horses. In the late 'twenties and early 'thirties arguments and bets were commonplace about whose horse could pull what, and it wasn't all idle chatter. People today would be absolutely amazed at the capabilities of horses. Unfortunately in the same way that it is no longer possible today to see a big passenger steam locomotive leaving a station with about fourteen coaches, using every ounce of tractive effort available to it in order to quickly reach running speed, thus enabling the driver to keep to time, so now it is with working horses.

We usually see on television working horses or cart horses, pulling, for example, a brewer's dray or a pair pulling a single plough. Although this can be heavy work the horses are not really pulling as anyone who has used cart horses over a period of time will agree. The horse, as well as the carter, knew where there was a bad patch of land, usually mud, approaching a gateway, particularly those used by cattle. If the place was unfamiliar to the horse it would sense the urgency in the carter's voice and manner, the hastening of steps, tugging on the bridle and more than a few clicking noises from the side of the mouth, and it would usually respond. If no sense of urgency was forthcoming from the driver, the horses seemed to react in one of three different ways. If the load suddenly brought a horse

The Junction Inn at Grange Court where the horses waited whilst the carters nipped in for a drink! The brick wall encloses a lawn. In earlier years this area was cobbled, forming a pull-in for horses and carts.
(Both D. A. Trigg)

to a standstill, some would just stop, another would just start plunging its way through the obstruction, sometimes getting away with it, but usually not. In the third example the horse would pull, giving an initial heave. It would go into a forward leaning position with tensed straight legs, do a fast walk, taking small steps, jabbing its hooves into the ground leaning still further forward with its belly half the normal distance from the ground, its chest and head also very low. The horse would struggle forward to firmer ground or to the crest of a hill, its breath coming in quick gasps. Coming to a standstill to catch its wind, it would take huge breaths causing its flanks and stomach to protrude above and below the shafts, huge drops of perspiration dripping from the full length of its stomach. The ears were either forward or straight up, the eyes large and staring, the nostrils dilated, while saliva was very evident in and around the mouth, the bit, and on the ground. It was for certain one such horse that a carter took to fetch a wagon load of coal from Grange Court station. This coal was one of several loads it would need to empty a coal truck in a siding. Having loaded the wagon with two or three tons of coal—exactly how much I don't know—the carter drove the horse and wagon to the Inn. Here he nipped in for a drink while he waited for his workmate to arrive with a trace horse, to help up Grange Court Pitch. The carter had not hitched the horse, which was a good reliable animal, and with that load it was not going far anyway. So he sat down with his drink, listening to the lunchtime conversation, occasionally joining in.

When a cart or trolley drew up outside a pub on a quiet morning there would be some pause in the conversation as people glanced in the direction of the door to see who was arriving or departing. When leaving they would try to put up a little show of trying to get away quickly in much the same way as someone in a car or on a motor cycle may do today.

On this particular morning, a noise was heard outside on the cobbled road. The carter heard it, as did several others and although no one looked out the group expected someone to walk in. No one came in, and the carter did eventually take the trouble to peer through the door to ensure his charge was behaving normally. He wasn't prepared for the sight which met his eyes—it caused his hair to raise his cap two inches! He shouted 'Bloody Hell' or words to that effect. Whatever it was brought everyone running out of the bar to witness a once-in-a-lifetime sight.

The horse had taken the load of coal up the first part of the hill and was just past the bridge. The carter, followed by two others, did their best to run up the hill in an effort to catch it, but by the time they got near the rear of the wagon, it was well on its way up the final steep part and had reached the point of no return. The horse, obviously out of its depth, was unable to dig its shoes into the road surface. Near the excavations on the site of a new bungalow, the group found, to their great relief, a couple of rocks. These were grabbed and they ran on as silently as possible after the wagon. Had the horse come to a standstill these rocks would be used as chocks behind the wheels, which could have prevented a disaster. Placing their rocks on the rear of the wagon they started to push, hoping against hope that by some near miracle the horse could last out long enough to reach the top. For the moment, however, getting a grip seemed to be its main problem.

The horse proved that it still had something to pull out of the bag for it started to weave its way for the last few yards, scrambling from one side of the road to the other, its heavy shoes beating an irregular tattoo on the road surface. It finally reached the crest of the hill,where finding the load was coming easy, set off home at a fast pace.

All three men, who up till now hadn't uttered a word in case the horse had stopped, all shouted at once. The horse stopped, the carter ran forward, grabbing the bridle with trembling hands, swearing at the horse with one breath and praising it with the next. He was beginning to realise how lucky he was to still have his job and home. More important, his reputation as a carter. It is easy to imagine what could have happened if the horse failed to make it. The load would have probably dragged it backwards down the hill with dreadful results. By no stretch of the imagination could the wagon be expected to keep a straight course for more than a few feet, so there were two possibilities. One, it could have gone down through a fence and off the road, dragging the horse with it. On the other hand it could have run up the embankment opposite, tipping the load. As there were very strong shafts on the wagon it would have no doubt thrown the horse on to its side or even its back, with serious results. Even if it had not broken anything, imagine trying to get near a horse lying on its side; it would only be possible to get at one side of the harness to free it, even then it would still be trapped by the shafts, with every kick and violent movement taking off skin and flesh. Just for good measure the boss may have appeared over the hill with his fast-trotting pony and float, no doubt heading for the Junction Inn, with the excuse of seeing how the coal hauling was coming along.

Very few carters could have lived down a situation like this, so he had good reason to be in a nervous state. Of course, there was still his mate, on the way with the trace horse, to be dealt with. He told him some pack of lies, about a stranger who was taking a team of six timber horses through to Huntley. This man refused to take no for an answer when his offer to pull the load up the hill was declined, and before our friend knew what was happening he had hooked a chain on either side and they had all trotted up the hill. This excuse held good for some time!

There are many such stories. Now to return to the railway.

Apart from a spell in the Army, I have always lived within a few miles of Northwood Green. As a toddler my whole life centred on Walmore Common, Northwood Green and Westbury-on-Severn.

It was June 1926 that I first saw the light of day, in a cottage in Ampney Lane. In those days it was just a muddy track.

'Grange Court Junction', 'Grange Court Junction', one or more of the porters would be calling as the doors opened and closed with a very solid clunk. The platform cleared quickly of passengers, no one arrived from Hereford this morning, everyone was off to

Gloucester. 'Close the doors please' would be quickly followed by 'Right away'. The guard, who usually glanced at his pocket watch, blew one quick blast, and gave a quick flourishing wave of his green flag at the same time. Smartly stepping into his compartment he would then close the door and lean on it, his head partly out of the window. As the train began to move, a cheerio to George Draper, a polite wave to the Station Master, his next action would be to close the window—by now smoke might be seeping through the opening. Grasping the thick leather strap, he would pull up the sliding section that encased the pane of thick glass. This strap had holes punched in it at regular intervals to enable the window to be secured to the desired height by pushing the strap over a protruding brass knob.

In the guard's compartment quite a few objects were provided for his use. His food box or a leather satchel, red and green flags, detonators, and a hand lamp, which he could change in a flash from white to green or red. A little corner seat to do his writing. What was perhaps the most important thing of all, the emergency brake, about the effectiveness of which there could be no doubt. The passenger compartments on these local trains often had no corridors, just a door on either side.

The reason for writing in the past sense is because the last train journey I made until recent years was from York to Gloucester, when demobbed in 1948. Things have now changed. I remember walking along corridors, seeing third class, second class and first class compartments. Also sitting looking at pictures of faraway seaside towns and beaches, to which the GWR ran, later realising that these resorts stretched from North to South Wales, London, Cornwall and Devon. What quaint scenes some of them were, giving passengers something to look at besides the forbidding notice by the emergency cord, which boldly stated that the penalty for improper use was £5. A small fortune in the early 'thirties!

Incidentally, operating this brake would stop the train, but not quite in the manner we see in films, where the trains with wheels tied, carriages and locomotive skidding along, showered sparks, until the whole train came to a halt with a thunderous shudder. In the compartment, as soon as the door was closed, I would heave on the big window strap and allow the window to slide open, then out popped my head. 'Keep your hand well away from the door catch', would come my mother's voice, 'and mind your eyes when the train starts'.

I could see the fireman looking out, now ready for the green flag and whistle. He finally got the tip; one blast on the engine whistle, and we were away with loud blasts from the chimney, quickly gathering speed towards Gloucester.

I would keep looking ahead as best I could but so much small ash was flying that I was soon looking through my fingers, trying to hear and see as much as possible. Soon we were passing the level crossing called Broken Cross, the point at which we crossed to and from the cottage, at the edge of Walmore Common. After several huge black clouds of smoke billowed from the engine, I finally gave up and closed the window, sitting down, rubbing my eyes, hoping Mum wouldn't notice and say 'well you were warned'.

On this particular Saturday morning, the Hereford-Gloucester stopping passenger train was being pulled by a 5300 class engine—useful for either passenger trains, local stoppers or goods. I discovered years later that as long as I could keep up steam pressure and water, they would certainly do what was expected.

The driver had just filled his pipe and applied a match to it as the fireman walked across to the driver's side of the footplate, reached up and shut off the steam valve that worked the boiler water injector. He then turned and swung the horizontal handle which controlled the water, which cascaded down on the track. The fireman reckoned he would not need much more water as the engine was going on shed at Gloucester. The fire was almost white hot and rather low because it was necessary to work the fire right down to the bars—the odd shovelful may have been needed.

Whilst at Grange Court the fireman had taken several quick glances back along the platform, satisfied that the guard was not quite ready to give him the tip. When he next glanced the doors were all shut and the guard was holding both flags furled in one hand, and was in the act of moving away from the Station Master towards his waiting open door. Then the train got underway, the driver opening it up three quarters. The old 5300 leapt into life, blasting away out of the station.

The advanced starting signal had dropped at the first motion of the train, the line was clear as far as the eye could see. The train passed the black steps, the driver and fireman were both looking through their narrow windows to check everything was clear at the Broken Cross. Now the fire was quickly checked and as it was low the fireman 'splashed a bit around'—this was the usual term used when a light layer of coal or slack coal was used just to keep the engine going on low fire. For several brief moments dense black smoke came from the engine chimney, then quickly cleared to a nice cloudlike exhausted steam. From a distance this looked like a string of white clouds with huge dots spaced out at intervals, climbing slowly skyward.

Passing Ley Crossing, the driver closed the regulator and the train coasted towards Oakle Street station, another scheduled stop. The driver moved the brake handle slightly, there was the sound of air rushing into the vacuum pipe—this would affect the wheels of the rear carriage first—another brief open and shut movement of the handle and the effect could now be felt on all the carriage wheels; finally the engine could be felt beginning to dig its heels in.

While all this was taking place, the driver had automatically pushed the reversing or cut off lever right forward in readiness to make a smart getaway, the fireman had swapped from the exhaust to the live steam injector, deciding to keep the boiler topped up.

The stop at Oakle Street was very brief, only two passengers joined the train for Gloucester. The 5300 began to bark loudly, starting a rhythmic rocking motion which I found common in that class, also on the 6300, 4300 and 7300s. This, however, passed as the train picked up speed; once again there was the clatter of light steel on heavy cast as the fireman threw four or five shovels full of slack coal into the firebox.

The arrival at Gloucester station was heralded by the usual noise, doors opening and shutting, people chattering loudly. Station staff shouting 'Gloucester' 'All change' and, of course, station luggage trolleys being pulled or pushed, their steel-banded wheels clattering over the joints in the platform paving stones. The fireman now jumped down onto the platform, walked to the front of the engine, unhooked the spare headlamp and took it to the rear, where he fixed it on to one of the lamp iron brackets. He then climbed down between the engine and the first carriage and disconnected the brake pipe, placing one end of the pipe on to the stop end on the carriage. The other end was treated likewise on to the engine, thus separating the engine brake from the carriage brake, before he shouted loudly to the driver, 'Ease up', which meant squeeze the buffers up tight. He undid the couplings and placed them on their appropriate hooks. The engine on pilot duty that day was now able to connect up on the far end of the train, to shunt the carriages in readiness for the

Oakle Street station was a small affair, though well-kept, as can be seen here. (Westrail Enterprises)

next run. Had the end of the pipe not been located on the stopper, the driver would have been unable to move the carriages as creating a vacuum would have been impossible. Likewise with the engine which had just brought the train in from Hereford, its portion of the pipe connection had to be correctly located, enabling it to set off for the engine shed. After shunting backwards and forwards several times, our engine was finally moved off the main line, safely in the yard. This yard contained quite a few pieces of track, covering all the service area—any engine being in the confines of this yard was termed as being 'On Shed'.

The driver made up his daily time sheets noting any defects the engine might have. The fireman, in the meantime, closed all the dampers, opened the firebox and topped up the boiler, then he and the driver gathered up oil cans, spanners, gauge lamp, flare lamp etc into the bucket, also coats and lunch boxes, passing various items to each other they climbed off the engine, before making their way to the time office.

Engines brought on shed left by the crews were run on to the track leading to the fire drop and coaling-up areas. The first of these was the fire drop—very hot, very hard work, even when the fireman had worked the fire down low, the little ash and clinker remaining going black or rather grey. The heat rising out from the firebox door was such that when the man dropping the fires inserted the heavy iron bar into the firebox in order to break the clinker into smaller pieces for removal by a special shovel, he would usually close the doors on the bar as tight as possible. While he jabbed at the clinkers with the bar, which also became increasingly hot, he held it with big handfuls of cotton waste. After inserting the shovel, which must have been nearly 12ft. long, again using cotton waste to protect his hands, the fire dropper proceeded to fish ash and clinker up, out through this comparatively small round hole. Each time it went in the shovel obviously became hotter. It was necessary to exercise care to avoid burning his hands.

By now the fire dropper would be sweating profusely, each time he brought a shovel full of hot ash out fine grey dust would leave the main bulk, lifted by the hot air around, only to land on him, sticking to his overalls and cap. What was worse, to his sweating arms, neck, face and eyes. Small wonder the men thus engaged seemed to make a hurried beeline for the nearest inn the moment they were off duty!

After having its fire dropped, the engine was passed on in turn, down to the coaling stage. This was situated at Gloucester GWR shed at the top of a large man-made mound with a set of rails running up this steep bank. These rails passed through the building or coal shed, out along a short viaduct—it was an event that always drew a lot of attention when some small pannier tank engine was used to re-stock this coaling-up station. After quite a few years, I would guess about six loaded coal wagons were propelled up this bank at one time. The wagons were drawn right back to the stop block, somewhere near Great Western Road, then full blast at the bank. On the first part of the slope, this little coal train travelling in reverse was probably doing twenty miles an hour, but this was down to a crawl after about 45 yards or so. Looking at this spectacle from the side angle at a 100 yard distance, it seemed there would be an almighty crash, when the leading truck struck what appeared to be a solid mass of bricks perched directly in its way on the skyline. After a few seconds I was always relieved to see the leading wagon reappear out of the far side, gradually approaching the stop block—this was situated quite high above the engines waiting below to be coaled-up. All brakes were applied on each wagon, the engine, uncoupled, would slowly rumble its way back down the bank, while the wagons could be allowed to slowly run down into the coal stage as required. When they were all empty they would be taken slowly down the bank with an engine.

Of course, one usually visualises these things happening on a nice sunny morning or afternoon, but some times it rains or it is frosty or even snowing. Then this operation could become something else. With the little engine's wheels slipping from the start of its run at the bank, the sand box handle was then wrenched back and forth. Sometimes there was some sand available, sometimes the delivery pipe was blocked with wet sand, in which case it would be necessary to go back down and restart.

The actual job of coaling the engines must, without doubt, have been one of the hardest—certainly the blackest—anywhere! I have seen these men come into this filthy black hole, which supposedly in these days would be called a rest room, completely black with coal dust—just the whites of their eyes and their mouths visible, if they swigged a mug of water.

In this dark compartment under the coal stage, simply lit by a poor gas burner, the most visible things were pieces of comparatively white paper which held their wartime bread and fish paste sandwiches. Some stretched out on the dusty benches to catch a few minutes sleep prior to starting the second part of their shift.

I never actually climbed up on to the coal stage, but I can imagine them having to drop the line of coal wagons down each time one became empty. Taking their little paraffin lamp out into the night on the ridge, where they may have paused to see if there was a glow in the night sky as Bristol took its almost nightly ration of bombs, the wagons moving down the slope before stopping them where required so that the coaling-up team could drop the side doors. This allowed the first flush of coal to come tumbling out, the brake would be secured, the dust partially blotting out the dim gas lamp, momentarily hiding the wagon from sight. The practice seemed to be to fill small iron trucks or hoppers, which were then pushed on rails to the side of the staging, there to be released over the coal tender of the locomotive. Another thundering noise, more coal dust spreading over everything around. This went on throughout the shift until eventually the wagons were all empty. The whole procedure of replacing them with full ones would then begin all over again.

Of course, this operation varied from time to time, some engines needing several tons more than others, and so the amount done on any one shift could be light or heavy.

As in many other jobs, things went on behind the scenes in busy engine sheds that passengers would not normally see or even think about which I suppose is only natural. I will try to list a few jobs and people who were necessary to make the engine shed function, though I will probably leave some unmentioned.

There was, of course, the Head Foreman who, to me at the age of sixteen, was a pretty awesome figure. His word was the be all and end all in that small world of the engine shed. That, of course, included the yards and sidings therein.

Next to him was the Shed Foreman, who I now realise had a mammoth task trying to provide engines in all sorts of emergencies. I only saw them in wartime but I imagine their job had been more dignified in peacetime, not to mention easier going, somewhat of a more administrative nature. For instance I have seen a foreman in his smart suit clambering up on to engines, moving them down in the queue to be coaled, to have fires dropped, acting as general ramrod, pushing things along or running to the turntable to help some driver, fireman, or shed hand struggling on his own to turn some huge locomotive. I have also seen an engine coming off the main line, due for some maintenance or refuelling, when the foreman has rushed out in pouring rain, jumped over rails, dodging things like shovels, fire irons and other obstacles, too many to mention, to rally the engine crew—instructing the fireman to start rebuilding the fire, take water, and jump the coal queue.

The driver to do a lightning check, oil the engine so that it can be back off shed as soon as possible—now this instance was very far from unique. The engine firebox was probably carrying a lot of solid clinker, which would affect the fire to such an extent that the fireman was going to be faced with a near impossible task of trying to maintain steam on the impending journey. In fact there must have been hundreds of engines throughout the country in that condition for most of their working times during the war years.

Next to the foremen were Time Clerks, who seemed to have a lot of authority, especially when it came to putting up duty time sheets for the next couple of days. These clerks must have had their work cut out taking much on themselves in the absence of the foreman. At the time I was only interested in what time of day or night I was due on. It must have put them about somewhat, collating drivers and firemen for duties way ahead, providing an engine crew about every quarter of an hour on a huge sheet of paper. Men failing to turn up for various reasons, whose places had

28

to be filled by inconveniencing someone else.

This roster sheet looked so impressive as it was completed, pinned up behind the glass partition, together with speed restriction notices, etc, for us to check on. It remained like this for a time, while the old sheets had been worked out, then suddenly it seemed to go haywire. For example, an engine crew booking on at 3.45am may have booked off after having worked sixteen hours, then by law must have twelve hours rest, so it can be seen immediately that the earliest they can be brought back on duty is 7.45am. So someone had to be on their toes. Of course, these people had their problems—long hours, covering absent colleagues, little food and general wartime conditions. Incidentally, if sixteen hours seemed a bit much, I can vouch that it would have been considered commonplace; I once did twenty four and a quarter hours at one stretch—this I will mention later.

Then there were Charge Hand Cleaners. These were usually ex-drivers who had been taken off the footplate for some health reasons, usually it was for defective eye sight, who were responsible, amongst other things, for detailing cleaners for their duties. As it was wartime these cleaners did anything but cleaning. Some were used as call boys, some boiler washer's mates, or shed labourers.

There were Fitters, who had no let up at all; they were really hard-pressed, working on three shifts to keep the engines on the road. I'm not able to say just how big a job they reckoned to take on but I've seen them replacing springs, brake blocks, pistons and connecting rods on the same shift.

There were Boiler Smiths, Copper Smiths, Firelighters, Tube Cleaners, Boiler Washers too! At that time there were women in the tool stores, supplying the bucket of tools for each engine that was leaving the shed. Last, but not least, was a scrooge-like character we knew as the Pay Clerk.

The amazing thing was that everyone, other than office staff, thought nothing of climbing on to any engine, moving it should it be necessary, though looking back I can't imagine 'Bladder, the boiler smith being able to squeeze up on to the footplate, but they were all 'drivers'.

How it all began

'You'll have to start as a cleaner, then work your way up to fireman, then if you pass your engineman's examinations, you may possibly become an engine driver', said my father one night. We were discussing what I may do next for a living. 'What you need to do is write an application addressed to the Head Foreman, GWR Engine Shed, Horton Road, Gloucester'. This I eventually did.

I had left the job I had been doing since I was fourteen years old—I was now fifteen years and ten months—hoping to earn more. Well, the wages weren't to be much—I believe about thirty shillings, less stoppages—but earn was to become the operative word.

After a few days I received a reply; having been invited to attend an interview at Horton Road Shed, I duly set out.

My knowledge of Gloucester did not amount to much, apart from Westgate Street, up over the cross to Eastgate Street, and Eastgate Market. So I set out to find Barton Street, Millbrook Street, leading to Horton Road, on foot of course; I really began to feel I was taking something on. Then I had to find my way home afterwards, making sure to board the right bus, out of several that ran from Westgate Street at the same time. These buses came over the old stone Westgate Bridge, up Westgate Street, turning right, round Quay Street, they then kept bearing left, back out on to Westgate Street facing the bridge once more, ready for their outward journey. It was nothing to see half a dozen buses arriving, waiting, or leaving. There were the Red and White, Bristol Blue, and several smaller private concerns, so anyone not used to travelling on these buses could, and sometimes did, find themselves on the wrong one. After all it would not have done for buses to have shown an invasion force one with Cardiff displayed on the journey board.

As the War got into its stride, this terminus became quite chaotic in the winter evenings, with everything in complete blackness, apart from the glimmers that were once head-lamps. Buses were delayed for many different reasons. With a half hour turn round, it was hard to tell the difference between one running late and the one on time, both leaving from the same destination.

There were buses leaving this part of Westgate Street for Cardiff, Newport, Coleford, Cinderford, Hereford, Ledbury and Monmouth, not to mention all the villages en route. Petrol was only allowed for essential journeys, where no public transport was available. Many people who had never travelled regularly to work before were now compelled to do so, thus placing an impossible burden on the buses, as on the railways. The bus office was on the spot, and open quite long hours, trying to deal with enquiries, handling left goods and shopping. At the same time it provided somewhere for people to shelter or find a seat, if they were lucky!

It was often a worrying situation if someone had to face perhaps twenty miles in pitch

darkness with bad weather, a stiff westerly sweeping up the Bristol Channel, plus ....
thought of having to come again tomorrow, the next day and so on. If about twenty people were left off the last bus usually an inspector would call out that a relief bus was on its way. Should you happen to be one of six or seven left standing when the bus drew out, full to the door step, you would suddenly notice that the door to the bus office was closed and locked with no one left to argue with! So you set off at a stiff walking pace, hoping that some lorry might happen along, and maybe give you a lift.

When I finally reached Horton Road Crossing I passed through the small pedestrian gate, joining several others who were obviously waiting for trains to pass. An LMS tank engine, which was shunting just inside the gate, pulled up clear of where we stood. As the others moved forward then stopped again, I did the same. Apart from two women, there were four railwaymen with bicycles carrying dinner boxes, two GWR firemen, a guard, and an LMS fireman. As I was eyeing them and their uniforms, wondering what I would look like, I noticed they were all looking with a professional expectation to our right, towards Cheltenham. Then, suddenly. as if from out of the blue, a huge drab thundering shape emerged from an equally drab background, consisting of dark ballast between the rails, a dark dusty signal box and a huge drab smoke enveloped building, which I later learned was the LMS engine shed. It came from the Cheltenham down line, crossing diagonally through the GWR main London line. I hoped the others knew what they were doing and as I stood still there, I realised that it was one thing to be standing on a platform looking at one of these things at eye level, but down here where I was standing, feeling rather apprehensive about which set of rails it was actually going to pass me on, it was completely different. The train rumbled past, blowing off steam, in fact to my inexperienced eyes smoke, steam and water appeared to be coming out of many places at once. From where I stood it looked gigantic, as indeed it was.

It was a huge LMS engine, type unknown; the ground shook as it clattered past, the brakes could be heard now on the rear carriages as it began to slow down, approaching the LMS station which lay somewhere over to my left. At last we all quickly walked across, passing through the opposite gate into Horton Road.

On my left was one side of a large building. It was the GWR engine shed. Turning left off the road I passed through a narrow gateway on to an ash path, at the end of which was a group of grimey-looking brick offices. The Head Foreman's office was the first door I came to, so delving into my pocket for my letter, written on railway notepaper telling me I should present myself on this day, at this time, scanning the note just to be sure this was in fact the time and the date, I knocked on the door; a loud voice bade me 'come in'.

The Head Foreman was rather an elderly man, big built, grey hair, and looking rather pale, with an expression on his face, full of worried expectancy; it seemed to say to me 'what now?' He took his reading glasses off, saw I wasn't one of the continuous bearers of bad news, or seemingly impossible questions, and appeared to find a slight relief in the fact as I stepped forward holding my interview letter. He took and read it, asking for confirmation that I was indeed who I claimed to be. I produced my identity card, he put his glasses on and checked it, then asked me a few questions about fitness and health generally. He also asked if I had any relatives employed by the company. I told him about my father and grandfather, also two uncles. I happened to mention my great uncle Thomas Norton, and I could see his name had some effect on his general expression; he began to look almost in a genial mood! 'Ah! he's one of my top express drivers', as though talking to himself. 'Right' he said, 'let's have a look outside'. He placed his glasses on the desk and ushered me through the door as a yard foreman hurriedly approached. He told the foreman to go in and wait, saying he wouldn't be long.

He pointed out several small objects which were usually attached to some building or post, also a couple of engine numbers; these objects weren't difficult to discern if you had a rough idea what they could possibly be, but as I was in strange surroundings they made me blink a few times. Then he concentrated on colour, these luckily I found easier. I remember the last object was a very small plate of some sort attached to the top of the gasometer in Horton Road, and in spite of smoke and grime from two engine sheds, it was white alright.

This terminated the odd interview, apart from telling me I would be getting instructions in a week or two about travelling to Swindon for further eyesight tests. I began to feel quite excited as I made my way back to Westgate Street and even managed to get on the right bus to Minsterworth. I had seen more engines grouped in one area that day than I had ever imagined existed, also the trip to Swindon promised to be even more exciting. After all, it would be necessary to travel on 'The London' better known as the 'Cheltenham Flyer', which was *the* train to be on!

It was, in fact, three weeks before the instructions and free pass to travel arrived at my home. I spent this time with my grandparents, who were living at Holcombe, near Painswick, going most days with an aunt who was doing her war job, driving a milk delivery van for Spoonbed Dairy Farm.

The day arrived for me to go to Swindon, catching the bus at Minsterworth into Gloucester, hurrying off up the street towards the GWR station. I was feeling quite important with the railway pass, which I presented to the ticket collector—I don't know if I thought he may for some reason reject it, but I do know I was relieved as he clipped it and handed it back. In answer to my question, he nodded and pointed with his clippers towards the platform from which 'The London' would leave. Not a word did he utter.

His dumb insolence hurt my pride a little to say the least, after all I wasn't a child to be fobbed off in that manner, I was sixteen years of age, full of importance and with luck, after my trip, would be destined for the footplate, and him a mere ticket puncher! This mood, however, passed quickly; the signals dropped on the upper end of the platform. In the next half minute or so the train arrived from Cheltenham, drawn by a tank engine. Whatever their class I knew them all later as 'Cheltenham Tankies'. I didn't know there would be a slight delay while engines were changed, so I quickly found myself a seat in the first available compartment nearest the engine; I was ready now for the trip to what I later discovered was the real home of GWR engines. I could see and hear all sorts of activity going on outside on the platform, so leaving my seat I went to the window and looked out, as I had done years before at Grange Court Junction. The platform was indeed very busy, so many different uniforms hurrying along, many half carrying, half dragging kit bags and cases. Glancing forward I suddenly saw the big engine that was going to take this train to London. It seemed to glide slowly backwards towards us, to be coupled up to the train, and as it made contact with the leading coach I sensed a sort of immense pressure as it compressed the buffers, so that the 'coupling up' could be done.

The platform noises continued with the constant clattering of the luggage trucks, as they trundled back and forth on the platform, doors were being slammed shut, while many people were talking or shouting in order to make themselves heard above the din. Steam was roaring from what I later learned was the safety valve, but at that moment I began to think perhaps they do just explode after all. In my ignorance I was wondering why we had an engine at both ends of the train. I didn't discover until later that the tank engine that on this occasion had brought the London train from Cheltenham, would now be uncoupled in order that the 'Castle' could take it out of Gloucester station in the opposite direction towards London. The London guard would then enter the train at the opposite end to where the Cheltenham guard had been, and so effect a complete turn round of the train.

During the last few weeks we had visited uncle Tom Norton, who lived in Alfred Street. He was pleased to know that I was hoping to start on the job and, of course, he was only too ready to talk steam locomotives. Most of his interests now concerned his most recent experiences on expresses, including the 'London' so with all this fresh in my mind I had an idea that the fireman may be very busy, especially at the beginning of the journey.

I could see the driver now constantly glancing towards the rear of the train, looking for the guard's flag. The engine had now finished blowing off steam as a result of the fireman topping up the boiler—how he would need it from Gloucester up through Tuffley, Stonehouse and Stroud. They would need to make the supreme effort up Brimscombe Bank on up until they finally emerged at the far end of Sapperton Tunnel, where, as the nose of the engine began to drop down the incline, the rear rose in consequence. At this angle the water in the gauge glass would be down so low that the fireman could be excused for wondering if the boiler was leaking. I heard the guard's whistle when it came, louder than I could have imagined amid all the noise; I saw the green flag way down the platform, very close into the carriage, I think the guard was probably standing on the step so as to enable him to get his flag high enough above all the heads. The driver gave a short blast on the whistle, and I was about to gain a new experience as the train moved slowly off on a fairly tight curve across through the scissors on to the up track.

It had been one thing to see one of these huge 'Castle' engines on the run down the South Wales line, but this was something different again, hearing this one blasting away on the stiff climb up over Horton Road crossing, past the North box, and on over Chequers Bridge towards Tuffley.

Sitting on the right hand side of the compartment, the morning sun was shining from the left. The train was casting shadows on to the down line, above which rose other shadows of varying dimensions that travelled away and over the roofs of the houses that backed onto the embankment. These were the result of the mass of billowing steam plus more than just a little smoke, which seemed to become less evident as we increased our speed.

At Swindon I found myself with a dozen or so other lads of about my age, sixteen. We were all trying to look rather important sitting in the waiting room. I don't recall anyone trying to make any conversation at all. After a few minutes, during which time we all appeared to be dividing our attention between the big railway clock high on the wall—roman figures, of course—the floor, and each other, my turn eventually came to go in before the company doctor. The emphasis seemed to be on eyesight tests. The doctor appeared satisfied at length and I was told by a clerk of some description that I would receive a letter soon. I was not told whether I had indeed passed this medical or not, but the doctor's series of 'Hms' and 'Ahs', 'good' and 'right', led me to believe that I must have done.

Call Boy

It must have been a week later that I received a letter saying that my application for a job as engine cleaner had indeed been successful. It instructed me to report for a 2 o'clock afternoon shift on the following Thursday. I was quite excited about this, but couldn't imagine how anyone would tackle the job of cleaning a locomotive. Incidently, I never did get round to it!

As cleaners, most of our time was taken up 'calling up' drivers and firemen, and advising them if there was any change in duty; this was something that happened quite frequently at any hour, all around the clock.

Then there was a duty as box boy; this was a job that consisted mainly of splitting up old sleeper wood, nailing it together in squares about eight by eight inches; these were then used for lighting up the engines—he also had the job of actually lighting the engine. In his hut there was a small stove kept going for the purpose of heating up sand, to keep it dry and free running. Another job we were given to do from time to time was boiler washing, plus, of course, general shed labouring, but as this was wartime no actual engine cleaning.

I was never very keen about the 'calling and advising' part of the job, it always seemed to be dark and quite often raining. I would set out from home on my bike— a good Raleigh Sports model with three speed and dynamo lighting—for Gloucester. This was about a seven mile ride by the time I reached Horton Road Shed. After signing on, we took one of the upright railway bikes which were of the old fashioned type to the last nut and bolt, with broad leather saddles, wide rims and lever-type brakes. To cap it all they were painted a horrible railway brown, and had detachable front and rear paraffin lamps.

As most calling up of drivers and firemen was done during the hours of darkness, we would give these lamps our attention first of all. Pinching lightly the little wicks to get rid of the burnt ridge on the end, we then filled the tiny well with paraffin, always overfilling and causing a spillage, no matter how hard we tried to avoid doing so. They were finally cleaned up with a piece of cotton waste pulled from a wad always carried by everyone on the job.

The most senior call boy would get the list from the office and study it. First he would check that the times ran consecutively, then he would sort them into their correct areas. It didn't take me long to realise that it wasn't because he was a keen worker that he took on this job with such enthusiasm, he had an ulterior motive— it was simply enabling him to pick the easiest, most spaced out for time, and the nearest to the shed. I have come back on quite a few occasions wet and cold, to find the old hand snoring in the little cabin we used. I found this particular aspect of the job to be quite miserable, trying and difficult in almost every aspect.

It was miserable because during the few winter months that I was engaged on the job it seemed to be exceptionally wet and dark. The darkness was made worse by the blackout. Not a light was to be seen all night long, except perhaps a solitary flicker from someone's cycle lamp, or perhaps a glimpse of the dim signal lamps as I crossed the railway at Horton Road Crossing. Imagine on one of these dark windy nights, when the rain never seemed to stop all night, after cycling from home to work (which used to take me about half an hour) I would arrive at the shed, exhausted and wet. If it was still raining when it was time for me to set out, I would put a fawn coloured railway cape over my shoulders and arms and set off into the darkness.

It was very difficult trying to find the correct street, let alone the house. It was usually impossible to see a street name by pointing a little orange flame towards it, and the piece of half-crumpled paper, which was by this time becoming increasingly damp, made things only worse. I found that I had to knock more than once on most occasions because, having been called over the coals for making too

Part of Gloucester shed as I remember it, photographed in March 1948. The pannier tanks still sport their Great Western lettering with 4659 standing next to the turntable. (Author's Collection)

36

much noise and waking the whole household, I began working to a set routine by starting off with a light tap, and then with short pauses my tapping got progressively louder, until I got some kind of an answer—and how varied these answers were. Of course, a thing like this could never be anywhere near foolproof. The drivers and firemen would book a call at the end of their previous duty, so if, after being called, any of them should happen to drop off to sleep again, and they could hardly be blamed if they did, because they were exhausted, I was soon to discover all they needed to say on arriving late for work was 'No bloody call boy again'. As no-one could prove them wrong the matter seldom went further. Anyway, perhaps I had missed them as I was usually half asleep.

Quite often we got several calls booked at exactly the same time, usually in different streets, so in these instances some were called too early while someone else was called too late.

There was always one thing guaranteed to wake me up, if only for a few minutes. That was on the one or two occasions that I shuffled up to a door with my shoulders hunched against the elements, leaned on the doorpost and went through my routine, only to learn that I was not even in the right street. The stuff that came through those windows by way of abuse alone is best left unsaid!

There were, of course, the day shifts, though how much day was involved depended on the time of year. These were six till two, and two till ten. On these days our time was occupied on whatever job the foreman cleaner decided on. Frequently there were advice notes to take out informing drivers and firemen to report for duty at a different time. This usually meant that the shed foreman and time clerk, as mentioned earlier, had found it necessary to juggle with the duty sheet since they had gone off duty. I forget which day of the week these sheets were put up, but it didn't really matter because we seldom knew Tuesday from Sunday. However, the names were entered on a huge sheet of paper which was then fixed up into an equally huge wooden frame, which was then hung up behind a glass partition. This duty sheet or roster looked very neat hanging there for everyone to study. The name of the driver was in one column, in the next, each opposite his mate, was the name of his fireman. Each pair of names were always together unless one or the other was ill, or a permanent change was effected. It didn't take anyone long to find out how important it was to keep the same two together for as long as possible, providing they were compatible whilst on duty.

There was a tendency for engine crews to loiter in front of the roster and their actions would often have been worth capturing on film as each person unconsciously went through his routine. On more than one occasion I was expecting someone to suddenly terminate this terribly tense atmosphere by breaking into hysterical laughter and diving head first through the window. I think everyone was longing for the day when he would see his name next to a time between eight and nine in the morning, but alas, like a win on the football pools, this seldom came about.

One man would sidle up to the window as though half afraid to look at what 'they' had cooked up for him, his eyes darting up and down the sheet until they focused on his name. He might be pleased at what he saw, so would grab his food box and quickly slink through the door, almost as though embarrassed by his good luck and afraid that should he hang about someone might decide to change it. The next man might scowl at the sheet for a full minute before making a dive for the sliding glass shutter on which he would rap sharply and when it was eventually raised he would pitch into the unfortunate clerk for having put his name for duty at some ungodly hour, for the umpteenth week on the trot. The clerk would make various excuses and it seemed to me that after each one he managed to keep repeating that he, after all, was only carrying out the foreman's orders. To which the driver would reply, with his head halfway through the shutter, 'I'll tell you half the trouble with this office and the way things are run here, there are too many rabbits, lumps of home

"Lady of Lynn' stands ready for its turn of duty as the trilby-hatted foreman, raincoat over shoulder, cycles in for his stint of duty, far right. The box boy's hut is to the left of the locomotive's buffer beam, behind it is the copper smith's workshop. (Author's Collection)

cured bacon and black market eggs finding their way through the back door.' Then he would grab his lunch box and make a dive for the door, naturally slamming it behind him.

At the onset of one such tirade the busy office had suddenly become very quiet, the girls in the tool stores suspending operations to listen to what was going on. Indeed the silence was complete and as it happened, timed perfectly for everyone to hear what caused the air to 'turn blue'. It came about with the irate driver trapping the tail of his raincoat in the door on his way out—it almost threw him off his feet. As he opened the door to release his mac, a big fireman, who cared for no-one, shouted 'Hey Fred.' The driver opened the door wider and poked his head round to see who had called him; his face was already a deep crimson as he snapped, 'What?' The fireman, as expected, said, 'Don't slam the door when you leave'. The driver took a step towards him, pointing his finger and trying to say something in a threatening voice. It ended in complete incoherence as he thought better of what he was trying to say anyway, so he backed, spluttering through the door, which he slammed, causing the office to shake and everyone to burst into uncontrollable laughter.

What sometimes happened was for drivers and firemen to stand in a group before the offending roster, while they argued and swore about the injustice of it all, while each would, from time to time, flash murderous glances in the general direction of the nervous-looking clerk.

Ironically, their real frustration usually began when on checking the list one day they found that at last someone had made a mistake; they were due to sign on at 08.00 hours. After checking to be absolutely sure they would go home feeling quite elated but alas, this was sometimes short-lived. The real trouble stemmed from the terribly long hours. There was a rule, as stated earlier, that each man must have at least twelve hours off between each turn of duty. Now, if he started at 08.00 hours and finished at 23.00 hours, he would find himself unable to report for duty again until 11.00 hours the next day. If on the next turn he did fourteen hours, then he would be due to start at 13.00 hours and so on. So it is easy to see that in next to no time he would find himself on evenings, then nights, and so it continued all through the war years.

Box Boy

The turn as box boy came round now and then, and this was still worked on three shifts. This, like so many other jobs, had its slack and busy times, but there was always something to do.

When the number of the engine and the time for lighting up was given to the box boy, all relative information was chalked up on a slate. He would set off at the appropriate time for each engine, carrying several lighters, waste and paraffin. This job only came my way on about three occasions so I was never very skilled at it. If I remember correctly, four lighters were enough to do the job providing everything went according to plan. Each of them was stuffed with a wad of cotton waste, which was then soaked in paraffin and a flame applied to each one, then as they began to flare up they were lobbed into the firebox of the engine, not too far forward, and as near the middle as possible. Next, some sizeable lumps of coal were picked out—these would perhaps range in size from lumps like a man's two fists, up to the size of a football—these were also in turn lobbed into the firebox. The object was to build them around and over the flaming lighters, but many a lump went astray. It often took two or three hundredweight of coal before the lighters were covered satisfactorily. When it looked as though the coal might begin to catch, the firebox was closed and the rear dampers opened. At this stage it could be safely left for a while, as the box boy attended to the next engine.

It didn't always work out that way, quite often the shed foreman would be breathing down the box boy's neck, while hurriedly brandishing his watch and telling him to get the engine in steam. Everything now was panic stations as the boy would go into his own particular routine, endeavouring to satisfy the foreman that not only was he doing the right things, but that he was also getting results.

The first thing to be done was to check the steam pressure gauge to see if any pressure registered. If it did he was in luck,. The blower handle would be turned, and depending entirely on the amount of steam available, a high or low volume of steam would be emitted from the chimney. This would have the immediate desired effect on the firebox, a draught of air would be drawn up through the dampers and begin to make the fire brighten up. After a few minutes the pile of, by now, burning coals would be gently disturbed with one of the long fire bars which every engine carried, though from time to time they had to be brought a fair distance from some other engine and the whole thing became a case of robbing Peter to pay Paul. The object now was to try and spread the fire as far over the surface of the box as possible, so that more selected lumps of coal could be added. There was, incidently, a very important thing to check and which had to be done before the fire was lit. It was vital

40

to ensure there was water in the boiler, without which serious damage and delay could be caused, so working the handle on the gauge would cause any water to bubble in the glass. Sometimes it would be difficult to see as the protecting glass was very thick and frequently discoloured, but once the water was disturbed it could usually be seen.

An engine in this condition, that is, an empty fire box and yet with some steam remaining, meant that it had at least been partially serviced, having obviously been rushed under the coal stage and its fire dropped, then quickly on to the firelighting area. On this occasion then, it was having to do without having its tubes cleaned and also missing its boiler wash. Even so the engine crew that would be taking it off shed would still be comparatively lucky. Quite often though it was imperative that certain engines were prepared and off shed in double quick time. On these occasions things really got moving. Someone, in fact anyone from the foreman to perhaps a cleaner with not may day's service, would bring an engine with plenty of steam and stop it alongside the engine being lit up.

There was a long flexible attachment, at the end of which was a length of metal pipe, bent at one end into a circle. Around the circle a lot of small holes were drilled, through which steam would rush. The flexible end was attached to the live engine, the circular end of the metal tubing was lowered into the chimney of the dead engine and the steam then turned on. The steam rushing out through the holes roared up the chimney, causing a powerful draught up through the fire bars, and the freshly-lit fire. The result of this operation was that steam was raised very much sooner than would otherwise have been possible.

One engine that was seldom hurriedly lighted in this manner was the one that was picked for the London run. There was usually plenty of time to light and prepare this engine; as they were important regular runs, a driver and fireman had at least an hour to prepare the engine. As mentioned before, the box boy was kept fully occupied between lighting engines, making firelighters and keeping containers filled with sand, which was situated over a stove to make sure it was thoroughly dried, so that there was a supply readily available for firemen preparing the engines.

Coaling the Mails

Yet one more job that was carried out in turn by the cleaners was coaling the mails. This was considered to be the plum job within the grade and was always looked forward to with eagerness. Usually two cleaners were sent together to do this job and as there were few mail trains passing through Gloucester on the Great Western each night, there was plenty of spare time to follow our own devices, which usually meant sitting in the corner of a dark cabin and nodding off, much to the envy of everyone else who were hurriedly going about their various duties.

About half an hour before a mail train was due to arrive, the foreman cleaner would fling open the rickety cabin door and thrust his lamp in. The effect of this yellow ray of light as it pierced the darkness of the cabin appeared, to our tired eyes, to have the intensity of a searchlight. 'Come on, you two' he would shout, 'It's time you were on your way to the station for the first mail. As he said this I was conscious of his hand going into his waistcoat pocket, from which he drew his railway watch, as though to emphasise the lateness of the hour, and though he shone his lamp on his watch I'm sure he didn't look at it—it seemed to be just a mechanical action which was common to all railwaymen with any authority. Although we weren't keen on being rudely awakened in this manner just as we had dozed off, we still preferred it to the other occasions, when he sent another cleaner to awaken us.

Usually, if this happened, we would never know who this person was. He was there and gone in a flash, pausing with the door open about ten inches, just long enough to lob in a large handful of smouldering waste, after which we would come to, coughing and choking, whereupon we would scramble to our feet, hurriedly clawing our way into the pitch darkness along the walls of the cabin, eventually bursting out into the fresh air, where we would spend the next few minutes cursing, gasping, and rubbing our eyes. After the smoke had cleared a little, one of us would venture back into the cabin, groping our way along the seat searching for our little lamp, which was already trimmed but as yet unlit. On locating this lamp, whoever had volunteered to make the attempt would once more make a hasty dive for the door. This lamp was known as a gauge lamp, and its proper use was for illuminating the water gauge glass on the engines during the hours of darkness. It was a small lamp; in the front was a plain glass, one side red, the other side green, and was for general use on the engine. It could be taken from its bracket and used by the firemen in the darkness, especially while stationary, and was also useful for picking one's way past obstacles when it was necessary to go to the signal box. But quite a few of these lamps were used around the engine shed by cleaners and other lowly individuals, while the foremen all carried the big interchanging lights, as used by the train guards.

Taking our lamp, we would set off as fast as we could, giving due care to where we were stepping. Apart from the rails, crossover points, signal rods, and wires, there were many obstacles that may not have been there when we last had occasion to go that way. Amongst other things there were fire bars and shovels, which, when stepped upon, had a nasty habit of rearing up handle first, causing anyone walking up close behind to trip and fall headlong. Another dangerous obstacle was the odd smoke plate, discarded by someone from an engine. In shape these smoke plates somewhat resembled a five gallon oil drum, minus top and bottom, and tapered diagonally, similar to the blade of a garden trowel when lying on the floor; it was just about shin high and very dangerous to walk into. The most lethal thing of all were the handles for operating crossover points. These were used extensively in shunting yards, engine sheds, or anywhere off the main line. These handles were about three feet high and very dangerous to walk into. Once we were out of the shed area, we had the added danger of trains on the main line. It was so easy to have your senses so occupied by a train starting out from the station, up past the engine shed, that you would be unaware of a train coming down, which would certainly be unheard until it was very close; engine lights could not be relied on as they were quite often unlit; either they had blown out, or, as was more often the case, run out of paraffin.

After several minutes of picking our way through these various hazards, we emerged at last into the pale platform lights, which cast wraithlike shadows of hand barrows, seats, or sacks of mail waiting for the train we were here to meet, along with several other objects.

As what appeared as a pale moving mass began taking human shapes, we began to derive some consolation from the fact that we were not the only idiots prowling around at this hour of the morning. I think that I can safely say that, in those days, the station platform was never clear of people, quite often there were hundreds, almost everyone in uniform of some description, even if only in overalls!

Anyone walking on to Gloucester station today could hardly be blamed for being unable to imagine the amount of activity that went on night and day, all round the clock. The uniforms somehow appeared part of the station, as no matter how many days or hours went by before I next approached the platform, nothing ever appeared to have changed.

The RTO office—a travel information office for the armed forces—was busy as always with perhaps ten people crowding round the little counter, waiting to make enquiries about trains and passes, with quite often a small queue outside the door. Some people would be casting anxious glances in the direction from which they thought their train may at any second appear.

Meanwhile a seemingly endless stream of people, men and women, not to mention railway staff, were entering or leaving the one-time refreshment room, now known as the canteen, where they purchased the only thing that was sometimes available—watery railway tea! I am not running the railway tea down really, I believe it to be a fair and accurate description, even so I can recall many times after we had been on duty approaching twenty hours, when my mate and I could have used half a bucketful each, but that is a later story. Many other people, who had perhaps already slaked their thirst, were sitting on seats, porters' trolleys, barrows or on their kit. Others were half asleep in every conceivable position, some stretched out, some curled up. Others sitting with their heads down between their knees appeared fast asleep. In this ghostly light some of the scenes were reminiscent of my recent visit to Pompeii. Naturally, while these people were engaged in the various pursuits, the one big thing they all had in common was never far away.

Every so often the station pilot would rumble down light through the station, only to pick up some coaches with which to make up a train, then blast its way back up in the other direction, disturbing conversations, and sometimes causing smoke to come wafting along under the platform roof, while in the distance an engine could be heard working very hard up the bank, coming from the South Wales direction with a coal train.

It came into view over the bridge that spans London Road, still pulling hard and making a terrible din that appeared to be echoing from one end of the town to the other; for just a brief moment the silence, when it came, was almost deafening in the other extreme. As the huge black mass loomed slowly out of the darkness with much hissing and rumbling, the injector could be seen spluttering steam and water alternately. The fireman obviously being otherwise occupied at the moment with the handbrake, was unable to adjust it, so that the water could be forced into the boiler and not spilt, as was now happening. As the fireman applied his handbrake hard, the buffers of each truck could be heard as it came over the bridge and started to run downhill, and banged against the one in front. Now, as the full weight of the train came against the engine the driver applied his brake. The brake shoes could be heard grinding against the engine 'tyres' (so called because these were replaceable, being made separately to the wheels) and long streams of sparks could be seen in the darkness coming from the direction of the wheels, as the engine ground its way toward the end of the platform where the engine crew would be relieved, provided their luck held. The crews could never be sure of this, as I was to discover later. The trucks were now passing, each one in turn bumping or banging twice as its two sets of wheels spanned the joints in the rails, the whole train now going slower and slower, until at last it stopped and a few of the trucks rebounded a foot or so, as the buffers decompressed slightly.

During the time this has been happening, the boiler has been topped up and the engine is now blowing off steam as another sound descends upon the comparative silence; a goods train goes smartly down through the station in the other direction, over the bridge and soon the three red lights of the guard's van disappear into the darkness as a driver and fireman make their way along the platform, to relieve the recently-arrived freight train in the station.

The lad I am working with on this job started to make some comment about the mail train being late when a clatter almost above our heads told us that it was signalled in. I glanced in the direction of Horton Road crossing and sure enough I could see the two dim headlights, one above the right hand buffer, one top centre signifying that this rapidly approaching train was an express, paper or mail train. Even now, as I stopped to look back, it was giving quite a lurch as it swung through the crossover points from the through road to the platform siding. If I remember correctly, these particular points were known as 'scissors' and it seemed to me a very apt description.

As though someone had fired a starting pistol, it seemed as if every person on the down platform moved at the same instant, as this beautiful big green, albeit uncleaned, 'Castle' came charging in, apparently in great haste, passing all the people who were hurriedly grabbing their various kit in readiness to make a dive for some spot on the train. Seats seldom came in anyone's priorities; the important thing was to get in through the first available door.

As the train made its way to the far end of the station, a bright stream of firelight from the engine firebox marked its progress. It lit up everything in view, not missing even a cigarette end. The brakes which had been partially applied well before entering the station were now making themselves heard; they varied from a high pitched squeal to a low shuddering moaning noise, but the important thing was that they were doing their job. The next instant the whole thing was at a complete halt.

The train seemed to be bursting its sides, as practically every door was thrown open and people began hurriedly entering or leaving. Weaving our way through this throng and heaps of mail and parcels, we ran the remainder of the way to where the engine had come to a halt by the water column. Stopping at a water column, with a long train of passenger coaches, called for great skill and attention to detail.

With an engine on a goods train it was always possible to pull forward a foot, or even reverse a little, in order to adjust the position of the filler hole in the water tank in relation to the water column. With a passenger train, especially a mail train in the darkness, it was very different. The driver needed to be right first time; he couldn't begin to pull forward or push backwards to adjust his position with passengers entering and leaving, and mail being loaded.

In order that the bag on the column could be left in the tank with the water running while the firemen attended to other matters, either pulling coal forward, making up the fire, or perhaps working the injector, the column arm needed to be almost exactly above the opening in the tank. Although water could still be obtained if the engine was a little out of position, the fireman would have to give the wet slippery bag constant attention because if the bag was entering the hole diagonally he would have to support the weight of water between the end of the metal arm and the point where the bag disappeared into the tank. If the distance was too great, he would be unable to hold the weight and the end of the bag would fly out, drenching anyone nearby.

Here was a scene which in those days was by no means unique, but never to be forgotten by the people present, at the same time never to be authentically re-enacted; perhaps it was the feverish way everyone worked, their hurried movements and gestures, whether giving information of importance or just making idle comment. Come to think of it, I wish it were possible to faithfully reconstruct that scene, partly for my own enjoyment, but also so that many thousands of steam enthusiasts, who have really missed something, could steep themselves in the nostalgic atmosphere which surrounded an incident such as this.

The Castle was rather quiet now; any noise there might be was coming from the injector and this was occasionally drowned by the platform activity. The rays of light from the flickering fire hole doors repeatedly stabbed the gloomy light on the platform, violently throwing shadows left and right, as the driver and fireman moved this way and that, while they busied themselves about the footplate and perhaps wondered if anyone was turning up on this trip to give some much needed assistance before they set off in great haste for Cardiff.

Nothing could be relied upon at this time, so the thing to do was not to hang about waiting for help, but rather, get stuck in before that annoying little rattling noise occurred, which always heralded the signal dropping, usually before you were ready.

Gloucester Central Station in November 1963 and a hive of activity. Small Prairie 4564 blows off whilst waiting for its next move. In front of it, platform staff off-load a Gresley pigeon van whilst in one of the centre roads Hall class 6993 stands alongside a parcels train of mixed stock.   *(B. J. Ashworth)*

46

In order to eliminate as much glare from the fire as possible, blackout sheets were fixed on hooks on the rear edge of the cab roof; on the coal tender were fixed large low-tensioned springs which held the tarpaulin fairly taut above that part of the footplate, which would have otherwise been fully exposed to the night sky, and naturally presented a pretty good target for enemy aircraft. These sheets sometimes caused the cab and footplate generally to get very hot when the fireman was working hard, and although it was possible to stick your head out and snatch a few quick breaths of cold air, there was not much to be done about occasional condensation, which, of course, made conditions less pleasant.

As we climbed onto the footplate the fireman disappeared down the far side. I knew where he was going and scrabbled up over the coal to the water tank. As I lifted up the heavy lid I could see the water pipe on the water column just about shoulder high; the moon was shining quite brightly now and there was a touch of frost developing. The fireman swung the chain towards me and as it rattled against the side of the tender I caught it, then as he released the catch holding the arm which would swing round and reach the tank filler hole, I began pulling it towards me. I grabbed the long leather funnel, which was known as the bag, pulling it through my hands as I would a piece of rope. I found the end and pushed it down into the tank. 'OK!' I said, and he turned the water on. As can be imagined, when there was a hard frost and the bag was frozen, it was different altogether, though in severe weather there was sometimes a fire devil beneath the arm of the column.

The driver was by this time down on the track, that is, on the right hand side of the engine. He had the flare lamp and oil can and was looking at the right hand big end bearing. He must have been a little concerned about it because it was the only oiling he did.

As he climbed back to the footplate, the fireman shouted 'Shut that injector off for us mate'. I didn't hear his mate's reply but the noise of the injector suddenly ceased, so he had obviously heard.

While all this was taking place, my partner was working like a trojan at the coal, hauling large lumps forward, breaking some with the pick and stacking them at the rear of the footplate to form a rough barrier against the coal he would stack behind. I could hear the water as it neared the top of the tank now, as it came right up it was visible in the moonlight. 'That will do', I shouted, and the fireman began spinning the control handle whereupon the water stopped. I pushed the still dripping bag over the side and then the chain which the fireman grabbed, and pulled the whole thing into a parked position. The fireman climbed back on to the engine and I could hear the engine crew talking as I scrabbled back over the coal to join my mate, where we quickly finished off filling the hole, afterwards straightening our backs before climbing back on to the footplate. The fireman began shovelling coal on; he immediately spoiled my mate's nice barrier and coal tumbled forward towards his feet. He put about a dozen shovels full on, pushed the shovel under and into the coal and then opened the firebox doors slightly, turning on the blower a little, so the smoke which had previously begun to get to us was suddenly no more.

As we stepped on to the platform the fireman swept the coal dust from the footplate. Using the injector briefly he then made everything nice and fresh with the scalding hot water from the pep pipe. We stood near the engine subconsciously waiting for the right of way. As there came a slight whisper from the safety valve, all along the train things now appeared to be as an ants' nest on a hot summer afternoon. Doors slammed at irregular intervals, and away in the distance the guard could be seen, still showing a white light, which we knew would change suddenly any second now.

The engine started to blow off steam with a sudden roar; this is always music to the fireman's ears even if it is sometimes a little rough on them. The steam shot straight up from the top of the safety valve, looking pure white against the moonlit sky, but was soon spent in the frosty air; the wonder of it was that as fast as it disappeared it was immediately replaced in such a constant stream that it looked to be a white solid column. There came the sound of the guard's whistle and glancing towards the rear of the train we could see a green light. I heard the fireman say 'Rightaway' and as I looked in his direction I could see he was winding his hand brake off quickly. The driver was opening the ejector that would create vacuum for the brakes; as it reached its maximum it began making a spluttering noise and was then shut off.

I could see a movement the driver was making by the reflection of the fire and it was obvious that he was winding the engine into forward gear. Then came one shrill blast on the whistle; I suddenly realised I was holding my breath—waiting. Even with our short service on the railway we had heard all this quite a few times before, but each time it exceeded our expectations. It was magic.

It seemed to me there was a noise crossed between a hiss and a thump as the driver gave the regulator a little upward tug allowing steam to meet the first available piston with a seemingly irresistible force which was followed immediately by the first exhaust blast. This caused all heads to turn in the direction from which it came, then came the second, third and fourth and so on. Each of these early exhaust blasts seemed louder than the previous, the sheer magnitude would have to be heard in order to be appreciated to the full, and each produced an echo that slammed back and forth from one side of the station to the other. For a few seconds it was hard to be certain which were the echoes and which was the original sound.

As the engine left the station precincts the echoes became less discernible, as she climbed the short sharp gradient over London Road bridge, the locomotive became silhouetted against the frosty moonlit sky. The exhaust blasts were coming a little faster—still as loud as before. Somehow it seemed to be taking over as it were, attempting to engulf everything in the immediate area. Looking back now I still don't believe that out of perhaps four hundred people on that platform, I could have been the only one who got a feeling like a small cold key being pulled up and down my spine on a piece of cotton, while my pulse felt as though my heart had moved up to the back of my throat. As the engine began to level off over the bridge and start a slight descent towards 'Over Junction' the noise suddenly seemed to hesitate, then open up again, perhaps a little less noisy, as the driver wound the lever back—this would help effect economy on the fuel, as is one reason for changing to a higher gear in a car. It also prevented half the fire being blasted out of the chimney.

As the last few coaches went gliding past us it was just possible to see a faint glimmer of light through the odd window, but very little, for the main part none was visible. The guard's van went by quite fast as the train began picking up speed, the guard still keeping a sharp lookout to see that everything was OK. Had there been anything seriously wrong he could have stopped the train with his brake, and I do mean stop! I have been told that if operated fully, especially with the engine still pulling, it would quite possibly break a coupling and part the train in two.

The red lights on the rear of the van climbed the bank silently, sliding from my view as we turned and walked back along the platform, picking our way once more through objects and people.

Everything began to settle down once again as though the events of the last few minutes had never taken place. Just then the peace was temporarily shattered by the station pilot, pushing a few coaches up the centre track.

We stepped finally from the end of the platform into the world of rails shining in the moonlight, ballast, signal wires, and crossover points. Pausing, we could now faintly hear the familiar note of the 'Castle' as she was pounding away up the incline from 'Over' towards Highnam Bridge, before dropping towards Oakle Street and Grange Court station.

The two tracks, the GWR and LMS, crossed each other diagonally at Horton Road. Unless you were familiar with the railway setup it was confusing to say the least, especially for anyone travelling from Stonehouse towards Gloucester on either the LMS from Bristol or the GWR from London.

After leaving Stonehouse the two tracks converge and travel side by side for a few miles before parting again at Tuffley. The LMS ran straight down into Gloucester, while the GWR veered off to the right, then swept left in an arc, coming to rest in the station, facing in the opposite direction. The high covered footbridge which once connected the two stations has long since gone, together with the old LMS Eastgate station.

As we picked our way on towards the engine shed, I heard an engine whistle. It was an LMS express just pulling out from Eastgate station heading towards Birmingham. I've no idea what type it was, but wondered at the vast difference in the sounds produced by the two engines.

The GWR engines, whether two or four-cylindered, produced four beats to each complete rotation of the driving wheels. This LMS engine, on the other hand, was a three-cylinder, so there were six beats to every rotation. Obviously the amount of noise made

49

by each exhaust depended how hard the engine was being worked. It was necessary to have a heavy blast on the fires of these GWR engines because they used slow-burning Welsh steam coal; this was why the GWR engines made more noise generally than others; it fell on the ears sharp and crisp.

The LMS was now going past Horton Road crossing and the engine could still be easily heard, though compared to the 'Castle' it sounded rather muffled. As mentioned they were apparently less noisy because they burned faster-burning house coal, consequently much less blast was needed on the fire. Indeed, I have no idea how much one of them could be coaxed or, for that matter, bullied into burning Welsh steam coal. I never experienced that situation on an LMS but have found myself with fast-burning house coal on one of the GWR engines on more than one occasion. This was no joke because although it burned very quickly and it was easier to keep up the steam pressure, the coal went up the chimney almost as fast as I could shovel it in.

I don't know how accurate the story was but I did hear of the fireman who set off for London on the 'Cheltenham Flyer' with a tender of house coal, not, I might add, from choice. The normal procedure, I was told, was that when the London train arrived in Paddington the crew would take the engine to the shed, have their food, take water, quickly fill the hole, look over the engine generally, do the oiling, then have a rest for the return journey.

Apparently on the run in question, the fireman was practically sweeping the tender out when they reached Old Oak Common, which meant them having little fire left either. On top of having all the usual chores to attend to, the crew also had to go under the coal tip, which left them with a dirty footplate and a thick coat of dust on everything they touched. This would have to be swilled away from the footplate, the tool boxes, shovel and fire irons. Then oily waste would be wiped over the pipes and all the controls. The fire would also have to be made right up in readiness for the run home.

By now we were crossing over several sets of rails that were part of the shed area, where there were several engines in various stages of lighting up, and some were actually prepared. We picked our way more carefully now, because we were back amongst the obstacles, finally groping our way into the cabin. The lamp had been left outside after having been extinguished, so as not to betray our whereabouts for a while at least. The cabin was not only very dark inside, it was also hot and stuffy, this being brought about by the little tortoise-type stove that was seldom allowed to go out. The long bench seats which ran the full length of the cabin on either side were empty. With a contented sigh coming from one side, and a faint grunt from the other, we slid down on to the benches, hoping it would be ages before the old chargehand would come down for us to go down to meet the Down paper train.

The next thing I knew was a lamp shining in my eyes, with the old chap saying, 'Come on Boyo, get down to that station. I'll see to it that you don't have time to sleep tomorrow night'. We clambered to our feet and got a light for our lamp, setting off once again for the station, where everything would appear like it did last time, through our bleary eyes.

It seemed very cold to us now after the stuffy airless cabin; my mouth tasted like a coal scuttle and I coughed a few times, partly because it was necessary, partly because it seemed the right thing to do. I pushed my hands down into my pockets as far as they would go, then with my shoulders hunched up level with my ears, stumbled after the other lad.

A well-loaded parcels train heads into Gloucester past Over Junction with 4-6-0 No. 4956 Plowden Hall in charge. The Docks branch can ben seen converging on the left, whilst in the middle distance stands Over Junction signal box and the commencement of the Ledbury branch.   (Author's Collection)

Italians and the Cleaners' Cabin

While on a day shift during my first few weeks on the job, and whilst still engaged on some of the jobs I have mentioned, I joined the new starters who were going to the cleaners' cabin to have their food. I understand that in pre-war days it was for the exclusive use of the cleaners—for there was quite a large gang who were engaged in exactly what the job implied, cleaning engines. We were, however, obliged to share it with the Italian prisoners of war, or go elsewhere.

Looking back, I can't think why we ever ventured into the place, but being rather young, plus the fact that time was approaching when we would tolerate anything, I suppose there was some excuse. It would have been an ideal setting for a nightmare. I got the impression that in the past the walls had been treated to the occasional smear of whitewash, but this practice had eventually been curtailed for some period of time; the way things were I couldn't imagine them being done again for the duration.

There were dark dusty wooden benches fixed all around the wall, and a huge bench-come-table near one end. This had a habit of changing ends, depending who the previous occupants were. The only light was a single gas mantle and the whole place had an almost anaesthetic effect on those who approached its portals, with tired eyes that had also been subjected to acrid smoke, seeping from chimneys of several engines in various stages of readiness, and perhaps only seconds earlier having squinted in the sunshine.

There were people in front of me and behind me and I entered somewhat hesitantly; it was not easy to see who was there for a few seconds until my eyes began to get used to the gloom. The floor consisted of large flat stones and I was standing in what had to be coal dust. Dressed in dirty overalls, it made little difference where I sat. I had made out two dim figures near one corner, and as I turned to put my bag on the seat, I suppose I realised that they could only be trying to light a fire, and yet when the almost blinding flash came, it caught me unawares. As the flames increased it lit up those black faces with eyes that seemed to get bigger and shine brighter every fraction of a second, except those that were watering from the smoke and a suspicion of paraffin vapour!

When my eyes became used to the conditions, I started in amazement at the scene. The fireplace was huge, it looked as though it could take a hundredweight of coal at any one time, and frequently had done. The dead ashes lay in a huge heap, stretching almost a yard out on to the floor; these I later discovered were occasionally taken away by wheelbarrow. The whole looked something like I imagined a miniature grumbling volcano would appear. There was, at that instant, a loud clatter of boots on the floor, as somewhere over in the darkness, a thin, normally white-faced man with glassy eyes, swung his feet to the floor; he had obviously been asleep and as he scrambled into a semi-standing position he stared uncertainly around, then sank back on to the bench and I thought to myself 'that poor chap must have thought he was in Hell'!

The fire was now settling down and someone came in carrying two big iron kettles which were placed on the fire with a long metal rod. In no time, it seemed, there was steam and water being emitted from both spouts. Tea cans were produced and everyone busied themselves with their meagre tea rations, making a can of tea as the boiling water became available, and before it could indeed boil away.

This was my first time in this place at a meal break and I didn't quite know what to expect. It was also my first encounter with Italian prisoners, who I had seen down in the yard supposedly shovelling ashes; I certainly didn't expect the events that followed in the next half hour, before I groped my way back out into the daylight to carry on with whatever job I was doing on that particular day.

There was a clattering of boots, then a lot of chattering in a foreign tongue as the door suddenly flew open. About six of these prisoners came in carrying a 'devil'—that is the name for an oil drum with one end cut away and many holes punched all around the sides and bottom. This they stood on bricks and iron rods, supported on anything suitable to keep the drum off the floor so that plenty of air could get at the fire built inside.

Others carried cooking pots, billy cans and frying pans; these they handed over to the person who was brought along as cook. They threw ready-chopped kindling wood into the 'devil' and soon had a small bright fire going. Luckily the cabin was rather lofty and there were large ventilation holes leading back into the main engine shed. It was always a matter of luck, or the way of the wind, whether smoke left this cabin and drifted into the outer shed, or whether the smoke from the engines behind came into us.

As I searched my bag for a bread and fish paste sandwich, I could hardly believe what I was seeing. I realised that this fire was in the middle of the cabin and that a large pan was placed on top of it. Into the pan went twelve persons' ration of butter for one week—three half pounds! As the butter melted potato scallops were put in to fry, and another pan containing sausages was placed on our, now vacant, fire, and yet another half pound of butter, and eggs, followed the last sausage; then coffee was made. When the coffee was poured I was amazed to see unlimited sugar and something I had not seen since before the war—Nestles full cream condensed sweetened milk.

By the time they were all settled with their sausages, eggs and scallops, bread and butter and coffee, we were all looking on, almost drooling at the sight and smell of

53

this practically unobtainable food. Most of us had ceased to delve into our bags—in the sight of all this, it didn't seem worthwhile somehow.

When the charge-hand cleaner stuck his head round the door and shouted something about starting work, it came almost as a relief. I had seen enough to unbalance me for one day, anyway the engines' smoke was beginning to prevail and the cabin was taking more than its fair share of it.

As we gathered our cans and bags to leave, one of these so-called prisoners leaned back, patted his bloated stomach, and said with a leering grin, something like, 'Issa goota for prissonairs', I answered, 'Yes, but I know something that would have done you more good before now, and it is usually administered quite cold'. As I left I promised myself that I would not use that place again; it was not only the Italians and their food, but also the smoke, dirt and lack of light.

We walked through the shed towards daylight. I said to a cleaner who was nearest me, 'What do you think of that lot then?' He said, 'What's that?' I said, 'That food they had in there—I thought they were prisoners of war'. He told me that was the usual procedure, that he was used to it and that no one was surprised any more. I said 'Good God, we are all going mad. That was altogether two pounds of butter he put in that pan, sixteen people's ration for a whole week'. He said, 'I would have liked to have got outside some of them sausages'. As it was obvious I was not getting through to him I thought I might as well let the matter drop, anyway the sunlight was affecting my eyes, so I had other things to occupy my mind. I wasn't really interested in things like sausages, potato scallops, eggs, bread and butter and sweet coffee!

Food Rations Again

I have mentioned the lack of food once or twice and casting my mind back I am trying to remember just what food was available.

I think I am correct in saying that we were allowed 2oz. butter, 2ozs. margarine, 2ozs. cheese, (4ozs. for manual workers), 4ozs. bacon, 2ozs. tea, 8ozs. sugar per week. Things like cereals, tins of spam, corned beef etc. were worked on a monthly points system. One person's points would allow one of these items for a month.

As the war progressed we would find that odd items were suddenly on ration. Milk was on ration and I think one of the final items was bread, which, of course, was far from white but we became used to it and there was usually enough to last the week out. So it can be seen why I always carried a handful of shallots and salt. Incidently, I think that salt was about the one thing that was not rationed.

There was always a railway canteen but we could never use it because we could be sent to relieve a train at any time. It was obviously well patronised by the clerical staff, who were doing mainly an eight hour shift, usually all on days.

Shed Labouring

A few days after this incident I was asked by the chargehand cleaner if I was interested in going on to shed labouring; two new cleaners were starting and I, or some other cleaner, could be spared for this job. As I already knew there would be a few more shillings in my pay and that I would do no more calling up, I immediately said that I would accept.

It still involved three shifts, so that meant that once more I encountered the prisoners, though not at very close quarters. If I was on two till ten, they left at four, so that was only two hours. While in the morning, six till two meant four hours. They arrived about 9am, and by the time they started their way to the job, with much haggling on the way, it was usually 9.30. Then they ambled away about one o'clock.

I was sent with the two older men down to the track, where the fires were being dropped. There were piles of cinders and some large pieces of clinker—these we had to shovel up into the wagons brought along for this purpose. When a fresh wagon was started things weren't too bad, we were able to have the side door down, but once the ashes had risen so that there were the odd few rolling back out, it was necessary to heave this heavy door up, and then the real work started. For a beginner engaged on that particular operation it was soon obvious that this was going to be one more never-to-be-forgotten experience. Apart from the physical effort needed to shovel this stuff over the side of the truck, the side of which must have been 8ft. high at least, I realised that this, as with many other labouring jobs, also needed a lot of skill in order to make a tidy job, not to mention the easiest way of doing it for, as usual, it had to be done for more or less eight hours. I attacked my bit of ash, anxious to make a good impression on these old hands—I didn't want them to be in a position to tell the chargehand or foreman that I was not up to the job and so risk going back with the other cleaners.

I was shown how to enter the blade of the shovel wherever I could, then instead of pushing vainly with my arms, to push the inside of my right knee against the back of my right hand, which was on the shovel handle; not only can almost all the body weight go behind it, a constant pressure can be kept on the shovel while the handle is wriggled from side to side, or up and down, then there is every chance of by-passing any obstruction. After a while I got the hang of this, and the result was that not only was I nearer getting the job done, but needed about a quarter of the effort. This has saved a lot of energy during my life, because whatever I have had to shovel I have found myself automatically using my knee.

There was still the problem of getting the ashes off the shovel into the truck—this took longer to perfect as it was not so simple to explain, in fact, had they not been able to demonstrate, I would have taken a long time to get used to it. I welcomed the chance to straighten my back so that I might watch how the job was done. It was surprising how much work they got through in the following few minutes, each tried to outdo the other. I, for my part, appeared almost spellbound by their efforts as I peered this way and that from one to the other. Each time they looked as though they were going to stop the demonstration, I would put on a sort of puzzled or worried look, so that they kept on a while longer until eventually, to avoid appearing completely daft, I intimated that I was ready to give it another try.

I was amazed at what I was able to achieve in this field with practice; I was able to shovel any substance with perhaps the exception of feathers, delivering a shovel full virtually intact. Water is not so easy to move by this method, but with practice one can get a surprise.

I may be asked who on earth wants to boast of being able to deliver a shovel full of sand, for example, 14ft., keeping almost every grain together? I would answer, from my present day observations, very few people. The point I am trying to make is that it should not be underestimated.

There was a more pleasant side even to that job—it wasn't always hot and sticky, with dust sticking to your arms, face, down your shirt and into your socks, making the ankles filthy. On a cold morning it could be almost pleasant with all the activities that went on in the yard. Each time something happened, be it a train going up the main line, or an engine moved on the shed, we would pause and look, usually making some comment about each event, before getting back to the job.

After I had been on the job for some weeks I realised that my first impression on the day that I had first reported to the shed, of how dangerous Horton Road crossing was, was justified. This crossing was very dangerous because, just for good measure, it would seem that there were also two LMS sidings, used quite often for shunting goods wagons.

It was quite tricky in daylight, but at night it was very bad. If the LMS were shunting it was necessary to take an opportunity to cross their track and stand watching the up and down signal, straining eyes and ears for anything looming out of the darkness; up traffic was no problem—they were heard without a doubt—but down traffic was quite different.

Imagine one of the worst situations, when it is a dark night with driving rain, an engine is shunting about 6ft. behind, and a train is coming down with perhaps one, or even both, of its lights extinguished. You watch whoever appears to be an experienced railwayman and stand by him, hoping he is stood astride the right track.

I was present on one occasion when several did get it wrong. Luckily I was well behind or I would have been trampled, when in the last few seconds someone realised they had all got it wrong and shouted, as he leaped back with his bike. I have

56

never seen so many bikes at one time being snatched up onto the hind wheels, or dragged by the handle bars, with the pedals scraping the gravel walkway. It could have been very bad, but I never did hear of anyone being hit.

There were many engines going on and off the shed, and we witnessed most of these operations while we straightened our backs for a few seconds.

An engine coming on shed usually attracted our attention by starting off from the station quite quickly, more so than had it been drawing a train. Then it was suddenly shut off, immediately beginning to make all sorts of noises within a wide range of hissing, whistling, and quite a bit of clanging before finally coming to a halt just past the points, near the small signal. Four short blasts on the whistle would result in the points and signal being set to allow the engine to come on shed. If it had to work the return trip, for example, to Cardiff, it would go on to the turntable to be facing in the right direction, all set for when the time came to go 'off shed'. The engine crew would have time to get their engine ready for the return run, taking water, shovelling coal forward, filling the hole, oiling and checking and finally generally cleaning the footplate generally before going back to the station to rejoin their train.

One thing I forgot to mention, which I suspect all crews do before all else—boil the tea can! The means by which the tea can was boiled was the use of the shovel— it was placed near the tip of the long blade and gently entered in through the firebox door, where it would boil in a matter of seconds.

The turntable fascinated me. It always looked, as did its surroundings, black and grimy, not to mention cumbersome, but when an engine and tender weighing well over one hundred tons was placed in a central position, it came into its own, showing what a beautifully balanced piece of engineering it was. One man could turn an engine on these turntables without undue effort, though it was necessary to dig the toes into the ashes in order to get it in motion initially.

The operation of dropping down empty wagons on the coal stage, as mentioned earlier, held my attention for some days. Indeed, I think I can say I was fascinated by it. There always seemed an element of risk involved, so much so that I was continually expecting something to go wrong with either the brake of the wagon failing, the man's brake stick breaking, or some other failure, be it mechanical or human. Though nothing ever went wrong with this operation, I found it a constant source of excitement.

The time came eventually when I no longer watched what was going on. I think I must have tired of waiting for one or two wagons to get away down the bank at full pelt, ending up somewhere in Great Western Road, having first done a mystery trip through stop blocks, parcel shed and fence.

This was my first experience of shovelling for any length of time. It hardened my hands after the initial, inevitable, blisters; it also started to tone up my muscles for what was to follow in a few months time.

Naturally I got to know the men I was working with better each day. I realised that although they were doing a thankless hard dirty job, day in day out, seven days a week, probably for the rest of their working life, there was a lot to learn from them.

They didn't appear to demand much from life as far as I could see. Outside their family life, cigarettes and beer seemed to be their only goal, both of which seemed to be difficult to come by. I learned later that in most cases those who did menial jobs around the shed were men who had at least one regret in life; they had failed in some way to get onto the footplate, or had been on and had been forced off by health, usually failing eyesight. The worst of it was that in most cases many had been fostering a burning ambition to be engine drivers, often from a very early age. Whatever the reason that led to their particular situation, it marred the rest of their life. Not only did they somehow appear--and were often felt--to be failures while socialising with their mates who had been more fortunate, but they gradually became the poor neighbours as they and their families began to drop out of their normal social activities, because their wages could in no way be compared with that of a driver or fireman.

I found myself eating my lunch at this particular time in the company of an ex-driver with defective eyesight. He had come off the expresses, but as he was very near to retiring I don't think he was very put out about it. He gave me the history of the men I was working with, which made me feel very sorry for them. As a result of these accounts of bad luck I began to admire them for the quiet resigned manner in which they carried on with the job, with few grumbles. When the time came for me to leave them to start a different duty, I realised I held them in rather high esteem.

Tom Evans and Boiler Washing

The move from ash loading to boiler washing came early in the New Year. I can't say I was sorry because the weather was beginning to get at me, not being used to it— admittedly we did take shelter from most of the falling weather, but this was unofficial and really depended on who was around at the time.

I was standing against the corner of the coal stage on this January morning, seeking some sort of shelter from a shower of sleet whilst directly overhead was a track carrying coal wagons. Some of the sleet was still falling on me and so I observed, was a lot of coal dust from the activities above. I was just beginning to wonder which was the greater evil when the chargehand cleaner came round the corner. He told me they were trying to make up one more team of two for boiler washing duties. This would still be labouring rate as opposed to cleaners' rate. Furthermore, without a shadow of doubt it would also be warmer—this turned out to be a bit of an understatement, as I soon found out!

I readily agreed to accept this new job, not that I liked the sound of it very much, but he had assured me it would be warmer than where I was at the moment. Looking round me I thought he must be telling the truth. He told me I would be working with Tom Evans; I told him that I had heard of Tom Evans but did not know him. He looked at me with disbelief written all over his face and said, 'Don't be so bloody daft boyo, everybody knows Tom Evans, now go and report to him'. With that I set off smartly in the direction of the shed, where I was pretty sure he would be found, but I could have passed him without knowing.

I asked the old ex-driver I had been eating my sandwiches with. He looked at me with a frown, applied a light to his pipe, then keeping his eyes on me, as he peered through the puffs of smoke, he said, 'If you really don't know Tom Evans come to the time office at 2pm. He is due on duty then—I shall be pinning up some notices on speed restrictions, I'll point him out to you'.

I thanked him, after confirming that I would keep the rendezvous. I felt I had made some headway towards carrying out my orders, then I suddenly began to feel like a bit of an idiot, after all I didn't even know Tom Evans, but apparently everyone else did.

At about 1.55pm I made my way to the time office, so that there was little chance of me missing my new work mate. In view of the difficulty I had experienced so far, I didn't want this to happen.

Standing in front of the engineman and fireman's famous duty roster, my eyes had moved about half way down, when the door opened and closed, someone raised the glass shutter and said, 'Book me on please'. Hearing a voice reply 'OK Tom' I quickly looked round and instinctively knew that this was the man I was looking for.

I can best describe him as a muscular version of John Wayne, with a pleasant face, fair thinning hair, dressed in shabby working trousers, light black shoes, and one of his short-sleeved, open-necked khaki shirts. He had already taken his jacket off—it appeared to make him uncomfortable, as ties do to men who don't normally wear them but find they have no choice when attending certain functions. Uncomfortable or not, he made me feel cold. I approached him to confirm that I was correct in my assumption that he was indeed Tom Evans, and he replied, 'Yes, who wants me?' I told him that I was supposed to join him on the job, starting on the afternoon shift next day. He told me to follow him muttering something like, 'We'll see about that'!

First he found the chargehand cleaner and after some heated argument with a fair bit of swearing, we all made our way to the shed foreman's office, where it all started again. It seems he had nothing against me personally, how could he? He didn't even know me. The real trouble was that I was fairly small, under-fed, and sixteen and a half years old. This was a man's job—he couldn't see how he could keep up a quota of three engine boiler washes per shift, helped by only a lad!

The foreman explained that there was no other way he could fix it to keep everything going, somehow they would have to put lads on this job whether Tom liked it or not. After all he said, 'You're as good as three blokes Tom'. 'I know that' came the reply, 'But I can't be in three places at once'. But that was not quite how he put it! He said 'Come on' to me and burst out through the door. I was trying to keep up with him, at the same time keeping at what I thought was a discreet distance.

We entered the boiler washers' cabin. He threw his jacket down on the long bench-like seat, and, grabbing a poker, attacked the little tortoise stove, threatening to wrench it from its chimney. Luckily it appeared to realise the perilousness of the situation and perked up no end, causing him to relent and throw the poker down into the ring of steel that formed a sort of hearth-come-base.

He appeared to calm down quickly, and talking quite calmly now he enquired my name. He seemed amused when I told him and wanted to know if I was a relation of Charlie Trigg—a well-known Gloucestershire jockey of the 'twenties. I said that Charlie was not a close relative but I knew him well as he was still living at Minsterworth and was now very deaf. (This led to some funny incidents, particularly on buses and in church, always causing great amusement amongst the lads.)

Tom said, 'I can't keep calling Douglas all day and night. 'I shall call you Jockey' and that's that'. So it began and I was known as Jockey for the rest of my time on the job. He asked if I hadn't any overalls and I said, 'Well, I've got these'. They were trouser and jacket type which were issued to potential footplate staff, as well as those actually engaged on the bottom rung of the ladder. 'They won't do', he said, 'Five minutes and your trousers will be full of hot cinders; they won't so much burn as irritate. No, you will have to have boiler suits', and off he went to demand some.

His hurried departure on his stilt-like clogs which not only increased his already

60

considerable height, but made him walk, or hobble, in an awkward manner, made him look a bit comical to me and I was suddenly conscious of laughing to myself. This caused a pair of footplate men, who were strangers to me, to look at me a bit suspiciously as they passed on their way to the foreman's office.

Next afternoon I reported for duty at two o'clock; we didn't use the twenty-four-hour clock much at that time.

Tom was already there, and he produced two sets of boiler suits for me. I thanked him, quickly putting on one set, all the time wondering where his were—he didn't wear them, just overall trousers, a khaki shirt and the very comical wooden clogs, covered in coal dust, grease and oil.

Tom lit the lamp, tossed me a huge piece of very sooty rolled-up hessian sacking, and said, 'Here, you'll need this. Right then, let's make a start.'

As I followed him out of the daylight into the dimly-lit smoky atmosphere, carrying my piece of sacking and one of the large spanners necessary for the job, I was not very enthusiastic, to say the least.

Boiler washing began with the removal of the mud hole doors. These were oval pieces of casting four or five inches long and about three inches across, on which a bolt or stud was fixed in the centre. These were situated at the top and bottom of the boiler; the lower ones were usually found between two of the wheels or else were accessible between the spokes, and the top ones were reached by climbing along the outside of the engine, hanging on by one hand and working with the other. After removing the nut and securing bridge, one of the bottom doors was given a sharp tap and the muddy slush and water rushed out, splashing anything in reach, before running off the walkway down into the engine pits. Once the initial deluge was gone, the rest of the doors were removed, then all the boiler plugs were removed, enabling us to start the actual washing out of the boiler. The amount of sludge that came out sometimes would need to be seen to be appreciated.

Large hoses were connected to those stand pipes in the centre of the walkway; there was a nozzle on the end which was small in comparison. When the water was turned on and boosted with steam, the force of the jet leaving the nozzle was rather hectic. I have had the pipe wrench itself from my hands when I have been half asleep, causing much havoc in the shed, with drivers scrabbling from beneath engines they were preparing and other boiler washer gangs shouting and running. Worst of all it upset Tom, causing him to throw himself into a frenzy.

After Tom had done the first part of the wash, pushing the nozzle in through each doorway and turning it in every direction until the water flowed back out clean, it was my turn.

Having been told what to do I climbed up the engine steps and worked my way along to the front of the boiler. The large smokebox door had to be opened, which would expose the blast pipe below the chimney, also the smoke tubes that ran the full length of the boiler to the firebox. The boiler plugs could also be got at from here, and at last I could see the reason for my piece of sacking. There were several inches of small dead cinders or unburnt particles of coal that had been blasted from the firebox, but had not gone straight up out of the chimney.

This was the nearest I ever got to being in a bake oven. By the time I had placed my sacking in the cinders, kneeling to roll it out the full length of the smoke box, I was already sweating without having started the job.

I carefully crawled backwards to get my spanners and a light, taking care not to disarrange my previous effort. It was sometimes necessary for me to exert every bit of strength I possessed to undo some of those plugs. Lying out full length on my stomach, the heat was so great it was only with difficulty that I could get my breath and the sweat running off my forehead into my eyes made it difficult to see anything.

My light was called a flare lamp, but the only flare it ever produced was when it was tilted too much, or toppled over. It was a very crude little paraffin container with a handle, a spout, and a large round wick. It was about two match power and very smoky, shaped somewhat like a gravy boat with the top covered in, apart from a hole about one and a half inches in diameter, through which to pour the paraffin.

The plugs all had to be placed somewhere safe, because on odd occasions when they had been knocked into the ash, they were very difficult to find. When all the boiler plugs had been removed, Tom would pass the end of the pipe to me and as soon as I had inserted the nozzle into the holes I would shout for the water to be turned on. The pipe would jump a bit as the jet of water shot into the boiler, then Tom would shout, 'Hold tight Jockey, I'm turning the steam on'—hold tight I did!

I would grip the pipe with all my strength, laying full length on top of it. It still caused my whole body to jump off the cinders for an instant. Just as I thought I hadn't done too badly, that any second from now Tom would turn it all off so that I could relax my grip, his voice would come echoing inside the smoke box, 'Don't bloody well go to sleep there Jockey, have you got the pipe in?' I replied that of course the pipe was in, 'Well wriggle him well about then, wriggle him well about'. I believe this was supposed to be funny. By this time I was in such a state I could have thrown a fit—here was a brass nozzle that just about fitted into the plug hole, how was I to wriggle it about? Apparently he meant it because whenever the boiler inspector found a bit of mud or scale that he wanted removed, Tom usually said it was my fault for not wriggling the pipe enough. When we had finished the boiler inspector would come on the scene. His too could be a hot job; it depended on how long the engine had been off the road.

He carried, amongst other things, a bright carbide lamp, a hammer and small mirror fixed to a wire rod. Squeezing into the fire box was no mean feat, especially when he got as far as his shoulders, where he sometimes had trouble getting his arm and his head through more or less together. At this stage he always got me worried, as sometimes his clothes all became rolled up, seemingly round his neck, and he sometimes looked like getting stuck there in this small solid ring.

In the warmer weather he probably had no difficulty, but this was winter and he had pullover, boiler suit, and whatever he thought he needed to keep out the cold.

I don't ever recall having got into a firebox myself. Had I done so I think I would have found it exceedingly claustrophobic, panicking before I was properly in.

Once the inspector was in, he proceeded to inspect the stay bolts, which appeared to be spaced about six inches apart as far as I can recollect. He would tap them with his hammer, looking for any faulty stays before he moved down to the far end of the firebox to inspect the brick arch and the fire bars.

The arch, made of fire bricks, was built down towards the front end of the firebox. Its main function was to prevent the fire getting heaped up against the tubes, and consequently blocking them.

When the internal inspection was finished he would come back out on to the footplate, grunting and struggling and gasping for breath, completely covered in grey dust.

Clambering down off the engine he would insert his mirror into each of the mud hole doors in turn, turning it this way and that, reflecting his light around inside the boiler with the aid of this little mirror—this was the part we were interested in. It wasn't often we were called back to have another go at an engine—in the first place we usually got it right first time, secondly he knew he would set Tom shouting and swearing as he glowered down on him, thirdly he always came to us at meal breaks for boiling water to make his tea and could just happen to be unlucky if Tom wasn't in the right mood!

When the job had been passed by our friend the inspector, we then had to come along and reassemble the parts we had removed. This involved applying graphite grease to the plugs before screwing them in securely, placing thick lead washers on the mud hole doors, then inserting them endways in before turning to fit in position.

These mud hole doors were, and are, very simple, but in my opinion, also very clever. Being a greater diameter than the hole they are inserted through they have to be oval, in order to pass through. When the lead washer is placed in position it is virtually out of sight until the bridge has been placed across the door; this bridge has a hole through which the bolt of the door passes; a washer and nut is then screwed on to the bolt. The whole thing is tightened with a large spanner, compressing the lead washer into a perfect seal. When this stage had been reached it was my lot to climb on to the footplate, then make my way along the walkway to a point near the top of the boiler, where I had left out the last plug.

Stretching down, I would take the end of the water pipe which Tom was passing up to me, then the pipe was once more inserted in this last plug hole so that the boiler could be filled. This job was very important because the box boy could just possibly come along and light up the fire without checking the gauge glass first, and that would have meant serious trouble. When we thought there was sufficient water showing on the gauge glass the last plug was smeared with the graphite grease, then screwed in securely.

At mealtimes, which incidentally were taken whenever they could be fitted in, we would wearily make our way to the cabin used by the boiler washers. All the cabins had one thing in common, they were all dark and dusty, but we soon got used to that sort of thing. The little gas mantle was a pitiful effort, but it was just about possible to see what to eat and what to leave—what with pieces of old newspaper and the inevitable balls of cotton waste, we had to take care.

As soon as we got in the cabin, Tom would take off his jacket, revealing his famous khaki open-necked shirt, and he would stoke the fire and look to see if today the little boiler was, in fact, boiling for making the tea. He was now an entirely different person, his whole manner would alter; the change in his speech was very noticeable.

It was obvious to me that he had received a good education, because he seemed to hold his own in conversation with everyone we met during the turns of duty, from foreman to coppersmiths and drivers, but I never heard and I didn't like to enquire why ever he was engaged in such a menial job. If ever someone was meant for something better, it was Tom. Once the tea had been made it was the practice to remove the copper boiler, which had obviously been made by Tom in working hours, but nevertheless appeared to be a very fine piece of workmanship. Then it was the turn of the frying pan.

From his jacket pocket would come several rashers of very fat belly bacon, wrapped in greaseproof paper. Now I am not suggesting that he was exactly engaged in anything untoward like the black market, but he seemed to get a 'fair quantity' not that anyone else would try to eat it anyway. Once this bacon began to frizzle the smell was out of this world, as the saying goes, the stuff dreams were made of, because at four ounces per person per week, dreaming was practically all there was to it. To all those going about their duty outside, it was bordering on cruelty as it wafted on the cold January air, but to me, it was near murderous as I watched him gently teasing those pieces of fat round the pan until they were beginning to take on a somewhat brown colour. When at last he removed the pan from the stove and took up his lump of bread, I suddenly realised that I had only taken one bite of my fishpaste sandwich and that it was still rolling around my mouth. Mealtimes now took on a new meaning. I even began to look forward to them again, as each time Tom took his last piece of scrumpy fat from the pan he would say, 'Here Jockey, dip your sandwich in this fat', whereupon I would do just that. I know it was, as we say, enough to kill me, but it was beautiful.

This had been going on for some time, both of us taking it for granted that I would take part in what would be a daily or nightly ritual, when one day I inadvertently ate my last sandwich before I was due to go down into the pan. Tom stabbed the last piece of fat with his fork, placing it carefully on his bread. 'Go on then' he said, as he took a bite at the bread with the morsel on top, causing a little stream of fat to run over his bottom lip and down his chin.

64

Seeing that I appeared to hesitate instead of making my usual dive toward the pan, he repeated, 'Go on', with a bit of agitation in his voice which meant that he could get annoyed if I didn't play the game according to the rules. 'I can't', I said. 'What do you mean, you can't?' Then I explained to him in what I thought was a suitably apologetic voice that I had foolishly eaten my last piece of bread. He looked very put out, then began telling me what a waste it was, to leave fat like that while half the population was going hungry at this very moment. He then said something I shall never forget. 'Well you can't waste it and that's for sure, so you had better take your socks off and dip them in'. As silly as it seems, it was a few seconds before I realised he was joking.

One afternoon on our way from the boiler inspector's cabin to the shed, after we had just finished our last boiler wash and been to see if the inspector would come to inspect it. Tom called in at the coppersmith's shop. I, of course, followed. I wasn't interested in his business but I had never been inside the shop before, so here was an opportunity.

I had often heard Tom mention someone he called 'Bladder' and the moment I saw him I knew to whom Tom had referred. He was indeed gigantic, with a huge red face, a bald head covered with dust and smuts from his fire, while down his forehead ran small streams of sweat.

As he stood in that gloomy shop, with the embers of the fire throwing reflections on his face, it looked like war paint on some African warrior.

While he carried on a somewhat wheezing conversation with Tom, I had a little nose around, looking here and there, ending up by the anvil which was quite near the fire; this was still bright as though just used and should have been a warning to me, but it went unheeded. On the anvil was a bar of metal, about an inch in diameter, measuring about 2ft. I picked this up then, using it like a drum stick, began tapping it on the anvil. After a while I realised it was rather hot—it had been left to cool a bit, before being taken to whoever it had been ordered by.

I didn't have time to throw it; I just opened my hand allowing it to fall to the stone floor with a clatter. Luckily for me, my most recent operation had been to smear graphite grease on the plugs then, on climbing down from the engine afterwards my hands had become coated with dust, so instead of being badly burned, all I had was hard silver-coloured skin which, when cupped, formed the shape of the rod. I believe that was the last occasion on which I picked up anything from an anvil!

Dangerous Assignments

Tom was well known for his dicey, but nevertheless, very courageous exploits with steam. This usually came in the form of leaking mud hole doors.

I was with him on only two occasions and that was enough to convince me that, foolish or courageous, he was certainly capable. There was no doubt in my mind that he was aware of the possible outcome should anything go wrong as he continually took these calculated risks. He was obviously a man prepared to go beyond the call of duty to do his bit for the war effort.

The first of these emergencies came one day as we were about to snatch a bit of lunch. We were walking towards the cabin when the duty foreman came running across from the direction of the turntable, calling out to Tom. It was one of the quick turn jobs, just a few tons of coal and straight back out onto a train that was due in an hour.

The foreman had been pleased to get this particular engine as it came on shed, but was taken aback to see a large jet of steam rising from the mud hole door at the top of the boiler. He was panting for breath as he caught up with us; he looked very worried and agitated but this didn't prevent him approaching Tom cautiously and asking almost apologetically if he would help him out of a spot. He told Tom that he had to get the engine out in an hour and that it was, at the moment, under the coal tip with the fire very low, and the steam being let out ready for us to fit a new lead washer when all the steam was out, but that wasn't what he meant. He really wanted to ask Tom to do something that he had no right to ask him to do; he wanted the job done while the engine still had quite a bit of steam. Tom knew this; this was why the foreman hadn't put someone else on the job, who was not about to eat his food.

Tom carried on somewhat about the boiler washers who had last worked on the engine, the weather, the war, the shortage of good quality bacon, and the foremen who always expected favours, but were not so quick in returning them. 'Tell them to leave the fire and steam alone and get the thing up here to me a bit quick', he said.

I was sent for the sack bag and the large long-handled spanner, which was used on the nuts when tightening the mud hole doors, while Tom disappeared into the cabin. When I met up with him outside the engine shed he had collected his piece of tubing which had been specially made for him. This piece of tube was about 30in. long, with a thread cut inside one end to enable it to be screwed on to the bolt of the mud hole door, which it would fit quite loosely so that very little effort was needed to screw it on or off. As I had omitted to bring one or two lead washers or gaskets with the spanner and sack, I was once more despatched into the gloom of the shed to fetch them.

I could see an engine coming up from beyond the coal stage; there seemed to be a lot of steam about it generally, then as it came nearer we could see steam leaking badly from a point at the top of the boiler near the cab roof.

The engine, which was of the Grange or Hall class, stopped about twenty yards outside the shed. The foreman came hurriedly down the steps from the footplate, almost losing his trilby in the process as it touched the handrail on the way.

I followed Tom up on to the footplate where he was taking stock of the steam, water and fire. The fire was very low, the water was visible in the gauge glass, the pressure was about 70lb. Tom checked the handbrake, then opened the injector, allowing steam to roar out from the pipe which was situated about 18in. from the ground. The steam was gouging a hole in the cinders, causing them to fly all ways, as they mingled with the coal-dust-laden water which splashed from the hole and was gradually increasing in diameter. All we could do now was wait until the steam had dropped to a level where Tom could rectify the fault.

While we waited he threw a few lumps of coal into the firebox, keeping them near the door, well away from the area of the lead plugs which were meant to protect the boiler in the event of too little water when they would melt, putting out the fire. When this happened the engine was said to have 'dropped its plugs'. I thankfully never had this happen--very few people ever did because water was a thing that was given a lot of attention whenever anyone was on the footplate. Apart from the trouble the company would give you, their engine would be stuck, having to have attention from boilersmiths at least—what was worse was the danger to the engine crew!

I would expect it to be a type of explosion in the firebox, as steam pressure capable of providing enough power to pull a train was released into a white hot fire. Even with the firebox doors closed I would imagine the footplate the wrong place to be—should the doors be open at the time, no one would stand a chance of surviving!

Apparently either the lead plugs or boiler stays blew on one of the Yankee engines that were supplied to this country under 'Lease Lend'. I'm told it happened somewhere in the Stratford-on-Avon area early one very cold frosty morning. The driver received a very badly scalded leg. The fireman took the full blast through a partiallyopen firebox door. He hurried nearly two miles to the nearest signal box, stumbled up the steps and collapsed on the floor, where he died while waiting about two hours for an old ambulance.

The signalman suffered from shock for a long time after seeing the chap stumble in through his door; the flesh was almost hanging from his face and hands, while the rest of his body seemed to be held together by his clothes and overalls. Everyone agreed it was a miracle that he had walked that distance in that condition. Fortunately that was the only explosion I heard of while on the job.

Returning to our engine with the faulty lead gasket on a mud hole door. Quite a few people had, by this time, paused to look as they passed to and fro. Here and there small groups of two or three would stand discussing what was probably going to happen, their faces full of expectancy.

Tom climbed up and down the footplate; first he was up in the cab checking the steam pressure, then he was on the ground looking up at the steam escaping from the offending mud hole door, with a deep scowling frown on his face. He was now very much the centre of attraction, as people came from the offices and tool stores, as well as those engaged in outside or shed duties. I suddenly began to feel very important myself, after all I was the Great Man's helpmate. I began copying most of the things he did, while keeping very much out of his way, at the same time willing my grubby white face to portray complete nonchalance as I peered here and there. At last the pressure was down to about 10lb. on the clock and I began to sense that, whatever it was going to be, was about to happen.

Tom climbed along the side of the engine, holding on to the handrail with one hand to keep his balance, while in the other he carried the long spanner, the sack bag and the piece of tubing.

He slowly undid the big nut—this he had to undo completely with the spanner until it finally fell off the bolt and rolled down the side of the boiler to land in the walkway where he was standing. There now remained the bridge which spanned the mud hole, and Tom flicked this upward and off, pushing the jaws of the spanner underneath it. 'Jump up into the cab and see what pressure there is now Jockey', shouted Tom, above the noise of the two jets of steam, 'then get ready to give me a lead washer when I shout'.

I clambered up into the cab, feeling very important now. I looked at the gauge— it was down to 7lb. so I hurriedly stuck my head out, shouting as loud as I could to make Tom hear. I quickly climbed down again, wanting to be sure that I didn't miss anything, as I made my way to the spot where Tom was standing.

He shouted to the foreman to get another engine alongside with the blower attachment; any engine as long as it had plenty of steam.

All eyes were on him now as he very carefully screwed the piece of threaded tubing on to the mud hole door bolt, holding the sacking so as to keep most of the steam from his hand. When the tube was at last well on the threads of the bolt, he looked down to see where he was likely to put his feet when moving quickly. Next, while holding on to the rail with his left hand, at the same time gripping one side of the sack bag, he held the other side of the bag between thumb and base of index finger of his right hand and struck the end of the tube with his right hand in a lightning swipe, at the same time swinging to the left as he went into a crouch. The sudden added noise was unbelievable, even with such a low reading on the gauge.

68

I think it took most of the audience by surprise, because I got the impression that nearly everyone stood back when it happened.

There was a loud explosive roar, as the vicious-looking jet of steam shot skywards from the door. I thought if only someone could balance on the end of that jet, they would be lifted about 20ft. into the air. After the initial blast Tom was back up alongside this jet of steam and taking the end of the tubing, which was lying almost horizontal, he turned it the same way as always when removing a mud hole door. As the door turned endways the steam pushed it out vigorously in spite of its weight, throwing Tom's arm into a wide arc, but he was gripping it hard so he didn't lose it. In a flash he ripped off the old broken and flattened lead washer, then grabbed the new one I was holding up for him to take and placed it on the door flange. Now, holding the tubing in his right hand, and protecting himself with the sack which was held in his left hand, with considerable dexterity he quickly located the door. Suddenly, everything went comparatively quiet. He said 'Come on Jockey' but I was already on the bottom step making my way up to the footplate, then along to where he was now holding the tubing with both hands. I passed him the bridge first then held the nut and spanner, ready for him to take. Quietly he took the bridge from me, then removing his right hand, slid the bridge down the tube until it reached his left hand whereupon he changed hands to allow the bridge to pass all the way down to the boiler, where it spanned the door once more.

The reason for the slack thread in the piece of tube now became evident; he supported the door in place with his left index finger and thumb while he carefully unscrewed the tube from the door bolt. As he started the nut on the bolt, quickly running it down with his fingers, everyone appeared to be relieved as they started talking and moving about—it was as though they had hitherto been transfixed to the spot.

Tom gave the word and the steam was turned on in the pipe that led from the engine standing on the adjacent rails, down into the chimney of our engine. As the dampers on the footplate were opened the small heap of fire lying near the door was spread out over the area of the firebox, then fair-sized lumps of coal were added at fairly short intervals.

During the next thirty minutes the engine underwent a transformation. Tom finished tightening the nuts down on the door bolt and there was enough steam to inject more water into the boiler—much to everyone's relief. We were now piling lumps of coal into the firebox in large quantities as the black smoke bore witness to our effort; it was now possible to take away the blower pipe from the other engine, as our engine's own blower took over. 'She's all yours' Tom said to the foreman, 'Don't get making a habit of it though, I don't want that too often!' The foreman expressed his thanks as Tom stalked away saying something about already having a pocket full of 'thank yous'.

We hurried to the cabin to make our tea, hoping that the urn would still contain at least a little hot water. The tea made, Tom produced the fat bacon and I couldn't wait to dip my bread in the remaining fat.

A few weeks after this incident, I was lying on my sacking in the smoke box of an engine, the warmth on this occasion almost sending me to sleep, when Tom shouted, 'Hang on Jockey and wriggle him about well, I'm turning the steam on now'. I gripped the pipe for dear life, but it never came and after a few seconds I was aware that the cold water had also ceased; then I heard voices.

It was the duty foreman's voice that I could hear—it sounded as though something was amiss—I daren't let go of the pipe just in case it was suddenly turned on again. I didn't relish the idea of having to lie back in black cold water, so I lay back where I was, holding on to the pipe (just in case) trying to hear what was afoot.

'Come on Jockey, bring the kit, we've got to go down to the station, it's another mud hole door. The best thing you can do, Fred, is to get on to Cardiff and find out what in the hell is happening down there'. 'I'll do that right away' said Fred Smith, the foreman, as he hurried from the shed, heading in the direction of his office.

I scrabbled out of my bed of warm cinders, then hurriedly climbed down to the floor, snatching up a sack bag in case Tom needed it. I stuffed the spanner into the sack before running to the cabin for my coat, as there was light rain falling, and it was quite cold.

Tom appeared round the corner, walking with a comical gait as he tottered along in his clogs, carrying his piece of tubing and shouting at me as he approached, something like, 'Where was I going?' I said to fetch my coat and did he need his? He told me he didn't have time for a coat as there was a Castle heading a troop train standing in the station awaiting our attention. He then set off at a fast walk towards the station, wearing only his short-sleeved khaki shirt and overall trousers.

We could see the trouble long before we were able to hear it; it was a slender white pillar of steam sprouting up through the drizzle, fading out somewhere above the station roof.

At last we could hear it, above every other noise around the station. It was almost like a normal safety valve blow off, but the closer we got the worse it appeared. It looked as though most of the station staff were out on the platform, as were the locomotive supervisors, staff from the Military RTO Office, Officers and NCOs from the train itself, and hundreds of mixed services, men and women on either platform, with many soldiers' heads peering from every window and door. I must say that they gave us plenty of room to work—no one, with the exception of the locomen and loco supervisor, was within twenty yards or so of the Castle.

I suppose the supervisor had little choice, while the driver and fireman, having been saddled with this embarrassing malfunction shortly after leaving Cardiff, now appeared to be treating it with a certain amount of contempt, while keeping a wary eye on the jet of steam.

The supervisor told Tom there was really nothing for it but to take the engine off, then shunt the train into a siding to wait for another engine of some description. He also said that the shed foreman had told him to at least let Tom have a look at it as the train was terribly important to the war effort as the troops on board were due to arrive at a certain destination at a certain time.

To get a closer look at the trouble from a fairly safe vantage point, Tom stepped up on to the footplate and, of course, I followed, determined to be in on the act once again. Anyway I had carried the kit, apart from being the star attraction's mate! After peering through the driver's window for a while he turned to me and said, 'See what you make of that Jockey'. I peered out looking at the base of the steam, then turning away from the window I said, 'I don't like the look of it'. 'Of course you don't bloody well like the look of it—neither do I, but look at the nut holding the bridge'.

I took another look and it took a few seconds for me to focus my eyes on the nut through the steam, then I saw what he was getting at; the nut was not tightened right down. 'Come on', said Tom, climbing down on to the platform, where one of his greasy clogs failed to maintain adhesion on the wet surface, causing him to nearly end up on his back and set him off swearing and scowling as he fought to maintain his balance. He threw his arms about, holding the long spanner like a flail, while the supervisor, thinking maybe Tom was going to strike him, hurriedly jumped backwards looking very embarrassed, as he adjusted his hat and spectacles.

With many pairs of eyes fixed on him, Tom approached the engine from the side. Stepping up on the walkway, he held on with his left hand, still holding the spanner in his right. Success or failure now depended entirely on whether the nut was cross threaded or even very tight; in either case it could conceivably turn the door, causing a disaster.

Resting the spanner on the handrail and the boiler's outer shell to make sure it didn't waver about, he gradually slid it towards the nut, adjusting its direction simply and smoothly by the slightest movement of his hand, till finally it was located on the nut.

This was indeed a unique sight. Imagine two crowded platforms, all eyes looking in one direction, all looking spellbound as they watched a tall muscular figure clinging to the side of this huge engine, his sleeveless khaki shirt now wet from rain and sweat, as he slowly tightened down the nut causing steam to belch in all directions, rather like the action of a very slow rotating lawn sprinkler. The thought occurred to me that he looked like some demon, who, having made some fiendish contraption, had suddenly found himself unable to control it.

To everyone's relief the lead washer must have been still intact, and it was obvious the amount of steam escaping was becoming less and less as Tom worked away at the nut. He was still taking the greatest of care not to allow the spanner to knock the nut or the bridge, causing it to become unseated.

I think that on this occasion he was a bit worried, it seemed to take everything out of him. He stepped out on to the platform, then quickly clambered up into the engine cab where he sat for a couple of minutes talking to the driver, but I believe that somehow through the grime he looked a bit on the pale side.

As the fireman started working on the fire once more, there was another roar of steam, this time it was good news to everyone who understood—the Castle was blowing off properly.

Tom climbed on to the platform, a reluctant hero, giving a single wave in response to applause from the biggest audience he was ever likely to perform to. He turned towards the engine shed, saying to me, 'Come on Jockey, what the bloody hell are you gaping at? We've got some work to get on with at the shed. I could do with a drink of tea though'.

All smiles as a troop train pulls out from a station—scene so familiar through the wartime years.
(Author's Collection)

The applause was not yet over, and Tom was forced to take the longest bow in history as the train, now very late, made an immediate start along the platform beating us to the point where we would need to cross to walk close beside the 'up road'. The Castle put up a terrific performance as it pounded and ground its way past us on the crossover points that took it out of the platform loop on to the main track towards London.

As it did so it encountered a single short stretch of rail that had been well and truly watered by the injector of a goods engine that had gone up through the station, and it slipped profusely.

Now all that remained were twelve carriages that seemed to take ages passing us, as heads were leaning out of each window, shouting, whistling and giving the thumbs up sign, right to the last compartment. At last the complete train had left the station limits; all that was clearly visible was the rear of the guards van as it passed the engine shed.

For once Tom started walking without telling me to 'come on'. He hardly spoke for the rest of the journey to the engine shed. I remembered later in the day the expression on his face as he was subjected to that long bout of praise and goodwill. It proved beyond doubt to me that his armour had at least one chink in it, somewhere he had a soft spot, but it was usually very well hidden.

We made our way back to the cabin where we made and drank a quick cup of tea before going across to the shed once again. As I climbed back on to the engine, shuffling and groping my way back to the smoke box where I spread my sacking before settling down full length on the now cold cinders, I once more got the feeling that I had been there before.

Over the next three months I became better at the job, or so I like to think. In any event I was not chased around and sworn at as often as before, so I'm assuming Tom also thought that I was more use.

Around this time it was more noticeable that I was gradually being treated more like an adult, rather than the boy. He would discuss the job with me, telling me the technicalities of the boiler inspectors' job, pointing out their faults and shortcomings which he quite often backed up with proof or demonstration, so I was convinced he knew what he was talking about.

On being made Fireman

I was now approaching my seventeenth birthday and was naturally wondering when I would get some information about how, or when, I would become a fireman. I mentioned this to Tom one day; he obviously didn't want reminding of something he was already dreading. I discovered that it wasn't that he was sorry to lose me, rather that he didn't relish the idea of having to train yet another useless kid, with all that it entailed.

A few days before my birthday I received a note containing all instructions about my medical, also a railway warrant for Newport. There were no lads going from Gloucester so I had my sightseeing trip to Newport and back completely uninterrupted.

I don't remember a lot about the actual medical except that the doctor was a big man, who had pictures of rugby teams on one of the surgery walls. I though he was without doubt in each of the teams portrayed. The eyesight test was rather tedious and prolonged. At one stage it found me going through a pile of wool pieces, trying to match some of them up. Everyone who bothers to look at a forest or wood in the summer is amazed by the many shades of green. Well, after my encounter with that pile of wool for the best part of an hour, I can assure them, there are quite a few reds and oranges also.

Before leaving Newport I was told I had passed for Fireman and would receive further instructions before my birthday.

I arrived back home very pleased with myself, looking forward to the big day. I began imagining just what it would be like to see my name on the roster sheet under the fireman heading.

During the last couple of days on the boiler washing things were rather quiet, as Tom, instead of shouting to me 'hang on' or 'wriggle him well about' would call out 'let me know when you are ready for the steam'.

The time came for me to dip my bread in the fat for the last time, on the last shift of that job. Tom, having wished me all the best, said, in not so many words that he was sorry to be losing me. In the end I was almost sorry to be going but that feeling passed very quickly.

I was now kitted out with overall trousers and jacket, serge jacket, black raincoat, black peak cap with the red GWR embroidered on the front and an oval metal badge, which had a King class engine on the front and a number at the back. I still have it to this day.

I was called into the Head Foreman's office. He told me that he had confirmation from Newport that I had been appointed Fireman and was to begin my duties the next night, working according to the roster sheet.

I left his office feeling quite important. Making my way to the time office I made an entrance I thought might do justice to an old hand. I closed the door louder than necessary, throwing a scowling frown in the direction of the time clerk's window. I made my way round a fixture that stood in the centre of the room containing notices of all descriptions appertaining to the job and finally found myself running my eyes through the columns of names until I found mine.

The name of the driver I was to join was George Kear. We were due on at 10.00pm. The job was shunting at North Box, that was the yard above Horton Road crossing.

I booked on for my first job, then looked at the drivers who were present to try and discover my mate. As it turned out there was only one apparently young driver there and as I was obviously new to the place as a fireman, we both correctly assumed each other's name as we introduced ourselves. Tearing off a piece of cotton waste from the ball he had just drawn, George handed it to me, putting his own piece in his pocket. He took up his railway box saying, 'Well, I suppose we had better make our way up to the North Box'.

I don't recall much conversation between us as we picked our way carefully, stepping over each rail and avoiding all other obstacles, while continuously looking round to make sure we were not in the path of one of the many trains passing in each direction.

As we approached the yard, all seemed pretty quiet, with no apparent shunting going on. I soon learned that the work was all squared up in good time, so that everyone, shunters and engine crews, could get ready to be relieved by the next shift.

I must have been on hundreds of engines in the shed, but to climb up on to the footplate of this small tank engine, which was in full operational condition away from the shed, was, on this first occasion, rather strange.

The handing over was always rather brief on the shunters. In the first place the men you relieved were always in a hurry to get home, and in the second place there was little fire needed, so no need to fill the hole. The engine obviously carried little coal and this, barring occasional large lumps which had a habit of jamming in the coal hatch, usually rolled forward so that the coal was always within reach of the long-bladed firing shovel. When the others had clambered down, having bade us goodnight, I hung my jacket in the corner together with my bag, then looked around in the gloom. The fire was very low so didn't produce much light, the gauge lamp on the water gauge was not much help either. Shunting was always spasmodical, so it was the practice to keep a low fire or the engine would have been blowing off unnecessarily.

We chatted a bit and gradually became more acquainted and I discovered that he came from the Lydney area. He guessed rightly that this was my first job as fireman. In a silly sort of way I was a bit shy about making any move in carrying out my duties, which I wasn't completely sure about anyway. However, I was keeping my eyes on the situation without it being too obvious. Once I located the steam gauge in the gloom, I flashed odd glances at it until I was happy about the reading. I gave a false shiver and leaned forward on my seat, spreading my hands toward the firebox; this gave me the opportunity to look into the fire. Commenting how chilly the night was becoming for the time of year, I stood in front of the fire rubbing my hands, a crafty glance to the left and my eyes were focused on the water gauge. I then turned my back to the fire, finally sitting back down on my seat—I had at least made a start and I was able to remain seated while we waited for the shunters, confident that everything was OK.

At about 11.30pm I could hear sounds; doors opening and closing and voices calling in various directions. Finally a shunter's lamp appeared on the driver's side of the cab and the shunter said 'OK driver, we had better make a start if you are ready'. The two exchanged a few words and then the shunter disappeared. George stood up, had a stretch, then said, 'Ah well' and looked first in the direction in which the shunter had just gone, then put the lever in forward gear, applied the steam brake and said, 'Take your hand brake off, Doug'.

We started forward pulling a large number of wagons up the gentle incline, so that they could be shunted back down hill. George had to watch carefully for the signal coming from the shunter's lamp and this gave me the opportunity to start working without anyone's eyes on me. I opened the rear damper, then placed about eight shovels full of coal on the fire where I thought they should be, closed the door and steadied myself as we came to a rather sudden standstill.

Generally speaking shunting is carried out in order to sort out the various wagons that have arrived at the yards as freight trains. These wagons are then shunted down different sidings to form yet more trains for various destinations.

The shunter signals the driver forward, quite often up a slight incline then, when the last truck is clear of the highest points, the lever is pulled, setting these points in which ever direction is necessary. Lower down there would be another set of points allowing the choice of two more tracks; they all eventually straighten out and run parallel for a distance that was great enough to accommodate a long freight train. In order to avoid continuously having to pull ahead of the incline, it was necessary to carry out some rather violent acceleration and braking. To this end the shunter would swing his lamp from side to side vigorously, the driver would open the engine almost flat out, propelling the wagons as fast as possible over the short distance available, and would be ready to brake the instant he got a red light from the shunter. The brakes would be lightly applied to begin with, then as the metallic wrenching sound eased, signifying that the couplings were taut and unlikely to snap, the brakes were slammed on hard. At the onset of this operation, the shunter was standing by the wagon to be uncoupled, his shunting pole resting on the buffers of one of the wagons, then the instant the couplings slackened he would press hard on the pole and flip the heavy iron link off the hook on which it had been hung.

Coupling up wagons was a little different. The shunter would stand with the third link hooked with his shunting pole, then as the buffers on the two wagons were about to touch, he would swing the heavy coupling up on to the hook, then quickly disengage his pole.

When the wagons had been brought to a halt by the engine, the released wagon or wagons would go running on quite fast, rattling over the joints in the rails and creaking on the bends until, with a terrible metallic bang, they collided with the ones already standing on the track.

The shunting yard was always a terribly noisy place, but in the middle of the night, when most activities had ceased, the blast from a couple of shunting engines, the creaking and snatching noises from the couplings, and the eventual colliding of buffers, it was something else. I, in particular, felt sorry for people who lived nearby who would be attempting to get some sleep.

The shunters had a pretty hectic time; one would be uncoupling and controlling one set of points, while another would be nipping smartly across the tracks to alter the points. As one lot of wagons cleared them, there was often another lot on their way down, to be sent down one of the other tracks.

I threw on some more coal; as the steam clock looked healthy I put the injector on, pleased to see the water bobbling well into the top half of the gauge. Whilst carrying out these various duties, I soon realised that I was going to take some time to get my 'sea legs' as it were. Each time George braked the full weight of the wagons dragged the engine—it felt like standing in a small boat suddenly struck at the stern by a wave.

The shunters said that was all for a while, so we decided to use a little of our precious tea ration to make a quick cup. It was after I had been to the water tap at the shunters' cabin to fill my can that I first learned just how quickly it was possible to boil a can of water, which held almost a quart. Leaving the lid off the can, it was placed on the tip of the shovel, then carefully entered into the firebox, while the shovel was rested on the base ring of the fire hole door. Within seconds the surface of the water became agitated, then steam began billowing from the can; at that stage it was best to withdraw the can and make the tea, a slight delay would halve the quantity and then it would be necessary to make another trip to the water tap.

I was surprised how cold it became in the early hours of the morning, no doubt caused more or less by being stood, or sat, with little to do but stay awake.

While I was working in the shed, boiler washing or cycling around calling up, I hadn't noticed it so much. I don't know what time it began to become lighter in the eastern sky, but it was very early and seeing daybreak was something I was becoming used to since starting on the railway. There was, of course, one consolation. However cold it became, we could always stand in front of the fire, except on the odd occasions when rain, sleet or snow was driving through across the footplate, and we had to retreat into our respective corners.

At a little after six o'clock next morning, our relief arrived—they were a welcome sight, as I was ready for home and bed. They clambered up into the little cab and as we took our belongings from the coat hangers in the corner, they put theirs in. After a few words, during which time the engine was officially handed over by George, we bade them goodbye and with collars pulled up high against the cold morning breeze, which promised a shower of rain, we quickly made our way back down to the engine shed and booked off. I had completed my first shift as fireman.

I arrived home at Minsterworth having cycled from Gloucester at about 6.45am, to find that my father had already been up sometime and had a roaring fire going, on top of which was perched precariously the black iron kettle. It was common then to have sooty kettles and sooty saucepans, because few working people in the country had any other means of cooking or heating, other than the open fire. There was no power or water in Minsterworth until the mid'fifties. I would sit by the fire and nod off, only to be roused by my father saying in a loud voice, 'Here, catch hold now or you will scald yourself'. I would take the cup of tea, only to place it down again on the oven at the side of the fire, having persuaded him to pass me a slice of bread to save having to get up and fetch it. I placed the bread on the toasting fork and watched, through partially closed eyes, as the bread slowly emitted steam, but seldom seemed to turn into a golden brown toast. When I ran out of patience I would smear a little margarine on then proceed to chew very thoroughly, occasionally nodding off. I could have just laid there and slept but I knew that soon my mother, brother and sister would be coming down to get ready for school, so with a great effort I took the remaining hot water in the kettle out to the back kitchen, or outhouse. Taking the handbowl to the pump, which was outside, I pumped some water to which I added the hot water from the kettle, in order to wash. After washing, I sometimes walked up the garden to have a look at the river; it was seldom the same two days running, so it seemed quite a natural thing to do. I returned to the house, and suddenly realised that here, once again, was the beginning of another day of my life. Here I was, preparing to go to bed, yet with these thoughts I would suddenly find myself wide awake—this happened many times. If I managed to sleep two or three hours I was lucky. This was more or less how I carried on doing shifts on the railway. Little did I know what hours I would be doing in a very few months time, they were to make an eight hour shift seem like a lunch break!

I had been watching with interest for several nights what appeared to be the normal procedure for this shunting operation, concentrating on the way George used the engine, also the lamps signals given by the shunters; should they be out of vision, then they would use their whistle, though this seldom happened in my short spell of shunting.

It was about my fourth night as fireman, when George said, 'Do you want to have a go Doug?' as though I had been firing for some while. I was quite surprised, but agreed without hesitation, trying to appear not unduly concerned. Once I got the hang of it I found the job very simple, just as long as I concentrated on the shunters' signals.

There were only three controls for me to handle; they were the steam brake, which was straightforward, on and off, a reversing lever, which demanded the only physical effort, and the regulator, or throttle.

I found the time going much faster while I was engaged in these driving sessions, because after the first night it became the regular pattern, with George and I taking turns at dragging the wagons up beyond the points, blasting them back down the hill as fast as the little tank engine would propel them, then after the initial tensioning of the coupling, slamming the brake hard, sometimes tying the wheels if the rails were wet.

When I had been with George a few weeks doing morning, afternoon and more night shifts, we came on duty one day to find my name next to another driver, so our acquaintance proved to be rather a brief one, but even in that short period I knew I had learned something about the job.

My new mate was a rather jolly little Welshman from Neath, his name—Bill Start. We got on very well; he was forever spinning yarns about his youth, about Wales, and various drivers he'd had as mates. I continued to take turns driving as I had with George, but I later learned that it was the usual thing, so I wasn't privileged after all.

It was about the end of August, and we had been getting quite a few sunny afternoons while on one of our two to ten shifts. One evening about 7.30pm we were having a break, enjoying a cup of rather weak tea, when Bill, who had been looking aimlessly in the direction of Eastern Avenue, looked at me with a puzzled expression and said, 'Were there any coal mines right here Doug?' I said, with a chuckle, 'I shouldn't think so, there is still some coal mined in the Forest of Dean, but not here, why do you ask?' He answered, 'Well there must be either disused coal shafts or holes of some kind, because I keep seeing people disappear from sight every now and then. Here you are, come and have a look. I can see four people walking across that stretch of grass, now you will see them disappear'.

Stepping over to where he was sitting, nursing my precious cup of tea, I followed his gaze out across this stretch of rough ground that lay somewhere between us and the buildings. These were the newly-built RAF Records Offices.

The grass was very tall and coarse and beginning to turn a golden brown; it should have been mown weeks ago. It would have been of little use, but as they say, it's an ill wind. 'I thought you said you could see four people out there Bill', I said, 'You're too late', he replied, 'there were four, but as you can see, two have disappeared into thin air'.

He had a wicked twinkle in his eyes and quite a grin on his face. 'Now watch carefully and you will see what I mean'. I watched the two people pushing through the grass, a WAAF and an Airman, obviously out solely for a breath of air, and to catch the last of the warm sun. Suddenly she flopped down as though she had been shot, and he was a very quick second. They were completely hidden in the grass and as I watched in disbelief several more couples came out from different buildings and followed the same procedure, though I must admit one or two of the girls seemed to hesitate for a short while. One or two seemed to need assistance in making up their minds, but the significant thing was they all eventually disappeared! I must have looked surprised or shocked or both. Bill laughed and said, 'Pulling your leg I was, I've been up here a couple of years or more now and weather permitting it's been going on all the time. It's amazing how bad it is for concentration, knowing that within two hundred yards there must be upwards of forty couples trying to catch a little sun and air, yet never being sure if that was the real reason for this seemingly non-stop promenading.' I drank my tea slowly while keeping an eye on events. The sun was getting lower now, with less warmth in evidence, causing me to wonder if things were becoming a bit damp from the dew that would certainly be found at ground level. 'Perhaps those articles they are carrying under their arms are waterproof capes.' I said.

Occasionally on nights we would complete the shift by taking a train of goods wagons, some, or all, of which we had shunted ourselves down to Over Bridge sidings. This was the source of some excitement for me as it meant actually going out on to the main line, passing through Gloucester station, with all the feverish wartime activity. After that there was the waiting beyond the river bridge at 'Over' on the main line, looking out for the flickering signal from the guard's lamp, way back in the darkness, telling us that the points and signals were right for us to propel our train backwards into Dock Branch sidings. Having completed this operation it was my job to put a red slide into one of the lamps for a rear light, so that we could run light back to shed, where I felt quite important ascending from the cab on the ash and coal road, leaving things like dropping fires, coaling up, and other menial jobs that may be necessary, to lesser mortals—that's how it was on my first trip to 'Over'.

The part I forgot to mention was Gloucester station itself. We came down slowing into the station, stopping at the signals adjacent to the point where we used to coal the mail. I had only a low fire because that was the general rule, plenty of steam on the clock, and so much water that it was up out of sight in the gauge glass. I failed to see that as the nose of the engine was higher than the rear because of the climb up over Worcester Street, that the reverse would apply once we started going down the other side. The little tank engine had to dig its toes in to get up over the bridge, using a lot of steam in doing so, but I wasn't worried because the water was looking good.

We began the downhill stretch to Over sidings when I suddenly got a shock, the water looked to be dropping in the glass as though there was a serious leak somewhere, it bobbed lower and lower until it was almost out of sight. I panicked; the steam was dropping too and Bill was still giving the engine some stick—I didn't realise we were still pulling the bulk of the train up out of the station. I hurriedly piled some coal on—too late of course—but things were getting worse. Bill didn't seem to notice anything wrong, or if he did, he didn't seem to care.

In despair I threw the shovel down, snatched my little seat down into position and sat down. Bill was still looking unconcerned, or that is how it seemed in the semi-darkness of the cab, so I thought I would draw his attention to the situation developing on my side of the cab. Then came the words that were repeated from time to time by Bill, as whenever my name cropped up, he laughed till the tears came to his eyes. I had shouted, 'Bill, I've got no steam, no water, and the bloody fire's nearly out—I don't give a damn any more'. All he did was burst out laughing, closing the regulator as we drifted down towards 'Over' on the gentle downhill gradient. The steam pressure rose higher and higher, the coal I had belatedly shovelled on had now been blasted to a white mass of fire so at last I put the water injector on, soon to see the water bobbing its way up the glass once more.

I had no lasting embarrassment over this incident, after all it was my first time on the main line, but after some months when I began to become a little more experienced, I did sometimes begin to wish it had never occurred. I learned more in that quarter of an hour, from Horton Road to Over, than all the hours spent in the shunting yard, but I feel Bill must have laughed many times about that outburst over the years. Needless to say I did several more weeks of nights before I left Bill, so each time we had to take a train to Over Bridge there was some ribbing going on; me trying to act as though there had never been any problem, while he would make much of peering through the gloom at the steam and water gauges.

I quite enjoyed my time with Bill. As I said, he was a very jolly little fellow, always finding something to joke about, seeing humour in most situations. A quality I'm afraid I have never been able to boast.

The Main Line

About November of the same year, when I had been firing for about four or five months, the duty foreman told me I was being moved up into the relief link. This was the third link up out of about six, but it was by far the biggest, having many times more men in it and working not only any trains that came through, but also covering anyone going sick.

The latter enabled me to gain some experience that would otherwise not have transpired.

If I remember correctly, there was what was rather unkindly called the 'cripple link'; these were men who had, because of accidents or some physical disability, been taken off the mainline footplate—there were quite a few of them, some working in the docks.

There was the shunting link, one at North box and one at Docks branch siding, with three shifts for each engine needing twelve men. Next the relief link where I spent the bulk of my time, except for filling in with other links during emergencies.

The top three links were all regular jobs, whether their engines were prepared or the crews prepared their own, either way each crew knew what job they were on, and could be pretty sure when they would finish. These top three were known as the goods link, light passenger link and the express link. They also covered the duties of station pilot, which was probably worked by the passenger link.

My name was written in next to a driver by the name of Ron Carlile; having booked on we sort of introduced ourselves.

Tom Evans was in the tool stores and when he noticed me he shouted, 'Hello Jockey, how are you getting on?' That was how it came about that Ron knew my nickname from the start of our acquaintance. I've no recollection of the first journey we did together, but I remember having a lot of help from him, both advice and practical.

It was quite a responsibility for a driver to take on an inexperienced lad as a fireman. It was not just this lack of experience though. The neglected state of the engines, dirty fireboxes making it near impossible to maintain steam, black out sheets, and wartime conditions generally, made things very hard for them.

In those early days, as long hours were suddenly thrust upon me, I became exhausted very easily, partly from not having the knowhow. I soon learned that it was one thing to make up the fire on an engine in preparation for going off shed for some particular train, this was done in a more or less leisurely manner over a period of an hour. It was something else taking over an engine 'doing rough for steam' as it was usually termed, which after a trip to Hatherley Junction near Cheltenham, could be facing the bank up to Andoversford.

82

On occasions like this, often having to start off before I was ready, I would have to drag out one of the big fire irons known as the 'pricker bar'. Some bar too, about a foot longer than I was tall, the weight of which I couldn't guess—I know it was far too heavy. After jabbing this bar as many times into the fire as was necessary to break up the clinker, one half of the bar was almost white hot. It felt too warm as I carefully dragged it from the fire, then with great difficulty proceeded to swing it up into the long rack that ran alongside the coal tender. The trouble was that because the heat was travelling upwards, I was having to hold the bar about 2ft. away from the position where my hands should have been, this didn't help much.

On these occasions I found I was left with a very low fire which would need a lot of coal to get it back into shape. After a while I would flop on my seat, unable to do any more whatever may happen.

Apparently, it had only been about three years since Ron had been a passenger fireman himself, so he obviously hadn't forgotten what it had all been about. Although I had been unaware of it at the time, he must have been watching what was happening, because he would suddenly say 'Come over here and watch her, Jockey'. So saying, he would grab the shovel and try and get some sort of shape into the fire. In spite of what anyone could do, there were times when the only thing for it was to stop at some signal box to get up steam and water. Quite often if it happened to be daylight, drivers and firemen on engines passing in the other direction would be looking out, hands cupping ears, which meant they could hear our blower being operated. It was meant to say 'What a Fireman' as they went through the motions of pulling a lavatory chain. In the first place they would not have been able to hear the blower because of the noise of their own engines, and anyway it happened to everyone sooner or later, such was the condition of the engine fires.

I must have tried Ron's patience quite a bit in the first few days of our association. For instance, when a distant signal was against us he would immediately close the regulator; I should have wound on the handbrake which would have brought all the wagons up together, holding them, enabling him to ease his brake off or increase it without a lot of jerking and snatching. Instead I was probably watching the scenery, just staring into space, or watching the water that might be escaping from the injector dribbling along the track. Either the injector would be faulty or I wasn't operating it properly.

This situation was, however, shortlived. It all came to an end very abruptly with a near disaster which shook me for a long time to come, and several years later I still had a dread at the thought of what might have happened each time I passed the spot.

We were pulled into the loop line at Beachley; as with most sidings or loops I ever saw, it was very exposed to the elements. We had been on duty about twelve hours with no hope of any food or drink, neither were there any prospects of going on to

83

Severn Tunnel, where we would have hoped to get relief. I make no excuse for my labouring the point about lack of food, just in case anyone might think, 'Well, why didn't the fool take a packet of crisps, a few biscuits, or some chocolate?' I can only say that they virtually existed only in the memory of those who had been able to afford them before the war.

I was perched on my seat, slumped forward with my head almost between my knees. We had been here several hours, the fire was low and I pulled my coat over my back and shoulders—it would have been warmer standing in the corner by the boiler, but I couldn't quite manage to sleep standing up. There was also a limit to how long I could stand on my feet!

I was awakened by a whistle and as I dragged myself back to consciousness I could see a light being held through one of the signal box windows. Ron had come round, either at the whistle or the shuffling of my boots as they slipped off the damper handles, where they had been resting.

I said 'I think the bobby wants us' (the signalman was known as 'the bobby'), so I took the gauge lamp from its fixture on the water gauge frame and climbing down into the dark windy world, I picked my way along to the signal box, climbed the stairs quickly, opened the door and nipped inside. This was the place to be, everything was warm and polished, a real home from home. There was a chair with a cushion in it, and a small polished stove filled very near to the top with blazing coals, because that was one thing there was no shortage of as long as you were on duty. It was a different thing at home, green apple or plum wood, or perhaps some driftwood from the Severn.

The signalman had a kettle, a small teapot and a couple of cups. He was wearing a tie and polished boots; a glance down at my appearance caused me to think that I had a nerve to step inside this little palace. I was relieved to find I was standing on the thick doormat, so no harm had been done. We exchanged a few words from which I gathered the whole system was blocked with trains below that point—by now, of course, trains were being held back in every siding back to Gloucester as well. He told me that our engine was wanted urgently down at Severn Tunnel Junction, so if I could uncouple the train and let the guard know, we would be able to run light to Severn Tunnel where we could leave the engine, hopefully to get a ride back to Gloucester. I thought to myself, 'What, a free ride back to Gloucester!!?' Corn in Egypt!

With my left hand sliding down the handrail and the lamp in the other, I hurried down the steps, my steel-tipped boots making metallic noises as they made contact with the metal treads in a clip-clopping rhythmic manner.

On arriving back at the engine, I shouted up my information to Ron, adding with a few oaths that I had to attract the guard's attention, then off I went. As I trudged along the edge of the high embankment, with the wind howling through the wire fence and the telephone wires overhead, the swinging lamp casting huge shadows, causing my

84

legs to accelerate along the wagons in front of me, then as the lamp came forward, they would fly backward out of sight behind me. I began to find the situation a little eerie; I was always nervous as a lad, especially in a place like this, anyway I was so tired and miserable that I half expected the Devil or something to step out as I passed each wagon. I estimated, by glancing backward in the direction of the engine, that I had now reached the point of no return, so should some fiend appear, I would carry on towards the guard's van.

When I reached the van I climbed up into the veranda end and opening the heavy door, I stepped into an oven. The stove was almost red hot in places, giving off such a lot of heat I could hardly breathe. I could hear loud snoring so shone my lamp in the direction whence it came, to reveal the guard stretched out on one of the long seats. Now here was a job I should have been engaged on, I would have had no sleeping problems when I got home because I would have been able to get a lot on duty!

I shone the light on his face and was surprised to see how quickly he awoke—perhaps he also was expecting the Devil! His feet swung off the seat and clattered on the heavy wooden floor, causing dust to rise that was clearly visible, even in the yellow beam of that little paraffin lamp. I gave him the message, to which he made no immediate comment, then rubbing his eyes he asked me what the time was. When I told him it was 3.30am he muttered something, I'm not sure what, but I believe I heard the word 'hell'. He gathered all his belongings and kit, then we set off into the night again. He brought his lamp which gave out quite a good light, so my return journey was quite well illuminated. Before leaving, the guard wound his hand brake on very hard, then locked the door; we also applied a few wagon brakes just to be sure.

Arriving back at the engine, the guard climbed up onto the footplate while I remained on the ground to uncouple the engine, after applying some more wagon brakes. This completed, I put a red lamp behind, a white one in front in the G class position, that was lower centre, signifying a light engine to a signalman or anyone else it concerned. I climbed back on to the footplate and settled once again on my seat, thinking that here at last we were on the point of making a move.

I soon lost interest in the conversation that was going on between Ron and the guard; in next to no time I was dozing again.

I must explain that up until that time I had seen very few road traffic lights. There was a set at Gloucester Cross, but even these were switched off most of the time as police constables relieved one another on point duty, directing the traffic very efficiently to the north, south, east and west. In my mind I thought of the amber as caution as it indeed is. My mistake was trying to relate it to a railway caution. At this time I was hearing of engine drivers being cautioned at various points of their journeys; when they talked of having got a caution at a certain location I very mistakenly imagined the signalman giving them an amber light, indeed the 'distant' as it is known, is itself a caution signal for a running train. In actual fact a signalman's caution to a driver was a green light held steady; it means roughly that it is all right to proceed with caution, but the driver should be prepared for the station, or junction, ahead to be blocked.

A whistle attracted Ron's attention; he couldn't see the signal box so he said, 'What's the bobby saying now Jockey?' I struggled to my feet to look through the window and there, through sleep-laden eyes I saw a light which appeared a bit on the amber side. I thought 'he's giving us a caution'—but what for?'

What with Ron's misguided trust in my abilities, plus my total ignorance of the facts, the stage was all set for the final act of an impending disaster.

When I told Ron we were given a caution he accepted it because after all, trains were blocked from station to station, so it would be natural for the next station we came to to be blocked.

I wound off my handbrake, having already attended to the fire, which was by now, of course, very low. Ron opened the ejector handle to build up the vacuum brake, put the engine in full forward gear and opened the regulator—we were at last moving. Passing the signal box, which was still in Ron's vision, we were travelling about fifteen miles an hour, when suddenly there was a loud shout from the signalman and a red light was thrust out from one of the windows. I have never seen anyone move faster or operate so many different controls in so few seconds as did Ron. From the first moment he saw the red light he slammed the regulator down hard, flipped the brake lever right over, knowing the vacuum brake would take a few seconds to really bite. Next he grabbed the reversing lever and heaved it completely back to its full extent, then opened the regulator right up, then closed it again. There were muffled blasts from the exhaust as the engine reversed the driving wheels half a turn before the brake took over. The engine appeared to lift slightly and then began to slide forward with the wheels tied. Anticipating this, Ron had already dived across to my side of the cab, bumping into me which nearly caused me to fall off the footplate, as I tried in vain to get out of his way before I could grasp one of the handrails to steady myself. He was already grasping the sand lever with both hands as he vigorously rattled it back and forth; luckily for once there was dry sand available and the engine ground to a shuddering halt.

There was a bit of a shouting match between Ron and the signalman, but it soon cooled—Ron never said much to me, I don't know if he was too shocked, or relieved that we had got out of it that easy. Of course, he knew that it was his sole responsibility, but at the same time he had every right to expect more reliable co-operation from me. As it happened we weren't going anywhere for a few minutes and as things went a bit quieter Ron said to me, 'You haven't been in this loop before have you Jockey?' I replied that I had not. 'Well get the gauge lamp and go and have a look at what is in front of us, then perhaps you will be more careful next time'.

I took the lamp with me down on to the path beside the track and walked slowly forward. Five or six paces in front of the engine stood the signal with its dim red light showing. Just beyond the signal was a catch point, or throw off point, the function this and all others was exactly what it was called; it was to throw the engine off the track to prevent it going on to the main line, possibly into the path of an oncoming train.

I was very shocked. Beyond and down the embankment my light was not sufficient to show exactly where we had almost gone but I saw this steep embankment later in daylight and realised that had the engine come off the track, ploughing forward a few feet, it would no doubt have rolled and we would have stood very little chance of surviving.

I resolved there and then that I was going to treat the whole job much more seriously in the future. I also vowed to myself that I would never again let Ron down by betraying his trust in me as a mate on a hard and dangerous job. After a few more trips it was apparently all forgotten.

The Guards Van

After the episode with the catch points whenever we approached signals that he couldn't see without stepping across to my side of the cab, he would say 'How is it Jockey?' I would probably be already waiting for the particular signal to come into view, then I would answer 'Right'O'Way' or just say 'On', in which case I would immediately wind my hand brake on and Ron would close the regulator at the same time. My winding on the handbrake would cause the wagons to catch up on each other, this chain reaction would continue right through the train until it reached the guard's van and this was usually a sufficiently hard bump to make the guard aware that the driver had not got the necessary signals, or had not 'got the road', as we said on the job. It was the guard's duty to use his van brake to assist in stopping the train if it was on a downhill gradient or if the driver indicated that he needed assistance, which he would do by giving three or more short blasts on the whistle, or sound the brake or danger whistle on the level run. I think the guard generally left it all to the engine, at least that was my experience during the many times I rode back home in the guard's van after being on very long hours.

As a point of interest, freight train instructions state that each brake van will carry the following items of equipment:

A set of side and tail lamps, oil can, hand brush, sand bucket, short drawbar and block, fire shovel, shunting pole, not less than two sprags, brake stick, door key, also red flag and detonators.

Signing on and the Cabin

With the exception of shed turns, when the duties were to prepare engines, we would clock on at whatever time we were due, draw some cotton waste, have a look at the notices and any speed restrictions, then walk quietly down to the far end of the station to the engine crews' cabin, next to the supervisor's cabin.

On arrival, Ron would report to the supervisor, then we would join in at the first vacancy that occurred in any of the solo games that were in progress. Sometimes there were as many as thirty men in the cabin, as two men were clocking on about every fifteen minutes in the relief link alone. They quickly mounted up should the odd delays occur, which was often the case.

It was a job to know when to make one or two cans of tea. We would sometimes hang on for as long as possible, say for five hours, thinking that if we were sent away on six hours, we would still have one brew left for any eventuality. Then in would come the supervisor and tell us we would be skipped. A lot more men had booked on since us, the number was now mounting so we were to go and report to the shed foreman to see if he wanted any engines prepared. On these occasions we could have rationed our food out more evenly had we known. It was all a game of chance.

There were some day turns which made a very pleasant contrast to the darkness encountered outside the cab at night. After having stared at a brilliant fire, like everything else in life, when the sun shines it all looks better.

It could be very pleasant to start out from Gloucester on a nice day. We were lucky to pass a station or signalbox without stopping; usually we ran into a loop line to wait for some fast train to pass, then we would pull out again, travelling on to the next station or box. This didn't always work out right, it was sometimes several hours before we moved. Quite a few trains were due for the examiner's at Bullo Junction, where we would take the opportunity to top up our water tank, sometimes boiling our can. Quite often making a can of tea was a sure way of getting going again. Believe me, it isn't funny standing on the footplate of an engine with a heavy train, starting out of a loop trying to drink scalding tea out of an enamel can lid-cum-cup. It splashes anywhere between the chin and the nose, but on most of these occasions where we did have a train due to be examined, it was possible to drink our tea before setting off again.

The examiner and the grease boy would start along one side of the train, then back down the other, the examiner walking along flipping up each cover on the grease box on each axle. If it had sufficient grease he would close the lid again, if not it was left for the boy to put in a dab of grease then flip the lid down.

I often found myself passing strange stations and districts in darkness, then suddenly, one day, passing them in daylight. These were nothing like I imagined them to be. It is amazing how quickly one came to recognise small country stations in complete darkness, apart from one or two dim signal lights and the odd glimmer of light through the blacked-out windows of the signal boxes.

Things like the height and position of signals, the position of signal boxes, the clanging echoes of the coupling rods from station buildings, or any permanent fixture or building that echoed before or after the station. These sounds made, perhaps while running easy or with the regulator shut, coasting down a slight gradient, would be very different on the way back up through the same station. Instead of echoes from the coupling rods, it would be the rhythmic exhaust beats as the engine strove to haul its train of waltzing wagons up the incline.

The ability to recognise stations and places became more easy with experience, until as a driver a man was able, and of course is still able, to learn 'the road' as it was known, over long distances.

For every train journey undertaken by a driver, he must have had a period of learning the road. He must know every signal affecting the main or loop line for the the complete journey. It must be much easier nowadays, as greater distances are travelled without seeing a signal. In the past they were round every bend as each little station—now long gone—sported sometimes up to half a dozen in each direction, with names like 'Distant', 'Outer Home', 'Home', 'Starter' and 'Advanced Starter'.

The Author, aged all of 17 years 3 months, and just contemplating another long hard shift.
(Author's Collection)

These amounted to hundreds of signals on a journey of a hundred miles or so, all appearing very different in daylight to night time. By day we were looking for the yellow and black 'distant' or 'warning' signals, while the stop signals were red and white. It was surprising how great a distance the outline of the signal was visible over, usually some distance before the actual colour could be confirmed. At night the 'distant' or 'caution' signal was orange, the stop signals red, or green. Looking back, this distant or warning signal with its orange light, was probably a contributing factor to my mistaken assumption over what I had believed to be a caution at Beachley.

Today a brilliant red or green electric light can be seen over great distances day or night, and must, I would imagine, be bright enough to light up the driver's face as he passes, or so they appear from the main road, which is as close as I have ever been, or for that matter, would ever want to be.

I want to remember the train as it was, that is why my last train journey was in the latter part of the 'forties when on the day I was demobbed from the Army I travelled down from York to Gloucester, never dreaming that in a few short years one of the most wonderful inventions the world has seen would be discarded, like so many worn out old boots.

It may be possible for someone to blind me with economics, even then I would be sceptical, but regarding reliability and safety, I could never be convinced that the steam locomotive is inferior to anything.

The number of accidents with the steamers were few and far between, understandably so. There were two pairs of eyes which constantly darted from the controls to the road ahead and in addition there was always the ATC (Automatic Train Control)—at any rate, we had these on the Great Western. I must admit that, unfortunately, not all companies had this. I suppose we took this valuable bit of equipment for granted, as we went our way, relying on its fail-safe factor.

I remember being jolted out of my complacency on one particular occasion. I know Ron was, too.

Fog at Bristol

We had worked a Stoke Gifford train. It was a foggy November night so we were relieved to get the engine to shed, after which we made our way on foot towards Temple Meads in order to get a ride home. The fog was not getting any better but Ron, who had travelled that way home many times before, was making good progress. He suddenly turned into a dark doorway while I came groping behind, wondering where he was bound. I wasn't left wondering many seconds, my nose came to the rescue as I got a whiff of beer and a pale chink of light showed me a partially lighted doorway. We passed quickly inside, closing the door again, so perfecting the blackout.

There were quite a few people in the large dimly-lit bar, where, in spite of apparently rapid conversation being carried on wherever I looked, there seemed to be little noise. So it was there that I first tasted 'Georges' Beer and also had my first real experience of a group of city dwellers who were under constant threat of bombing raids. There were only two Royal Engineers in forces uniform, all the rest were cvvies, though like us, some wore overalls or other uniform of their trade. However dressed each person could look at the other and know that each in his, or her way, was doing some essential work towards the war effort.

Most looked tired, everyone a bit underfed, all appeared tense to varying degrees. They didn't look scared or terribly worried, though worried they must have been; more keyed up, as though waiting for something to happen, but they were not likely to be caught napping should it come. I then realised why I thought the place rather noiseless. While engaged in their rapid, rather disjointed conversations, I could see they were subconsciously listening for the sirens. In Bristol at that time it was not so much if, as when.

As we left the pub and made our way through the still thick fog, I felt no uneasiness about the journey back to Gloucester. We had, after all, encountered quite a bit of fog during recent weeks. We had plenty of time, so we walked slowly towards the station, Ron swinging his box, me with my dinner bag on my shoulders, my hands as far into my pockets as possible, collar turned up against this murky weather.

On reaching the station we saw at a glance that it was crowded as usual, mainly with service personnel, sitting, standing, leaning, hurrying. It could have been any station, it was as though they were part of a giant theatrical group who were determined to put on this staged performance for us at every large station we visited.

Walking towards the front of the train, we discovered that we had just been a little too leisurely in our walk from the pub as we were unable to find a seat, or indeed standing room in the corridor, so we eventually found ourselves talking to the guard, who said we could ride in the parcel van next to the engine, a thing we had done several times before—and since.

Ron knew the LMS driver, who was a Gloucester man, and while they exchanged a few words, including the fog, which apparently was now dense outside the station precinct, I could see the fireman still shovelling coal into the firebox while he topped his boiler. He shut off the injector and everything was quiet for about half a minute, then the 'Stanier' blew off steam. The fireman opened the firebox door a little, then turned the blower on about a quarter of a turn to get rid of the smoke. I could sense the atmosphere was leading to a climax. The station seemed quite bare now in comparison to the previous activity, the stage was clearing yet again and soon another group of actors would perform in this seemingly non-stop drama.

The parcel trolleys were moving away from the train, then the inevitable slamming of many doors, a crescendo that eventually died away to the odd one or two, as late arrivals managed to push their way into the corridor with difficulty only to find that shutting the door was even more difficult. I didn't know who it was, but some inspector type railwayman came up to the driver saying, 'You are 'right away' clear to Gloucester'.

Ron and I clambered in on top of the parcels, doing our best to get comfortable. Ron seemed uneasy about something; I could tell by his general attitude. The driver sounded his whistle, which, incidentally, seemed appropriate for the weather—it sounded as though the fog had got at it before we had even started. Then we moved away from Temple Meads.

The performance was not yet over. We were now in the orchestra stalls for the finale. As the Stanier hammered its way out of the station it gave a brief slip on the damp rails then settled down, pushing its blunt nose through the thick fog—the music was good.

It proved to be a fast ride, the parcel van was rocking and swaying about quite a bit. It crossed my mind that we would have been better off in a carriage near the rear. It seemed as though Ron had read my thoughts when in the next instant he said 'I tell you Jockey, I don't like this'. I said, 'It ain't that bad—I've ridden in worse vehicles than this lot'. He replied, 'No, not this van, you fool, I mean the bloke coming up to the driver and telling him 'right away' to Gloucester'. I said, 'Well, what's wrong with that?' He said, 'This is a bloody Midland engine on the front'. The penny dropped at last. Neither this engine, or any other to my knowledge, apart from the Great Western, had 'Automatic Train Control' fitted. So there we were, just passing down through Charfield at anything between 80 and 90 miles per hour, the driver having been told he had the road to Gloucester. Should anything big lie foul to the track, the only things that stood between that train, loaded with hundreds of passengers and disaster, were the possibility of one of the engine crew just happening to catch a glimpse of a glimmering signal light, or the efforts of whatever fog man happened to be on duty with his detonators. I was very relieved a few minutes later—it seemed a few minutes anyway—when I realised the driver had closed the regulator and was coasting down through Tuffley, still at some speed. At last we could feel and hear the brakes being applied and as the engine started to blow off we entered the LMS station, where, as we travelled alongside the platform, I suddenly became aware of all the usual echoes, both from the steam, the brakes and the metallic conrod noises. I knew we had arrived safely.

Automatic Train Control

From that night on I began to appreciate how lucky we were to have engines fitted with ATC. It worked from a metal ramp between the rails, which made contact with a metal shoe on the engine. These ramps were situated some distance from the distant signal so that in adverse weather conditions the engine crew had time to look out and catch a glimpse of the light as they passed.

When approaching the distant signal which was against us, a siren-type noise would be emitted from the ATC box and at the same time there would be a hiss of air rushing into the brake system, which, if left unattended, would eventually apply the brakes completely.

Usually, in good visibility when the driver could see the signal plainly, he would override the action of the ATC by holding up a little handle so making it unnecessary to replenish his vacuum brake. When approaching a distant signal in the off position, a bell sounded in the cab, making no action necessary by the driver as no brakes were being affected, the ramp having had a negative effect on the apparatus. There is no doubt that it made the job less hazardous in bad weather, and also a lot easier.

My first two motorbikes

At this time I had been the proud possessor for two or three weeks of an old Coventry Eagle 150cc two-stroke motorbike. It cost me the princely sum of £15. The idea was to get me more easily to and from Horton Road engine shed—in the event I must have pushed it nearly as far as I rode it. My father was right when he said the first time it failed to start that the chap I had bought it from must have seen me coming.

On the second or third time I rode it to work, in darkness of course, I was just going up a slight incline above the 'Apple Tree' at Minsterworth, when I was suddenly jolted from my drowsy state by a terrific bang, followed by a rapid hollow popping and hissing. For an instant I couldn't decide whether this thing had at last excelled itself by finding some previously almost non-existent power and consequently overdone it, or whether I was perched on my seat on some engine, being rudely brought to my senses by my foot slipping off the damper, which often happened. As the engine ceased to turn over, the lights failed, causing me to drop my feet to the road as I came to a standstill.

On this occasion my luck was in; it was only the spark plug which had blown out. Fortunately those old machines had the plug lead screwed on securely so I managed to retrieve it in the darkness, from where it was hanging down by my footbrake.

When the engine had cooled a little I screwed the plug back into the cylinder-head. It started up first kick, going like a bird for the remainder of the journey to work. I was thinking, 'well I'll soon put that job right, there really isn't that much to petrol engines,' but I soon found out there was more to it than replacing a spark plug.

At that time I knew very little about motor-bikes or cars. I didn't think that was anything to be ashamed of because these things were uncommon before the war. Only the doctor, better-off farmers, or the local squire owned a car, usually older people of a mature age. As we all know there are few houses today, rich or poor, that don't have at least one car or motorbike in the garage, or more than likely on the road, so people have the opportunity to obtain basic mechanical knowledge at an earlier age. On reflection I believe the ignition points were the main fault with that old bike, that was before I got about it!

At whatever time of the night or morning I was due to leave for work, my mother always got up with me. She would make a small fire in the open grate, boil enough water for a cup of tea each, then make what she called toast. Anyone who has tried to make toast by holding the slice of bread on a toasting fork, quickly offering it to any small flame that presented itself on any one of half a dozen pieces of kindling wood, will have some idea of the result. 'Crisp Hot Bread'—that is always provided it hasn't slipped from the fork too many times, when it was apt to take on a greyish look.

Mother always waited a while after I had pushed the bike past the window towards the road to see if it would start. On the many occasions that it failed to fire, when mother thought I had run up and down the road enough times, swearing and threatening to set fire to the thing, she would emerge in her nightdress to help push. One night, after running out to begin pushing the bike as fast as possible, her slippers flew off just as the bike started. Producing a light of sorts, I could see her footprints on the frosty tarmac road. I always think of that incident whenever Good King Wenceslas is sung; the bit about the footprints in the very sod!

Things began to get worse with this bike. I nearly gave up trying to ride it, even had I been fortunate to live at the top of a hill there would still have been the problem of getting back up, so I kept vowing to run it into the Severn.

Then came the time when some learned chap, I forget who, told me about a wonderful rejuvenating effect which an operation known as 'decarbonising' would have on a bike, so I resolved to have a go. It was as though the bike was aware of what may be happening in the future, because it started performing altogether better than of late. When at last I managed to find the time in daylight to start this job, I became aware of the fact that I had no tools available, with the exception of a medium-sized hatchet, a rather heavy hammer, and a very strained shifting spanner, but I knew someone who might have an odd spanner or two that I might be able to borrow.

I very cleverly clamped the adjustable spanner on to one of the cylinderhead bolts to get a rough idea of the size, then set off to see what I could borrow. I ended up finding someone who had several box spanners. I borrowed the lot—I did try to measure up which one was nearest to the gap I had originally set out with on the adjustable, but with the three sixteenths of an inch or so play on the jaws of the spanner, I could see it was not going to work out so I was most relieved to be offered the whole set. The piston head certainly looked in a dirty state so I pressed on, scraping the carbon away with my pocket knife from the top of the piston, the cylinder-head, and exhaust ports, though it was not a good job without emery paper.

I carefully disconnected the piston, using a couple of old darts to remove the circlips, before tapping out the gudgeon pin with the big hammer, using an old railway bolt which had come in a piece of firewood for a drift.

While putting things back together I was imagining the sort of performance I was going to achieve, in view of how well it had been going of late. Now, at last, it was ready for the big test.

I had seen some of the older lads of the village tinkering and riding their bikes on a Sunday morning. One would go tearing up the road, then as one or two of his mates watched, he would come down the road flat out, trousers flapping, shirt billowing.

One thing I did notice for sure was that it seemed the done thing to roll up the shirt sleeves, the shirt was always unbuttoned at the neck, while a ladies' hairnet kept their brilliantined hair in place.

All that remained was to pass the lads (and any of the neighbours who happened to be standing, shaking their heads) as fast as possible, usually looking whitefaced and savage as a tup, just for good measure. If they were not pleased with the way their bike had passed the saluting base, perhaps a little slower than desired, or if it had misfired once or twice, they would return usually with the left knee stuck out at almost right angles to the bike, constantly ducking their head half under the petrol tank, while with the left hand they either tickled the float chamber needle or checked to make sure the petrol was turned fully on. I am quite sure that often they weren't checking anything, but I suppose they thought it was the right thing to do.

Occasionally they would give the right hand side of the bike their attention just to make a change for the benefit of the onlookers, though this tended to cause some people to head across to the wrong side of the road. Neither was it easy, apparently, to keep the right hand on the twist grip while trying to get your head down inside, or outside the arm, so the left side still remained favourite.

As this was a weekday I had no audience, which in the event was just as well. No hair net, but I did roll up my shirt sleeves and unbutton the neck of my shirt; one thing I had just acquired was an old leather flying helmet, so I donned it. Looking at my reflection in the kitchen window, I thought it just the thing, with straps left hanging down.

Determined to make the gravel fly, I wheeled the bike out to the road where I quickly swung my leg over on to the kick start; it started about the third or fourth kick and as I sank bank against the saddle I steeled myself for a neck-snapping experience. Well, the kick didn't come with the first gear, second gear; found me relaxing a little, with top gear I found myself leaning forward in an unconscious effort to urge it on, while the bike chugged to a standstill. After a few more morale-sapping attempts, I scooted my way through the garden gate, stepped off the bike and let it fall into the box bushes.

Soon after this event I happened to mention all this trouble with the bike to a man who was riding one of the early type mopeds, that was the standard cycle with the little power pack; it was fixed behind the saddle with a direct drive on to the rear tyre. This man was thinking about buying something a little heavier when he could afford it, but in the meantime, having had some experience with motorbikes, he would call in and see if he could throw any light on my trouble. He called in soon after this, with some spanners in his coat pocket, with which he started to strip the engine. He then looked and poked about a bit with a screwdriver and a piece of stiff copper wire, which he pushed even down behind the flywheel, in the inlet, and exhaust ports, and down the exhaust pipe. Eventually he told me that he was unable to see anything wrong and replaced the cylinder, assuring me that it should be all right.

The results were about the same as before. We both had a go at the thing but eventually we were exhausted with kicking and pushing. I didn't want to know any more about it anyway, so I let it fall into the box bush again.

'Tell you what' he said, 'I like a bit of a challenge, so I'll make you an offer of five pounds, just to have something to tinker at to see if I can do anything with it.' I jumped at the deal but I told him there were no comebacks as he knew the score, to which he readily agreed. Next day when I arrived home from work my mother produced a large white five pound note—he had come and taken the bike. I must say I was quite relieved that it had gone, but I was still quite worried about selling something as useless as that. Two or three days later my young brother told me that he had seen some man riding past on a motor cycle just like the one I had sold, but I assured him there could be little chance of that, adding that it was highly probable

A busy scene south of Cheltenham Lansdown station looking towards Gloucester. The lines going off to the left went around the southern suburbs before climbing up to Andoversford and splitting, either to Cirencester/Swindon or Kingham . A triangle was completed by the line from the Gloucester direction.
(E.R. Morten)

97

that he would be returning it, expecting his money back.

The same evening a mate called in to see me. He told me that the man I sold the Coventry Eagle to had got it going well, which I was quite relieved to hear. Then I was told that this man was telling people what a mug I was for having put the piston in back to front. Of course he had noticed it straight away but kept quiet. Still, I was quite willing to pay to learn.

It was back to the pedal cycle for a few days, until Ron said that I should try getting lifts on goods trains to and from Oakle Street Station, which was the local station at Minsterworth, leaving me about a mile to walk home, so I thought—why not?

As I've mentioned before, we were now doing excessive overtime which took some time getting used to, but after a while time didn't seem to matter. The sooner I finished work the sooner I had to start again. There was nowhere to go and little to do; even when some function did take place I was usually on my way to work, or coming home, so the fact that I would need to leave two and a half hours before I was due to sign on duty was neither here nor there. The chief delay usually occurred at Over Junction, where goods trains were turned into the loop line, sometimes having to wait hours for relief in Gloucester Station, so they remained waiting at Over.

I tried this method of transport for a week or so, but I soon began to see that it wasn't going to work. No doubt in normal times this could have been done on a regular basis, apart from the odd driver who didn't feel like easing up at Oakle Street for me to jump off.

Of course, it could be difficult getting on at this station. An unco-operative driver could take a lot of convincing of the coincidence between me wanting a ride and the signalman having to check his train because he hadn't got the line clear for him. There was one occasion when I was most embarrassed by the driver and fireman muttering between themselves, each throwing scowling glances towards the steam and water gauges, to the fire, then at me, to be repeated every few minutes as the engine strove to get some heavy coal train moving again, so eventually discretion bade me stop this caper.

I soon bought another motorbike. This time it was right up to date, a 1939 BSA 250cc. Although three years old anything made during the year war was declared was about as new as it was possible to get.

My first semi fast

I had been on the main line a few months now, mainly with Ron although on the odd occasions it had been necessary to be with other drivers, usually for one shift. I was getting to know a little more about the job but I had not been on anything faster than the usual goods or freight train, the speed of which obviously varied a lot. At that time our station cabin, where we used to wait for a train, was a dimly-lit piece of old carriage at the end of the platform nearest Horton Road—terribly scruffy and untidy, it was known as the 'bug house'.

Ron and I were sitting there early one morning; it was our turn next for a job. We had booked on at midnight and it was now about five thirty in the morning. I was beginning to nod and as usual having difficulty in keeping my eyes open. I won't mention the fact that I was feeling a bit low in temperature and quite hungry! In my usual despondent frame of mind, I was getting closer to nodding off completely. I remember thinking along the lines 'God in heaven, there must be somewhere, an easier way of making a living. Surely there are jobs somewhere, where it is necessary to have daylight and warmth, sunshine even'.

The next thing I knew there was a sudden rush of air, I was bathed in light which was warm and in my confusion I thought my wishes had been fulfilled—behind all this there was an angel who had come to take me away. The angel was saying to my mate, in a familiar voice, 'I want your mate, Ron'. I was waiting for Ron to say that he could not have me and when he didn't I quickly roused myself, and as I did so the warm light became a paraffin lamp and as I began to focus my eyes beyond the lamp, the angel became the Podgy Inspector, who wore black boots, thick grey flannel trousers and a brown sports jacket. He looked uncomfortable at the best of times, with bow tie and bowler hat, but at this hour of the night he was out of this world. 'I want him to go to Cardiff with a train of tanks The fireman has been taken ill—the driver rang from Stroud where he had to stop to telephone. He is having to drive and fire as his mate is lying in the corner, with possible appendicitis'. Looking back now in an age where it is possible to be kicked to death in a crowded street without anyone lifting a finger to prevent it happening, it makes me glad to have experienced the other side of human nature, as I witnessed the willingness of everyone to help in the few minutes that special tank train was in the station.

People on the platform began to sense something was about to happen as doors leading from the street to the station were being opened wide, some dim lights were shaded or put out to prevent any light shining on the station approach.

When the old ambulance was backed up to the door, two men came hurrying on to the platform carrying a stretcher and people on the opposite platform began stirring to obtain a view of the ambulance men. There was obviously much conjecture in their conversation as to just what was going to take place at this hour of the morning.

Then the train was thundering down over Horton Road crossing, coming on down past the engine sheds and my heart gave a jump. I realised the engine was carrying 'C' headlights which meant that it was vacuum fitted, or brakes on every wagon, which in turn meant (and this was the most important) the driver was going to have to do what was known as 'run um', travel fast.

I was more than a little worried as I had not had any experience of speed on a locomotive. I was under no illusions about what might happen, or of my capabilities. If the inspector had changed his mind and come along with an older fireman I should have accepted it as common sense, after all what mattered was getting the tanks to the embarkation point on time.

The engine came to a grinding halt opposite the station exit, instead of pulling

Tanks were carried on special wagons, low-built to accommodate the height of their load. Notice the chains used to secure them. *(Author's Collection)*

right up to the signal. It looked a useful engine of the Manor Class, I forget which. I could make out the outline of the tanks and I thought, 'Yes, there is some sort of weight involved here'.

Now, even in wartime, passengers, whether forces or civilians, don't jump down onto the track and stumble across the rails to where a locomotive, belching steam, is towering above their heads, but they did that night. The two ambulance men clambered down on to the track, making their way uncertainly up on to the footplate, but the gangway between the tender and the engine was too narrow for a stretcher. The patient couldn't climb down, he was far too ill, semi-conscious and groaning with every breath he took. This was no problem—in response to shouts from down on the track, where quite a number of men had followed the ambulance crew, the stretcher was pushed out and down into the semi-darkness. A sea of hands, as about a score of servicemen tried to get their hands under it. The ambulance men and the driver got the patient on his feet and brought him backwards through the gangway

A typical wartime scene with armoured tanks being transported to a seaport for shipment to the Russian front. *(Author's Collection)*

down into the gloom. Holding on to the rail with the one hand, and the patient's wrists with the other, the ambulance men, one on either side, steadied him backwards until finally, with a groan, he sank on to the stretcher, which was sloping slightly down toward the footplate, so lessening the depth necessary for the man to be lowered before his back was supported by the stretcher. This was all made possible by many arms being stretched up to the limit. Some were tall enough to get their full hand to it, with others it was just the tips of their fingers.

The stretcher seemed to float across from the engine, up on to another dozen or so outstretched hands that were on the platform, and through the door. In fact they were at the rear of the ambulance by the time the two ambulance men had managed to find their way off the engine. Once more the old cliche, 'What a pity it takes something like a war to bring the best out in many people'.

As the stretcher disappeared into the darkness I quickly climbed up on to the footplate, by this time being as fully awake as I was ever likely to be. The driver was up in the tender working furiously away, shovelling coal forward in an endeavour to fill the hole as far as possible. I thought he was doing well as he looked about 60 years of age to me. He greeted me with a brief nod and said, 'You are with me to Cardiff then mate?' I nodded as I took the shovel and started building up the fire. It was very low by this time, having lost a lot of ground while the fireman had been getting steadily worse. The driver had had to fire and drive from Stonehouse; still, he had done very well.

Luckily the engine turned out to be one of the few I encountered which had been well serviced, the fire was bright and burning evenly causing the safety valve to blow about half a minute after the boiler was topped up.

The signal came off, we had the road. The driver said 'Right, let's get going mate'. I was already winding my handbrake off, I had seen the signal but I was hoping he had not as every few extra seconds were helping me to get something in reserve. It was still only about five minutes since the train had come to a halt, so most of the service personnel on both sides of the station were still on their feet, milling around the platform in the vicinity of the engine.

They seemed interested in the feverish activity going on on the footplate, it was almost as though they were expecting another invalid to alight, but they were at the wrong station, they should have been in Cardiff a little later! They couldn't complain though, the Manor made a wonderful start up the incline towards London Road Bridge. She did slip briefly by the water column where the rails were usually wet for most of the time when the bag on the column, still dripping water, was swung away from the engine tank filler holes to its parked position. This caused a lot of noise and a multitude of sparks showered the rails at a point to the rear of where each of the six driving wheels made contact and strived to regain traction, while overhead clouds of billowing smoke and steam made the dark sky even darker.

Until that noisy incident, our departure had been to the accompaniment of whistles, waves and wisecracks, but these were now some way behind as we descended toward Over Junction. I stuck my head out once to catch the signal on my side and as the cold air hit me I ducked quickly back in, shouting 'Right o Way Over mate'. I don't know if he acknowledged it or not. We clattered under Over Bridge, then opened up a bit along past the sidings, soon we were on the incline towards Downs Bridge. He really opened her up then and I was worried. I grabbed the shovel, which was stuck well under the coal, steadied myself and waited for the instant I felt confident enough to rip the fire box open, slam in a shovel full of coal, then balance myself, one hand on the loaded shovel and one on the firebox door handle.

Passing under Downs Bridge was the last landmark, with the exception of Chepstow Bridge, I remember seeing until we arrived at Cardiff—I certainly didn't have time to look out for any more signals. I was used to throwing half a dozen or so shovels full of coal on at a time, but as I was having difficulty in staying on my feet I had to be content with continuously holding the shovel, trying to pop one in whenever the possibility presented itself, which didn't seem to crop up often enough. I even found myself dragging the shovel with me as I tried to get the exhaust steam injector going. I thought if I let it go I'd probably never find it again! I estimate that for every twenty shovels full I managed to get into the firebox, I would miss with one, which would strike the edge of the sliding half doors, shooting the coal in the direction of the driver's feet. He shouted out 'Bloody hell mate' once or twice, after which he changed it to something else, which I never did quite make out.

We had been travelling some time when he shouted across to me 'We'll take some water here mate'. I replied, in a voice I knew he couldn't hear, 'Well I suggest you begin dropping the brakes into her then'. Thinking we were stopping I began to heave a sigh of relief at the thought of getting time to gather myself, but the sigh never ran its course. As I went to put my head out to see where we were the engine gave one of her many kicks, causing me to fall against the side rail giving my head a nasty bang. I turned back to the gauges again, and as I did so the driver let out one more oath, then turned round to the water scoop handle, furiously winding it down. Once again the penny dropped—I had never taken water on the run before—and I stood back in amazement as the water indicator quickly bobbed its way towards the full mark. The driver shouted 'Right, see if you can wind the scoop back up, she must be full now'. I wound as fast as I could, then once more grabbed the shovel, doing my best to get some fire in the box, but I seemed to be losing although the steam and water seemed to be looking all right. I thanked my lucky stars to be on a good steamer.

Somewhere behind me I was once more aware that dawn was bringing a pale world outside the cab slowly into focus.

A few minutes later I was able to see why the driver appeared to have grown a good deal taller than he was when we left Gloucester and also why he appeared to be shuffling his feet for most of the journey; he was standing on a six or seven inch layer of coal! Suddenly there were more signals than I have ever seen at one time, this was, without a doubt, Cardiff. I realised we were coasting in so I quickly shut off the exhaust injector, then turned on the main steam injector. The water showed a bit low in the gauge now, as it always seemed in the habit of doing when the engine was no longer pulling.

We were relieved at Cardiff, but before the fresh crew climbed up into the cab I managed to scrape some of the coal from the driver's side, then while the injector was still on I used the pep pipe to swill the footplate off, which completed the clean up. The hot water and steam cleaned every corner and crevice; it was quite a transformation.

The fire was very low now, I really don't know how much further I could have gone without being in trouble and I was thankful to hand the job over to someone else. I stepped up on to the coal in the tender and managed to slide and shovel half a ton into the hole before the relief had arrived. I apologised to the fireman about the fire. He didn't seem worried. He was a big Welsh chap in his 'twenties and he replied, 'Don't worry about it, she'll be all right Boyo'. I slithered back down over the coal on to the footplate, feeling a weight rise off my shoulders.

I walked with the driver towards the station. It was now daylight and being able to look around me I began to realise this was quite a busy place, somewhat bigger than Gloucester. After giving me directions to the platform from which the Gloucester passenger train would leave, we parted. He to book off, me to walk bleary-eyed to the station where I found a vacant seat; I soon dozed off.

There was no chance of sleeping for many minutes, too many trains were on the move. The noisiest was the station pilot, it kept hurrying backwards and forwards, in and out of the place with coaches that were being moved around, to make up trains of various lengths and types for different destinations. I got up and sauntered into the Church Army tea room and paid twopence for a cup of tea of sorts. Needless to say it wasn't very good, however, I was glad to drink it. There was, of course, no food to be had.

At last there was the Gloucester train standing at the end of the platform waiting for the signal and 'right o way' from the guard. At the front, blowing her head off with steam was 'Chepstow Castle'. How nice it all seemed in broad daylight. Now I could never have been described as a glutton for punishment, in fact I don't think I ever had what may be described as an appetite and I can't offer any explanation as to what went through my head as I stood looking at the engine and general activity on and around it.

I didn't know the names of the driver or fireman, which was nothing unusual. We all knew each other by sight but as the express men were never around the cabins, or around the shed, we only got a glimpse of them leaving with a train, or arriving back, or perhaps in the time office, but this didn't deter me. I walked up to the engine, greeted the two men, then stepping up on to the footplate asked them if I could fire the train back to Gloucester, just like that.

The driver looked me up and down. I'm not sure he liked what he saw, I know my eyes were black and half sunken into my head, I must have looked ready to drop. Certainly a good meal would not have gone amiss. He said, 'I don't know about that—have you worked a passenger before?' I replied hesitantly, 'Well no, not exactly, of course we don't get much chance of that, but I have just worked the Tank Special down'. He said, 'I'll tell you what, you can ride on the footplate as long as you don't get in my mate's way, then you can see how it is done'.

I accepted his offer, and I was now having to pretend to look disappointed because I was just beginning to realise what a fool I was, to imagine I could ever have made a reasonable job of working that passenger all the way to Gloucester. I was still only seventeen years and six months—not very big either. It's not often possible for anyone to be happy at having a request refused.

Everything looked good on this quite pleasant morning, at least I could see what was going on, both on the engine and the platform, where the usual slamming of doors was in progress. Through the firebox doors, which were slightly ajar, I was able to see that the fire had been made up so that there appeared to be barely room for a shovel to pass between it and the top of the smoke plate, while the coal was heaped up in the hole, readily available whenever the fireman should make a start.

The water was up out of sight in the gauge glass, so when the Castle blew it just kept blowing because there was no way of using the surplus steam, which was quite a revelation in itself as far as I was concerned. However, this was really short-lived and as the signal came off there was the usual shrill blast from the guard's whistle and we were off.

As this huge engine pulled away from the station the sound emitted from the blast pipe was almost deafening, while the massive clouds of smoke-tainted steam that came with each exhaust shot skyward, drifting on the breeze a little before quickly fading, only to be replaced by the next. As I stood on the hinged curved plate which spans the gap between the engine and the tender, the oscillation took me rather by surprise. I was forced to make a grab for the handrail to hang on. Previously I had only stepped on these plates briefly as I moved around the footplate on other engines I had worked. I had, on several occasions, felt a slight thrill when starting off with a heavy goods train, or climbing steep inclines through Brimscombe, or up to Andoversford, but these feelings were always cut short by the task in hand.

On this occasion though, all I had to do was hang on and look over the side of the engine as we blasted our way clear of the station. It was then that I experienced what I can only describe as an ecstatic feeling of power, for a few seconds it appeared to occupy all my senses, the sound of the exhaust beats, the sight of the billowing exhaust steam, the smell and taste of smoke, as it can only smell when produced by a steam locomotive working hard. The rolling motion caused my own weight to be constantly transferred from one part of my feet to another, while through my hands, as they gripped the rails firmly, vibrations flowed as an electric current, all appearing to culminate in my spine. It is impossible for me to describe accurately my emotions on that and quite a few occasions after, but people who have worked steam locomotives will know the feeling.

It turned out to be not only a very pleasant experience for me, but I also learned quite a bit, not least the mistakes I had made on the way down on the tank special.

We had travelled some miles when I became aware that there was not one bit of coal spilt on the footplate from the shovel, this I thought immediately was because the fireman could see what he was doing. Soon I realised the main reason was that he knew exactly where he was; he knew every signal and every curve of the track. There were many between Lydney and Gloucester, so he could quickly shovel six or eight shovels full into the fire, then stand back and hold tight to keep his balance. I don't think I would have done much better than I did had I gone down to Cardiff in daylight, not knowing the road. At least the darkness hid my embarrassment somewhat, when I began to realise what I was doing.

We arrived at Gloucester, running down to the far end of the up platform. The fireman uncoupled the engine from the coaches and we set off for the engine shed, and the turntable ready for their return journey.

The driver said, 'What did you think of the ride up?' I told him I had enjoyed it and said if I happened to meet them somewhere again, I would like to travel with them on the footplate. 'Yes', he said, 'Next time you can earn your fare by giving my mate a free ride'! On this occasion I was thanking my lucky stars that the driver had said I could come for the ride and watch his mate.

As I mentioned earlier, food and sleep were the biggest prob!ems at that time. As for myself, I don't know which of these two were in the shortest supply. It was possible to do with less and less of both over a period of several years, but I think it was sleep, or lack of it, that wore me right down. Food would vary, one day I felt relatively full, the next quite hungry, it depended on what could be found to cook up at home. Manual workers got a little extra cheese each week, I think it was four ounces, certainly not more—but I hated cheese. There was a scheme for fattening a pig for killing at home—you joined the pig club, thus enabling you to get a small ration of pig food, to be used with vegetable scraps, but it was necessary to forgo the bacon ration for a year, so you couldn't afford to ask the neighbours round for a bacon supper. Pig meat, which could not be kept for many days unless salted, was shared to some extent. This was repaid when the pigs were killed by neighbours. Incidentally, pig meat is a thing missed by many people, not least myself. Pork is, of course, available but that is not the same. Those small elongated joints that were cut from the backbone of large bacon pigs were beautiful to taste; the backbone which is quite scarce now was also very sweet. We found the tea ration was rather inadequate to put it mildly; we were issued with one quarter pound and one tin of Carnation evaporated milk every month, at the engine shed. I still can't imagine how we were supposed to keep milk for a month once it was opened. I took it home to be used up, while I took a little cows' milk in a bottle, but, of course, even that was rationed. There are two words that came very much to the fore during the war years, even now they both give me a queer feeling in my stomach, accompanied by a feeling of annoyance, to put it mildly. These words were 'rationed' and 'queue' whatever you did, or wherever you went, one, or both would crop up. If you were entitled to a ration of something you still had to queue for it and what was worse, ration book or no, there may not be any left for the time being after you had queued. I don' t want to give the impression of grumbling about situations that existed, even if we were unable to get a scrap of food of any sort after we had eaten that which we had brought from home, while factory canteens, restaurants and large stores were able to dish up good cooked meals. What's that saying about 'all being fair in love and war'?

The Mushrooms

I was regularly plagued with nasty chills and sore throats, and blamed the varying conditions of the job. One minute I was sweating and the next feeling cold or even shivering, and, of course, I was riding my motor bike home in all weathers with no proper kit; just a buttoned-up railway jacket or a mac, which was hardly sufficient to keep out the elements. It was while I was suffering from one of these chills that I found myself stuck in Over down loop on an engine at about 6.30 one autumn morning. We had booked on early the previous evening and had been on duty about twelve hours with no sign of us moving; there must have been a train, or perhaps two, in loops and sidings all the way to the Atlantic coast. I must have dozed off for suddenly I awoke with the usual start as my foot slipped off one of the damper handles, where I was in the habit of resting my right foot, because from my small wooden seat I had difficulty in reaching the floor.

My throat felt terrible. I couldn't attempt to clear it, neither was I able to swallow my saliva. I thought I could easily lie down and die and I almost did just that a few moments later when feeling desperately hungry I grabbed a shallot from my bag. Peeling it with my teeth and sprinkling it with salt, I popped it in my mouth and began chewing ravenously. As I tried to swallow I thought that the world had come to an end. My throat felt on fire and I tried to cough but had great difficulty in getting air up or down—as I said, I thought my time had come. I never did manage to get any of it down and felt very disappointed, savage and still very hungry. Ron didn't make things any better by rousing up with a start and saying, 'What the hell is going on Jockey? For God's sake have one of these Woodbines and get it off your chest'. I felt too ill to answer.

It was daybreak now, and sheep in a nearby meadow became restless after a hard night's sleep. They moved a few paces and began nibbling the grass. I was thinking something like, 'you lucky Ewes you!' when I realised the grass was not the only thing growing in the field beside the sheep. Unless my eyesight was becoming impaired by the fact that I had great difficulty in keeping my eyelids up, then those whitish blobs were mushrooms.

Quickly climbing down the engine steps I jumped on to the ballast, half slid down the line embankment, through the wire fence, and ran across the field towards the mushrooms as though someone might beat me to them. Needless to say, the sheep scattered in all directions then made off to a far corner where they stood in a group, all eyes on me. I ran around grabbing the mushrooms, placing them in my cap with such feverish haste anyone would have thought I was expecting to be shot at, or at least be chased off by an alsatian.

I took all I could find—about a dozen or fifteen—then hurried back to the engine, clambered aboard and started peeling the spoils. Ron said 'What have you got there Jockey?' 'Mushrooms', I replied. He said, 'Good Lord, Corn in Egypt'. When I had finished peeling I ran the injector and using the pep pipe I swilled the shovel clean, leaving half a shovel full of water in which to boil the mushrooms. They were thrown into the water, then I gently pushed the blade of the shovel through the firebox door, where, even though the fire was fairly low by this time, they were nevertheless soon boiling fast. After two or three minutes I considered them cooked and carefully withdrew the shovel. I became aware of a terrible craving for something hot and savoury as I got a whiff of the mushroom aroma, and began wishing I had just one small piece of 'Tom Evans' fat bacon! Having poured off as much water as I dared from this very long shovel blade without risking the loss of some of the mushrooms, I placed the shovel on the footplate, propping it level so as to retain its contents. When I had liberally sprinkled them with salt from my salt bottle I began eating with my fingers from the shovel, each one scalding my fingers, then my mouth. I was making rather a pig of myself, blowing my fingers and loudly sucking cold air as the mushrooms reached my mouth, but who cared? Except Ron, who looked at me with disgust and said, 'Good God'. Those soft hot mushrooms were like a soothing balm as they slid down my throat and I was actually making some sort of progress at swallowing again. With the last one eaten I sat back on my stool licking my lips and wiping away the water that had escaped down my chin. I must have looked and acted like a cat that had just eaten a mouse!

'Did you enjoy that lot?' asked Ron. 'I did' I replied, 'I could eat another shovelful if I could see any about', and lapsed into a comfortable silence.

About fifteen minutes later the train in front of us in the loop moved out on to the main line, departing towards Oakle Street station. We then received the signal to pull forward to take that train's place. As we did so I opened the dampers and made the fire up a bit as it looked as though we may move at last.

We crawled forward to the end of the loop, the main line signal came off, (signalling go) and soon a fast train was passing us, gathering speed towards Downs Bridge (the bridge joining Minsterworth and Highnam where it crosses over the railway lines). Ron said 'I should work her up a bit Jockey because I reckon we shall go when that fast one clears Oakle Street'. Thereupon I started seriously on the fire—although I had done a bit to it a few moments earlier, it was nevertheless still rather low.

I had kept the water in the boiler well up the glass. As soon as the steam pressure clock came up to the two hundred mark and the fire, with the aid of the blower, was looking very bright, I was more or less ready. As Ron predicted, the signal came off with a clatter, as they always seemed to do, and so I wound the handbrake off and we were on our way, laboriously pulling out of the loop on to the main line, then onto the incline towards the bridge. Glancing backwards from time to time, I was waiting to see the complete train out on the main line when I should get a signal from the guard that the train was intact and that he was safely on board-- then I would say OK to Ron and we would get seriously under way. On this occasion it took longer than usual, even after I had received the tip from the guard I carried on as though I had not yet seen him, leaning over the side and looking back I was attempting to hide the fact that I was being as sick as a dog! I could feel the perspiration on my forehead and I felt terrible, but at least I could swallow for a while.

A Near Go

One evening, during the hours of darkness, we took over a train which we were to work as far as Stratford-on-Avon. There we would hopefully be relieved, to be able to work another train or, should we be a lot over our working shift, get a ride back home.

On this particular evening there was a driver who, being new to the Gloucester area, was having a period of learning various routes, or roads—it was known as learning the road. As Ron was getting briefed by the supervisor it was decided that this driver should come with us. Somehow instinct would tell me as I approached an engine on a train like this if it was good or not, steamwise of course. Well, this one was obviously one of the bad ones, needing fire and tube cleaning, plus, in all probability, boiler washing. The fireman said 'You've got to keep at her mate'— that is like a hospital sister saying a patient is 'rather poorly'.

We crawled away from Gloucester at a snail's pace, up over Horton Road crossing towards Cheltenham. I could see this was going to be another of these outings which I associated with utter exhaustion to achieve little. With cotton waste in each hand I reached into the darkness and dragged out the long rake bar which was more the shape of a long old-fashioned key, a long bar with a sort of blade on the one end forming the letter L, with a handle on the other end. In daylight, without the blackout sheets mentioned earlier, it was possible with a little care to swing it to the left, over the coal and tool box, and drop the end down somewhere behind the driver's feet. The blackout sheet meant that I had to feed the bar back past my right shoulder, being careful not to overdo it while the far end of the bar was scraped across the footplate past the driver's feet and so into the fire.

On this trip it was much worse; there were two pairs of feet and legs to manouvre past. Luckily for me we were still going no more than ten to fifteen miles an hour as I entered the bar into the firebox, pulling, pushing, and raking at the clinker in

110

an effort to move it or break it all up. The clinker was too thick and later I had to use the heavier pricker bar to break it up. In the meantime I had discovered that this long rake wasn't going to do the job, thereupon I began to pull it out. The first 3ft. was red hot and the rest was very hot at the point where my left hand, with the ball of cotton waste, was positioned.

The drivers were talking and peering forward through the window, obviously looking for the next signal for our passenger to note. It was not always that the strange driver was the learner. For example, if we reached a destination and it was necessary to take the engine to shed and your driver didn't know the road, then occasionally instead of them sending a fresh crew, they may just send a driver who became a pilot man.

To get back to this near disastrous evening, as the red hot bar came clear of the firebox, I shouted 'Watch out for the bar', but they didn't seem to hear me and went on talking and looking out. I was carefully pulling the rake backwards, concentrating on keeping as much distance as possible between them and the bar, and my left hand was creeping further down the bar as I fed it back past my right side. I could see the smoke as the waste started to smoulder and I knew that was the limit, all I had to do now was to get it past their feet and I could drop it down on the steel footplate for a few seconds to ease my arms. I couldn't believe what happened next for it was over in a flash, there was a not-too-loud bang of steel-on-steel as the bar was slammed against the handrail leading to the footplate. I was thrown hard against the side of the cab where I stood for a few seconds—we were still chugging up the slight incline—the firebox door was wide open, the drivers still engrossed in whatever it was that was being pointed out at the moment, but the difference was that the large, partially red hot bar was no longer with us. I had done the almost impossible—struck a signal or some other solid object with a bar on a moving train and had sustained no injury. When I came to realise properly the gravity of it I was shocked into silence for the rest of the trip. It was some weeks before I mentioned it to Ron. Needless to say he was most concerned about it; all I could think about and still do, was how lucky I was that the blade, or spike (about nine inches long) was obviously pointing away from my body as it was whipped from my hands. I was careful after that but I realised it shouldn't have happened and that few people had the benefit of an experience like that for their future guidance.

The Long Shift

One cold miserable January afternoon I gathered my flying helmet, scarf, canvas leggings and proceeded to dress up against the cold as best I could. Taking my dinner bag to which was attached my tea can, I said goodbye to mother and wheeled my motor bike out. As previously mentioned, I had now progressed to a 1939 250cc BSA with coil ignition, and coil ignition was something new to me. It was tidy looking and a very pleasant bike to ride providing you weren't looking for any exciting speed or acceleration. I had little trouble until the battery began playing up and it failed to start her on one or two occasions.

However, one of my learned friends informed me that unlike a bike with the magneto, I needed power in the battery if I was going to start it anywhere near normally—but batteries were unobtainable. Soon ideas began to come thick and fast until I eventually eliminated all but two; one was to try and stop on a hill—the idea was that as the dynamo was working well it would, when run fairly fast downhill, generate power to close the points on the cut out, or avc, as it was known. As I couldn't guarantee a hill the next idea was the most useful as long as I didn't weaken, or just collapse doing it. A paper clip, or a bent brass terminal off a double cell cycle lamp battery was inserted between the contacts and the bike was then pushed at a furious pace in second or third gear and she would then start. The foreign body was then removed and secreted about my person until the next time. This particular day I went through the usual preliminaries and after a quick sprint along the road she was away.

On reflection I now realise I was accepting this as normal, but I was no sillier than millions of other people throughout the world, who, because of the war and consequential dire shortages, accepted every tribulation that was thrust upon them. I never once worried about a battery, which would have made life a lot easier for me, because I knew they were just not obtainable.

I booked on at 3.45pm. Ron was already there checking speed restrictions and all relative notices. We lingered a couple of minutes, then took a steady walk down towards the station and the relief cabin, there would be no point hurrying anyway. For the first four hours we waited, joining in one of the several games of solo whist that were in progress. We made our first can of tea and had a bite to eat. All evening, men came and went, but gradually the cabin began to fill; there were often occasions when there was no one in the cabin when we reported, and the supervisor would direct us to a train that was already waiting for its crew to be relieved before it could proceed on its way.

At about 10.30pm I was no longer sufficiently awake to play cards. I was sitting on a bench in the corner frequently nodding off, jumping back into full consciousness every time I leaned down too near the bench. Ron, who was still playing, shouted 'Are you going to put the can on Jockey?' 'I suppose I might as well', I replied, and taking the can I ambled off for the water, wondering if I would remain awake long enough to drink it. We had done seventeen hours on the previous shift and as usual I hadn't been able to get more than an odd hour's sleep. We drank the tea as soon as it was ready, and ate any food that was left, for now was the time we could usually be sent up to the engine shed to get some engines prepared as it was now too late to be sent away. No one enjoyed this because although we had not done any work on the shift, we were still tired and ready for home. It was unpleasant to go and get dirty and have to clamber hurriedly up and down the steps of a cold dead engine, looking for tools, checking sand, and making up the fire in the darkness after having kept clean for once. However, it was was not to be on this occasions; the supervisor came in about 11.15pm and looked round for Ron. His eyes caught mine and said, 'Come on' as he walked towards where Ron was playing. 'You'll be lucky' I shouted, 'You can have Ron but you're not having me tonight'. I was going home on time for once. As he was leaving after talking to Ron, I shot him one of the glances usually reserved for time clerks.

Ron told me that he wasn't prepared to go away at this time but the 'gestapo', as the supervisor was known, had said it was a very small job so he had agreed to do it. We were to walk to the North box up beyond Horton Road to relieve some men who had been on for very long hours, we would be taken off outside the cabin when we arrived back here with the train. Still protesting and muttering under my breath, I took my tea can along the platform to where there was an outside tap and as I rinsed out the can I called the supervisor, and the railway generally, everything I could think of and ended up by swishing a can of water at the supervisor's window as I walked away. Ron was waiting as I got back to the cabin, so when I had hung the can on to the bag by one of the straps, we set off reluctantly into the cold darkness, heading past the shed to the North box above Horton Road.

The driver and fireman were very pleased to get relief and after telling us about the condition of the engine, to which we replied that it wouldn't affect us because we would only be on it for a few minutes, they hurriedly climbed down from the engine. We heard the shuffling sound of their boots on the ballast receding quickly into the darkness. I wasn't very interested in the state of the engine as long as the water, fire and pressure was OK, that was it. The previous fireman had made a good job of filling the hole, he had certainly had plenty of time in which to do it. An LMS train started out from Eastgate Station, running up to the crossing and crossed the GWR track diagonally toward Cheltenham. As it cleared the crossover, we got our signal, so with great relief and hurried actions we got the train gently moving on the slightly falling gradient towards the station. Our mild elation at being on the move was short-lived. As we were both keeping a look out down over the crossing, the signals of both stations were all in view, the LMS slightly to the left and the GWR straight in front. Suddenly we saw several green lights appear. Then more green lights appeared beneath the existing ones--we were signalled right through Gloucester. 'They've got them all off Jockey' shouted Ron. I said, 'Yes. I can tell you something else that will be off when we reach the station, and that's me!'

We ignored the signals, pulling up through the station very slowly and coming to a halt outside the supervisor's cabin, where we sounded the engine whistle, whilst shouting various things at the cabin. When the supervisor could stand it no longer he emerged from the door looking very sheepish.

By now I had jumped off the engine and clambered up onto the platform, heading for the cabin. It was lucky for both of us that he came when he did, five seconds later I feel sure his nose would have made contact with the door—it had been my firm intention to kick it open just to see if he was awake, as we were supposed to be. We

Drifting into Gloucester Central station and heading for South Wales, the fireman has just topped up the fire of this 2-8-0, causing a cloud of black smoke, but it will soon disperse. In the foreground are the familiar signal cables and point rodding which, in the blackout, would trip the unwary or even those who regularly walked along the trackside. The crew would be anticipating their relief in the station in a few moments time.

(N. E. Preedy)

114

had a very heated slanging match on the platform during which I told him in various terms that he was a two-faced liar; he in turn threatened to get me suspended. I knew he would not do me a good turn like that, he knew I would have welcomed the rest. By this time many forces personnel on both platforms were taking an interest, some were moving closer so as to miss nothing that may occur, though one or two women apparently decided it was more prudent to keep in the shadows once they had sampled the language that was flying! 'Come on Jockey, I want to have a word with him', said Ron, so I jumped down from the platform and crossed the two up tracks. As I was about to stomp my way back up onto the footplate, I heard some shouting and the waving of a lamp from the signal box--I believe it was called Gloucester South—enquiring 'what in the hell was happening?' I was in the right mood to tell him. I stood with one foot on the bottom step asking him who he was and when he replied the obvious—that he was the signalman—I shouted, 'Well then, wind your—neck in'. With that I scrambled up onto the engine and slumped in my seat. I was fuming. Ron then climbed down from the footplate saying, 'I'm going across to have a word with the sod now: and he quickly crossed the track, placing his fingers on the edge of the platform. Ron leaped up from the track, then it started again but a train came into the station from the Cardiff direction, so their words were unfortunately drowned!

Ron returned after several minutes looking rather angry. He said 'What are you going to do?' to which I replied 'I'm going home, they must have men to relieve us, there was a cabin full three quarters of an hour ago. Ron said 'There are only three sets of men left and they are urgently needed. They want us to go as far as Over Junction, there we can change over with two Severn Tunnel men. We should be back here in half an hour or so. Eventually I agreed and we set off in great haste with a lot of noise, wheels spinning and sparks flying, as we crossed London Road bridge. As we coasted under Over Bridge we could see the headlights of a freight train in one of the up loops so we approached slowly, pulling in to the down loop. Stopping as near to the other engine as possible, after ensuring that our train was far enough inside the loop to be clear of the main line, we hailed the crew and told them we were to change over. Their reply was of the nature that had we been in a court of law, it would have been necessary to write it down and hand it to the clerk of the court! The crew added that they intended to go on to Gloucester to ride home on the first mail train heading for Cardiff.

The signal dropped, the freight train was quickly under way, leaving us with a train facing downhill away from home, which we certainly didn't want but there was no way out now, we had been done once again! We just stood there in the dim light afforded by the gauge lamp and flickering fire, staring at one another in shocked disbelief.

After what seemed ages Ron looked at his watch and said, 'Here we go again, it's five to twelve'. We still had to reach the signal at the end of the loop line so slowly we made our way towards the end. As we approached the signal came off for us to proceed out on to the main line. With that I once more started shovelling as Ron gave the regulator a vicious jerk upward and the rough old 5300 class did its best to respond. I told Ron that I thought they seemed anxious to get us away from Gloucester. The events of the next half hour seemed to prove me right. Letting us out of the loop turned out to be a little premature, because on arrival at Oakle Street station we stopped before the signalman waved us forward to the box. It appeared that he should not have accepted us from Over sidings because Grange Court Junction could not take us off his hands and there were no loop lines or siding at Oakle Street apart from a short siding on the up road for station business—local farming, plus the odd truck of house coal.

The signalman said 'We've got a problem'—this I found laughable. He told us there was a goods train coming uphill and when it had passed we were to pull on down the length of the train past his box. He would signal when we were far enough, then we must push back over on the up track to enable the down mail to go past us.

The goods train came through and we then carried out the signalman's wishes. I felt annoyed that just two orchards, one field and the main Cardiff road as it passed through Minsterworth was all that was between me and my bed. There I was, nine hours on duty already, still waiting to head away from home. Eventually we moved off from Oakle Street for Grange Court Junction, where we were to spend another couple of hours until the paper train passed. We then moved on down to Bullo. Here we had another long wait. Next we stopped on the main line at Awre, and eventually Lydney, where things began to happen again.

It had turned very cold during the night; we had noticed this on those occasions when we were stationary, but at Lydney a nasty north east wind was blowing down over our coal tender and we couldn't escape it.

We stopped on the main line and the signalman was waving his lamp, trying to attract our attention. 'The Bobby wants us', I said to Ron, 'I will go along to see what he wants'. I hurried to the signalbox, shoulders hunched against the cold, conscious of how snug it was as I entered. He told me that he had an urgent instruction for us, we were to push our train back right across the up track. Then with the cooperation of the guard along with others, our train had to be pushed into a siding and left. I commented 'That's the best thing that can happen, now we can run the engine back to Gloucester light, otherwise we will never get home. It's fourteen hours now and we are still going away from home, with no hope of moving by the look of things—by the way, it's just starting to snow'. I began to shiver at the thought of running fast, tender first, in this cold all the way to Gloucester. I did not believe

116

I could stand it. I closed the door, ran down the steep steps, making sure to slide my hands down the rails on either side, then trotted back to the engine, thankfully clambering back into the warmth of the cab, where, standing as close as possible with my back to the fire, I told Ron the news.

Naturally he was as pleased as I was and with a grin he said, 'That just shows what they can do if you stick to your guns to put the wind up them'. 'What did you say then?' I asked. 'I told them that we had both had enough because this was not the first time we had been tricked into going away late in the day. I told them if it got too late we would drop the fire and leave the engine where it was'.

We should have know better. Things weren't in the habit of turning out in our favour as we soon discovered when our train was safely off the main line, tucked away in the siding.

I had nipped smartly off the engine with my gauge lamp (it was definitely snowing now) and pointed its faint glimmer where I thought the brake handle on the first wagon ought to be. Hurrying from one wagon to the next I dropped half a dozen brakes as hard as I could, inserting a safety pin in each, then I uncoupled the engine. I put one headlamp on the tender; unfortunately we would have to run tender first, to class G, one light bottom centre signifying a light engine. Next a red shade for the front lamp which would become the rear when we rejoined the main line, ready for home!

The guard came walking along towards us and the ray of light thrown by his big lamp made the snow look worse than ever. He pushed his box up before him and climbed up on to the footplate.

He placed his box and lamp right out of the way in my corner, then as he rubbed his hands by the fire we began discussing our good fortune in a very light hearted manner.

As we waited expectantly there were these two lights coming through the snowflakes in the distance, which, by their jerking, swaying movements were obviously being carried by people on foot. There was nothing out of the ordinary about that apart from the fact that I was not expecting them, we just wanted a light from the signalman nearby. There was, however, something else I had no explanation for so I called Ron and the guard over. 'What in the hell is this in aid of now?' said Ron, as we stood together, straining our eyes to try and make out what the lights were that flashed on and off, this way and that, at frequent intervals.

It was a very bright electric torch which produced a long concentrated beam, but we wondered who could get them, or the batteries for them, except the police. 'Well, of course all the Yanks have got those sort.' said the guard. He was dead right, its bearer was a Yankee Major. There were three people in this group and all three were carrying a layer of snow on them. They all came up on to the engine for a warm and temporary shelter from the worsening snow. The two civilians turned out to be a shunter and a railway inspector, of which department I never did ask because I wasn't interested, just completely fed up and bewildered. The time must have been around 6 o'clock.

Apparently there was this ammunition train which had been loaded somewhere up in the Forest of Dean and brought to Lydney for urgent movement to Cardiff. I was thankful we wouldn't be going all the way with it—fancy taking an ammunition train to a place which was liable to be bombed at any time of day or night. Ron hadn't been past Severn Tunnel for some time so he couldn't take a train to Cardiff until he had familiarised himself with the road. That would have been his story anyway, and he would have stuck to it should they have tried to pull yet another one. It is said that truth is stranger than fiction! As I followed the progress of the light from the shunter's lamp, backward and forward in that snowstorm, finally latching on to a short train of wagons, I had no difficulty in believing what the old adage implied, but how much longer could this train of events continue?

Our guard went off to obtain details of the train we were about to set off with; it was customary for them to tell the driver how many and how heavy the load was. Any gradients likely to be encountered were taken into consideration when forming a train, where one class of engine may be capable of taking a given load unaided, another may require a banker. I didn't expect any problems with this lot although I couldn't see how many wagons we had. I think the rules wouldn't allow any more than seven of this explosive nature in one train. The guard returned, clambered up on to the footplate as quickly as he could, stamped his feet and brushed away at the layer of snow on his coat and cap. He gave Ron the load details, saying also that he had six American privates and a sergeant riding in his van—and we were definitely being relieved at Severn Tunnel Junction. Hearing a whistle, we looked out and were just able to see a light shining from the signal box, it waved from side to side so we moved quietly forwards towards it. The signalman told us that we were to proceed out on to the main line, so as to be in the queue as it were, but he had no idea when we would move. Apparently it had been snowing heavily for some time down below and they were having difficulty in keeping the points clear of snow. After returning to the main line we crossed over on to the down track, moving slowly down through the station, over the level crossing, to be stopped at the outer home signal, just up the slight incline leaving Lydney. It was about 7.30am now, still very dark, still snowing very hard, and the rails were now barely visible. We were stationary yet again.

I saw the reflection of a torch light on the snow; next a voice called out so I leaned towards the side of the cab very gingerly, trying to keep the bulk of my body in my warm corner beside the boiler. With the help of a few American phrases, and various oaths, which we were soon all to be familiar with, he explained that he was forced to get to the lee side of the wagons, where he was going to have to undo all his clothes in order to do an urgent job for himself. As though he hadn't got enough trouble, he was worried that we may move off leaving him in the snow, before he was ready to climb back into the guard's van. We assured him that we would not pull away without making sure he was aboard. As he made a dive for the partial shelter afforded by the wagons Ron said, 'Blast his horrible luck'. In what appeared to be about one minute later we heard him shouting and shining his torch—he hadn't been hanging about long! Not long afterwards we got the signal, then with the odd spell of slipping on the deep snow we made our way to Beachley once more, where we stayed until daylight.

It was a bright dawn for the time of the year, the snow storm had passed and it looked as though we could be in for a nice day, but for a very cold breeze that felt as though it had only just left the polar regions. At about ten o'clock Ron took a hazardous walk to the box to see what the signalman had to say. As he climbed down off the engine I said, 'Don't be long, our ride home will be leaving Newport about now'. He said, 'How do you reckon to stop it then? With detonators?' When he returned after about half an hour, he told me some bad news. It appeared that Newport had received a lot of snow. The station was blocked and they were having to use snow ploughs. I never did see a rail snow plough working though Ron told me it was quite fascinating to operate one of these, or just to be in a position to observe.

Apparently two useful engines were coupled to the plough, then they would blast away as hard as they could, charging into the snow drifts. If they didn't succeed the first time in breaking through, having come to a stop with their driving wheel spinning, and sand ground into the rails emitting smoke and sparks, they would back up some distance and charge again. It must have been some sight—some snow drifts too, to have resisted them.

Two men who were part of the permanent way gang then appeared, trudging through the snow along the track. They were stationing themselves at the signal box in order to free the points and signals for movement in and out of the loop line.

All this time since leaving Lydney, our guard had been doing well with the Yanks, sharing their haversack rations; all we saw was a cloud of cigarette smoke from their 'Camel'—or were they 'Lucky Strike'?—whenever they came out on to the van veranda.

When at last the points were cleared of snow and we got the signal, I was taken by surprise with the fire, but I would not have worried if they then had to wait for us. In any case we were now becoming low on water; we didn't think about it during all the fuss in Gloucester, and at Lydney we were occupied with other things. I didn't see a water column anyway, so I was trying not to waste any by allowing the engine to blow off while standing. We passed through Caldicot and dropped down to Chepstow; as we rumbled across the bridge at five miles per hour the river looked very black and rather forbiding against the snow. I found myself giving a shiver as I imagined how cold the water must be.

At last we reached Severn Tunnel Junction, I didn't know at the time but it was around midday. We were relieved, then climbed down into the snow on the platform, which must have been nearly a foot deep, at any rate it was well over the tops of our boots. Trudging after Ron and the guard, I felt in a daze and very weak. I slumped on a bench in the corner of the engine cabin and closed my eyes involuntarily as Ron said he would enquire about the passenger train.

The next thing I knew Ron was shaking me, telling me to hurry up as the train was leaving Newport, so we had better get back up to the station. On the way I enquired about the time from my two companions. It was the guard, taking out his pocket watch, who gave me the answer. 'Twenty minutes past two'. I was so shocked that I don't think I even answered.

After the warmth of the cabin I now felt thoroughly chilled, standing with sodden boots in the snow on the platform after having walked all the way from the shed.

Luckily the train soon arrived; for once we managed to get a seat and I could hardly believe our luck as the train pulled away from the station and my eyes closed. The next thing I knew, I was once again being roused at Gloucester station. The clock said ten minutes to four and we were allowed ten minutes walking time to the shed, so we clocked off at four o'clock. I made that twenty four and a quarter hours actually on duty, plus fifteen minutes travelling time each way to and from Horton Road. In all that time I would have eaten my normal four cheese or fishpaste sandwiches, drunk one and a half cups of tea (the can held three cups to share) on two occasions.

After my stamp and income tax, about thirty five shillings, had been stopped, I took home about five pounds twelve shillings for that week. I believe that around that time, that is up to 1939 and into the 'forties, a top rate passenger fireman's money was about nine shillings and sixpence a day, or about forty-seven-and-a-half pence. Incidentally we were due back on duty at 0400 hours next morning.

Grange Court Again

It must cross the mind of anyone reading this account of my experiences on the railway that it was nearly always dark with inclement weather—certainly that's how it seemed to me! There were, of course, some hours of daylight, and some nice days, too. I seemed to miss them in the end. I recall one nice summer's evening while taking a train downhill we pulled into the loop at Grange Court Junction. It was exceedingly hot and I wasn't much of a beer drinker, partly because it was, of course, very scarce—incidently don't be fooled by TV programmes where the Yanks are buying beer and spirits unlimited. Most pubs had a notice saying 'Not more than one half pint will be served to anyone but regular customers'! On this occasion I thought I could use a drink. I said as much to Ron who said that he felt the same and it was hurriedly decided that I should run as quickly as possible along the track to the goods yard, past the station, along the station drive to the pub.

By the time I got there I was just about ready for a drink and being more or less a local, also recognised for the job I was on, I had two pints. Paving the way for Ron, who wasn't a local, I told the landlady that I would hurry back so that my mate could get a drink. By the time I reached the engine I felt like going back for another pint, because I had sweated half the beer out of me already. When I was about fifty yards away Ron climbed down and hurried towards the pub. As I approached the engine I realised we had broken a very important rule—we had both left the engine unattended. Ron said, as he left, 'Give us a blow up if we get the road, I'll be listening for it'.

As I was somewhat keyed up waiting for the signal, keeping the fire up, and wondering how long it would take Ron to get back, I heard a familiar rattle as the main line signal came off; I was relieved it wasn't ours. Half a minute later I could hear a fast train approaching quickly from the direction of Oakle Street. In a few seconds I was able to see it as it rattled over the points at the far end of the loop. It sped along the length of the train, through the station, disappeared out of sight under the bridge, and then suddenly there was silence. This lasted for a few moments until the train was well away from the high bank, which carried the lane up over the bridge, I was then able, once again, to hear it roaring in the distance.

I was wondering how long it would be after our signal came off, before the signalman would be looking out, wondering why we weren't moving—it would take Ron three or four minutes to get back to the train so I made a decision. Once more a signal rattled and as I looked out I could see it was ours, but I couldn't prevent my eyes straying to the catch points on the rails; the were closed all right so why was I waiting?

Giving a long blast on the whistle I slowly wound the hand brake off, another quick look at the signal and points, I peered into the low evening sun to see if there was any sign of Ron—but not as yet. I opened the ejector to build up a vacuum in the brake, put the engine in full forward gear, then after a last dive to left side of the cab to look at the signal, I gave the regulator a tug. The engine moved forward taking up the slack between the wagons. I gave another long blast on the whistle, then feeling the engine hesitate as the weight came against her, I opened up the regulator some more. She began to bark quietly and the wheels began squealing on the sharp curve in the rails as I turned out of the loop on to the main line. Rightly or wrongly, I was now committed to carry on up to the station—where Ron had better meet me or there would be an embarrassing situation! I would have to stop at the end of the platform before disappearing under the bridge. The train was stretched right back beyond the station, through the goods yard, with the rear end snaking its way round into the loop.

Ron hurried from the inn in a direction that would take him down through the station yard and sidings at the end of the loop where we had originally stopped. As he became aware that the train was now heading through the station he changed direction towards the station at an easier pace. Crossing the platform, he stepped

Grange Court Junction where Ron's drink gave me the opportunity to bring the train in on my own - strictly against all the rules! The Junction station was always tidy and well kept in my days, creating a friendly and welcoming atmosphere to all who used it. The train depicted is a Gloucester-Hereford service, which is crossing from the main line to the branch. *(Author's Collection)*

on to the second step, then up on to the footplate as though it was an everyday occurrence. Just for good measure I gave the regulator another jerk which made her dig her toes in, and bark quite loudly, causing us to be completely engulfed with steam and smoke as we were travelling so slowly whilst passing under the bridge, towards where Westbury-on-Severn halt was once located. I asked Ron if he managed to get a drink but nothing was said about my having brought the train up to the platform; another rule had been broken—the train must not move on to the main line without two men on board. As this was the first time anything like this had been attempted by me, I was feeling quite pleased with myself. The important thing seemed to be that Ron had been able to regain some confidence in me as a mate.

Some of the men known to me from childhood were still on the job, we frequently saw them when we happened to be travelling downhill in daylight. It was quite common during the winter months for these men to shout for coal as we passed; this was bowled off on to the track in huge lumps where it would break up and fly in all directions. If a fireman was too busy or the coal too small, they would hail the next train along, but they were never without a good fire to sit by at lunchtime.

Quite often we saw my father, who was a 'ganger' at Awre during most of the war years. He used his old bicycle to travel ever day, including Sundays, from Minsterworth to Awre. He would walk the length, hammer on shoulder ready to knock in any loose wooden keys he might find. Every weekday he would walk his own length of track from Awre to a point near the old Severn railway bridge, then back to Awre. On Sundays he had to walk to Lydney and back. I remember my younger brother, Dennis, who was in his late teens and very fit, went along one Sunday morning 'for the ride'. When he arrived home he was nearly down from exhaustion. He has never forgotten it, small wonder my father never appeared very active during the evening. We couldn't mistake him anyway; he was a very big strong man, only about 6ft. 2in. in height, but he sometimes appeared nearly as wide, weighing nineteen stone at that time. He was still in his forties then. Later he was transferred to Over Junction, where he remained until retirement.

While I was still a child, quite a few years before I was destined to begin working on the railways, I heard many terms appertaining to the job, very few of which I understood.

Sunday work meant 'Relaying', then there was 'Fogging','Packing', 'Slewing', 'Fishplates', 'Keys', 'Sleepers' 'Chairs', 'Grass burning', 'Points deicing', and so on. Gradually I began to learn a few of them by the time I started on the job.

One evening he came home and said 'We've had a day today, the white-wash train came through. I had one dab. Poor old 'Webby' was nearly in tears, he got three'. I don't know if the white-wash train is still run for the purpose of testing the eveness of the track, if it is then that would support the argument that some of the simpler ways of doing things are the most reliable.

My father was rather annoyed one evening when I related a conversation that had taken place in the train on my way from school. As I mentioned before, I travelled back and forth between Westbury-on-Severn Halt and Grange Court Junction. At that time I was aged about six years and travelling each day I was soon to know one or two people by sight. Some would even get into conversation with me. Among these people there was a man and a woman who travelled together, both tidily dressed and well spoken. By the fact that they were travelling home at that time of day and I later deduced, that they had to be teachers. I told them that we played a lot of football at school and that I was a very good player. They asked me how many goals I had scored that day, I answered quickly something like eight goals. They appeared a little sceptical at that figure—I think they knew I was spoofing and thereafter made a point of asking 'How many today Douglas?' They were obviously enjoying this bit of daily intrigue and in my naivety I thought they believed me!

On the day in question there were two railwaymen travelling in the same

Another view of Grange Court station, looking towards Gloucester from a carriage window.
(Author's Collection)

124

compartment with my two regular companions. On boarding the train at Westbury Halt I moved along the coach to where my acquaintances were sitting. I sank down into the vacant seat and looked from one to the other. The original two promptly greeted me, then after asking the inevitable question and receiving the usual rash answer, they introduced me to the two workmen by saying, 'This is Douglas, he is a wonderful footballer—as you've heard, he's scored ten goals today'. One of the workmen asked my name and when I told him it was Trigg they asked, 'Do you know Tom Trigg?' 'Yes, he's my father'. They seemed very interested, saying that they knew him well and had worked with him many times. We were now nearing Grange Court Station so I gathered my dinner bag and prepared to make my way to the central doors of the car. They all said 'Goodbye, see you tomorrow', and as I turned to leave one workman called out 'Hey Douglas, ask your father who was the young man, on his first day at work on the railway, together with another lad, oiled the lengthmen's hut instead of tarring it? Don't forget'. Assuring them that I would ask the question I climbed down on to the platform, giving them all a wave as the little train pulled out of Grange Court Station.

When I asked my father about the incident that evening he looked very surprised and rather annoyed to discover his long forgotten past had caught up with him! In later years, when this subject was once again brought up, he attempted to vindicate himself by saying that the other young lad was already engaged in oiling the hut, he was just sent to help him.

During my period on the footplate Father would always know when I was passing on the train, as would all my relatives and friends, for we would give my code on the whistle. As he stood back, putting his hand up to us, we usually passed him with Ron's two hands round my neck pretending to throttle me—the expression on my father's face always said 'That's it, carry on'!

After my first few days on the main line I realised that if I was going to let people know I was passing Minsterworth in either direction, I would need to sound something different on the whistle. For no special reason, other than that it could be drawn out and would be different from any other whistle likely to be heard at Oakle Street, I chose the letter L in the morse code. So whenever anyone heard a rather drawn-out dot, a long dash and two more dots, they recognised it and knew where I was. Some years later this particular whistle was to give me a sudden happy surprise, bringing back many memories, some happy, some not so good, but taking on a new significance by working in the opposite direction.

Oliver Plank's Pint

The occasion I referred to in the previous chapter, where Ron and I both left the train for a pint, was a very exceptional and isolated incident. Neither of us were too concerned about beer, though we did have the occasional pint if it was available to us. There were, however, people who were a lot keener and one such person was Oliver Plank. He was a goods guard who we sometimes met up with during the course of our duties. It was between nine and ten o'clock one dark evening when the supervisor gave us a train for Cardiff, which was on the main down track in Gloucester station. Next to the train, against the platform, there was a passenger train, with all usual activity and noise, looking as though it may roar out of the station any second; it was standing where we used to coal the 'mails'. Now any betting man, knowing the way things were at that time, would have put his shirt on us not going until after the passenger—there was no likelihood of the signalman turning us loose in front of it.

In not so many words, those were Olly Plank's sentiments as he hurriedly told Ron that he was going for a quick one, saying, 'Give us a good blow up and pull out steady, so that I can jump on the van as it passes'. Whereupon he quickly dived out of view round the front of the passenger engine. He had been gone about two minutes, if that, when to our astonishment we saw the signal was off for us. We didn't hear it, with all the noise, it may have already been off half a minute. It may be thought that with all the delays and general chaos that a minute or so wouldn't matter, but it did and drivers had to accurately book times of arrival and departure. Ron gave a long blast on the whistle, which may have caused one or two railwaymen to wonder what it was in aid of and I slowly wound the brake off as Ron said, 'Well, we have got to go, it's up to him to be on the job'. We made such hard work of pulling out of the station that we could see the signalman looking in our direction, probably thinking he had made a wrong decision in letting us go.

During wartime the glass in the signalboxes was painted black. The signalmen had small holes where the paint had been scraped off at vantage points, in any case they were only using dim paraffin lamps that wouldn't throw much light. If necessary, providing there was no air raid warning in progress, signalmen would slide a window open to get a good look at the train and communicate with the driver or guard—this he did as we gave another long blast on the whistle. I was able to see that he was the one I had given advice to about the length of his neck on the night we had the argument with the supervisor. I found myself repeating it, not that he could hear me for all the noise going on. I was constantly sticking my head out to see if there was any sign of the guard's light. As we went over the brow of the hill and began dropping down towards Over, he would be out of sight until we approached the bridge so I gave it a rest. At the bridge there was still no sign and we were signalled into the loop as we expected. As we slowly approached the end of the first part of the loop, the signal dropped off for us to pull up on the far end. While we were still halfway along the loop a passenger train went hammering past, pulling away after its thirty miles per hour check, under and over the two bridges, under the road and over the Severn.

I still couldn't get any answer to my lamp from the guard. I suggested to Ron that we stay put and ring up the station. I thought he might well have managed a lift down on a passing train but as the only train due was the passenger and that had already gone, that idea was out.

Ron suggested we should carry on to see what happened. He reckoned that as there were no serious gradients, and with us having the knowledge that he may not be on board, we should carry on as normal. It seemed the only thing to do because if we had begun making enquiries at Gloucester, they may have had people searching the track, holding up traffic vital to the war effort and causing Olly very serious trouble.

We were now signalled on to the main line, and made a gentle start out of the loop so that there could be no possibility of breaking a coupling. I was, by this time, in the habit of looking out for the guard, whenever we started off. I did on this occasion and I could hardly believe my eyes—there was his lamp. I shouted, 'He's there Ron'. Ron came over to have a look, but neither of us could understand what was happening. Ron said 'Oh well, thank God for that', giving the regulator another jerk. We carried on to Bullo, where we were signalled into the loop, possibly for wagon examination or else the road was blocked with trains down beyond this point. These thoughts ran through my head as we turned into the loop. 'Nip back and ask Olly what happened, why he couldn't give us the tip Jockey. Tell him he had me worried back there, not knowing what was up'. Taking my gauge lamp I made to climb down to the ground thinking, 'Sod Olly and his beer!' Half way down I heard a rattle just above my head and without looking climbed back up. I knew we had the road again. Having released my handbrake, I took the gauge lamp and waved it furiously. There came an immediate reply from the guard's van—things were improving.

It just so happened that this trip turned out to be one of the few exceptions when we would run to Severn Tunnel with hardly any hold-ups, so we had no chance of contacting Olly until the time we were relieved. Having handed over the engine at Severn Tunnel, we waited for him to walk down the platform as the train pulled slowly away. When he eventually appeared, limping out of the darkness, we could hardly believe our eyes; he appeared to have a gigantic boot on one foot. He was shouting and swearing at us, accusing us of pulling away from Gloucester in a hurry, causing him to sprint across the track where he caught the heel of his shoe in the crossing. Only by wrenching his foot out of his shoe had he managed to grab the handrail of the van as it sped past. He had a badly bruised big toe, having caught it against the top step of the van as he stumbled in before collapsing on to the bench, panting and coughing. When he eventually got his breath back we were already pulling out of the loop at Over, where we first got the tip from him. Searching in the locker under one of the benches he found some tools and rubbish, some kindling wood, newspaper and of all things, some corrugated cardboard. He managed to wrap the cardboard round and round his foot in an effort to protect it and keep out the cold. Finally he secured it with a piece of string found in his bag. We tried to assure him that his accusations couldn't be further from the truth, telling him of our embarrassment during our departure, with half the railwaymen at Gloucester wondering what we were up to. Whether it was the beer, the lack of it, or the loss of his shoe, or maybe a combination of all three, I don't know but he limped off into the darkness, still blaming us. I was fed up with the whole thing and telling Ron so, I said 'If that is all the thanks we get for worrying about him and me having to keep sticking my neck out in the cold, he can go to hell next time!'

As we reached the cabins two guards came out of the doorway leading to the guards' cabin. They naturally enquired about his foot and he told them, blaming us yet again. The two guards walked off chuckling to themselves after having previously pretended to be sympathetic to his face. It ended by Ron telling him that he didn't want to hear any more about it. Next time he was with us, to make sure he was where he should be or we wouldn't turn a wheel, and someone else could sort it out. He added that instead of losing his shoe, it may have been his life as he could have slipped and knocked himself unconscious, where he could have been found cut to pieces.

A few days after that we heard he lost a day shift, travelling home to Worcester for money and valuable clothing coupons to buy some more shoes—his pint cost him dearly!

The Yanks

As mentioned earlier, an American-built locomotive suffered a boiler explosion, killing the fireman and badly scalding the driver. I cannot remember if we had any of the WD locos stationed at Gloucester; we had them on shed from time to time, of course and we were booked on them occasionally with trains we relieved. These engines looked huge and it seemed a long climb up into the cab where everything was just that bit different from our own locomotives. I believe these were 2-8-0 class, the driving wheels being not very large, perhaps somewhere between a 2800 and 5300. Apart from the odd boiler weakness and the unfamiliar controls, the 2-8-0s had another trait that made them rather unpopular. Instead of the regulator working up and down as on British engines it was designed to pull towards the driver to open and push towards the boiler to close. It was a ratchet and lever type similar to a large lorry handbrake. The ratchet was reasonably efficient once it was realised how important it was to make use of it. Luckily when the first incident occurred there was two men on the footplate. A young lad, or indeed a man on his own, may have ended up in Horton Road or somewhere down in Great Western Road. It was discovered that if the boiler was topped right up, in most cases the regulator couldn't be closed once it was opened and if the ratchet lever wasn't quickly released you had full throttle!

This particular engine had been prepared in readiness to go off shed, the boiler having been topped up by the box boy, as was the usual practice with British engines. As the driver grasped the ratchet and the regulator in one hand and began opening the regulator, it flew out to its fullest extent. He had no chance of releasing the ratchet as it was at the far side of the regulator from him. His fingers were still gripping both handles as he was thrown backwards off balance, momentarily actually holding the regulator wide open!

We found the steam brakes on these engines always left something to be desired and apparently the engine in question was no exception. The brakes were applied at once but this engine had a full head of steam, not forgetting the water, and it was completely flat out with the brakes taking little effect for some yards. For about five minutes the engine's wheels spun in forward and reverse, as it slithered and ground its way back and forth on about sixty yards of track. The driver and fireman were nearly exhausted from their effort of no sooner straining to pull the lever in one direction, then they had to immediately push it in the other—they looked scared too. Everyone was out in the yard watching; the poor head foreman was running backwards and forwards, each time the engine changed direction he would take three or four steps after it. Each time he paused, looking worried to death, the engine would come charging back towards him, belching black sooty water, which was covering everyone, while small hot cinders rained down like black hail. Eventually it blew out the excess water and the driver was able to close the regulator, half afraid to open it again when the time came.

There was another feature of the controls that was different from ours and one that had made it more difficult for the crew to control the engine during its rampage. The reversing lever itself was too short to give enough good leverage in an emergency, it was also pivoted at too high a point. After this incident engine crews were constantly aware of the water gauge.

We had a nasty experience with one of these engines while coming down through

129

Sapperton Tunnel. We had been pulling fairly hard up into the tunnel, to a point where enough of the train was over the top to start coasting. In next to no time at all we were picking up speed down through the tunnel, so I wound my handbrake on as far as possible. Once more poor leverage because of very small handles caused it to be rather ineffective, so Ron applied his brake a little, enabling me to tighten mine considerably. These engines always seemed to make a lot of metallic clattering noises when they were coasting, but coming down through that tunnel in pitch blackness, except for a flicker of light from the fire, with huge drops of water finding their way on to your arms and face, was some experience! To cap it all, Ron had his little torch, looking first at the regulator, then leaning out looking at the wheels. One instant the engine appeared to rock and jump violently, as the wheels spun on the wet rails, next, as Ron applied the brake, we got that smooth riding sensation when you know the wheels are tied. 'Look here Jockey', Ron shouted. I crossed over to his side of the cab, gingerly peering down into the darkness to where his small light picked out the skidding wheels. 'Now watch', he said as he moved his hand to the steam brake and released it, whereupon the engine once more shuddered as the wheels began to spin. He then applied the brakes again.

We were now travelling much too fast, gradually getting faster all the time. Coming out of the tunnel I estimated we were doing about thirty miles an hour, if not more. As far as I was concerned we had a runaway train under our feet. The situation looked better out in the daylight, but things were still coming towards us too fast. 'Can you see the guard's van yet Jockey?' 'Yes, its just cleared the tunnel', I replied. As Ron still struggled between the brakes, still trying to close the regulator, he told me to give the guard the danger whistle and to keep it up until we got some help! With all the bumps he should have known something was wrong. Luckily the guard was awake—he told us later he thought we were going rather fast but decided we would let him know with the whistle should we be in any trouble. The guard should have been helping us to hold the train down a bank like that anyway, and we were thankful that no sooner had the third blast on the whistle faded than we felt a light tug and knew that he was doing his stuff.

'We've got to shut the regulator or we are going through Brimscombe whether we have the road or not', said Ron. We both began struggling to shut it, but being so high up we couldn't push as hard as would have been possible had it been lower down. Suddenly there was a movement;the next thing we knew it was closed. For once we were glad of the ratchet which we felt sure would prevent it from opening again until we were ready. That would be sometime ahead—we were still going too fast, though we had slowed down soemwhat, partly as a result of the guard helping. We were now on dry rails, and most important, the regulator was shut! We clattered through Chalford and I glimpsed the distant signal at Brimscombe. It was against us. I shouted to Ron whose reply I can only guess at! Nearing the distant signal Ron seemed to be getting more in control again though having once let this train of wagons weighing hundreds of tons have its head for a short while, it was going to take some stopping. The stop signal was against us, and although we blew for the main signal several times, that's how it remained. We were calling the signalman everything we could lay our tongues to, he could have called us on to the box and that would have given us another forty or fifty yards. I reckoned that we were going to overshoot the signal by about four or five lengths of the engine, this was not only going to cause some embarrassment, but possibly some explanation of an official nature. It was, in any case, going to be annoying to say the least, after what we had just experienced with all Ron's struggling with the controls.

I suddenly had a dangerous silly idea which would cause another infringement of the rules, ie getting on or off a moving train. I climbed down to the lower step and jumped, landing on my feet though almost coming to grief because we were going a little faster than I thought. There was no time for reflections on what I had done—the rear end of a long 'Bogey Bolster' was passing, with its ratchet-handled brake. I snatched this down, running alongside the wagon as it passed me, and along came the next. I tied the wheels on this huge long wagon loaded with poles and then I couldn't believe my luck, there were three of them and as I snatched the third down, again tying the wheels, the train came to a halt with half the engine past the signal. I released the brakes and climbed back aboard. Nothing was said—I'm not sure that Ron wasn't too occupied to notice that I had been off the engine at all.

We had quite a few trips on 'Yankees' and it seemed as though once these locomotives were moving as long as you kept at it, then they weren't too bad. The engine certainly helped with the War Effort. Anyway I seemed to remember some saying about a 'Gift Horse'. I'll remember them most for their whistle. It was more like a siren and on dark nights it was easy to imagine myself crossing vast tracts of prairie, especially when travelling back through this valley through which we had just descended. That incident took place in 1944, but even now (1992) when I hear a freight train whistle in an American film, it takes me right back to some of those nights when we had taken one of them to Swindon. Hopefully we would have the road through Brimscombe, where we would start opening up, to obtain a good run through Chalford, up the bank. We would pass Chalford making a terrific clatter, then on up towards the steep part of the climb where we began to slow down. Here the old 'Yankee' would have to start pulling whilst, quite rightly, I had to keep shovelling. As we approached the tunnel we would be travelling very slowly, the exhaust noises travelling all through the valley. Even this was drowned as Ron gave a long blast on one of those never-to-be-forgotten whistles. Inside the tunnel it was another world. To begin with, no matter what was in front of us, we would never know, because it was completely black. The exhaust beats and all metallic noises were now very much louder, many noises that had previously been inaudible in the open air would now fall on our ears. If we managed to keep underway things weren't too bad, but if we did too much slipping, there could be breathing problems.

Cold air came to meet us down through the tunnel, and our smoke and steam were normally left behind though it would begin creeping after us, up the hill. If the engine slipped in the tunnel on the wet rails, or just slowed right down to a walking pace for whatever reason, the smoke would get us. At any rate it used to get me. There was little that could be done then, no actual work, that's for sure. The fire couldn't be attended to. A lot of luck would be needed to find the injector controls; if you did it was too smokey to adjust the flow of water in order to get it working correctly. I would sit down with my head as low as possible, hoping any fresh air which happened to be around would be down there, with my handkerchief held to my mouth with both hands. In this position I would paradoxically try to get air through this handkerchief, whilst at the same time trying desperately to avoid breathing at all!

Eventually, with any luck, although still in the tunnel we would pass the highest point and begin to make a little more headway. If it was daytime we would see a faint glimmer of light in the distance, then gradually become aware of cool air seeping up through the gangway encircling our ankles. Down near the track, which was now quickly becoming more visible, the smoke was thinning out, the small amount remaining now confined to the tunnel roof. The more we picked up speed the clearer the air became, and as my handkerchief was no longer likely to help me, I put it away, always thankful to be out of those situations. What a shock it could be to find hardly any water registering in the gauge glass now that the engine was facing down hill!

Tuffley Races

I would imagine most people in Gloucestershire who have ever been interested in, or connected with the railway in the days of steam would have heard of the occasional Tuffley Races. They were between the LMS expresses coming from Bristol to Gloucester, maybe beyond, and the GWR from London to Gloucester, which unfortunately had to make a stop at Stonehouse.

On the occasion when I was to witness my one and only race, I was one of nine train men travelling back from Swindon. Being unable to get in a carriage, not even in the corridor, we were sitting on anything we could find in the mail van, right next to the engine. I mentioned before that it was the engine crews' recognised duty to work the fire right down on any engine destined for the engine shed. This, plus the stop at Stonehouse was a double handicap on the Western train, which I expect sometime led to it being beaten to Tuffley, but not always.

It was a beautiful sunny evening and as we were on double summer-time it was often light at 11.30pm. It must have been between five and eight pm. As usual I dozed off on the way down but, as the result of a slight jolt when we stopped at Stroud, I slipped off the mail bag I was sitting on and when I opened my eyes I realised where I was for the first time since leaving Swindon. There was another young fireman in the group, and he was still sleeping soundly. Surely no one could feel more tired than me, perhaps it was just that he had a clear conscience. The inevitable game of solo was in progress and in view of the way the cards kept sliding about they must have been keen.

The last lap, I thought, as we pulled away from Stonehouse. It sounded by the loud bark of the Castle's exhaust that the same thoughts were going through the driver's mind. There was one other fireman in the group, he was a little older—in his mid-twenties. Near the top of our link, he would probably move up in the near future. However, he was sitting on a box or crate with his back to the engine, on the left hand side of the train.

As we approached the spot where the GWR and LMS tracks converge, we were picking up speed very rapidly. It crossed my mind that we were probably going to get a good turn of speed for the last lap—how right I was. The cards were just being dealt. The rhythm of carriage wheels on the rail joints was almost taking hold of me again, but all this peaceful scene was suddenly to be shattered.

The fireman sitting on the crate was dividing his attention between the card game and what was happening outside the window by his right shoulder.

Suddenly he jumped to his feet, then grasping the bars on the window he leaned towards the window, staring out. 'Look up then, here we go—here we go'! he shouted excitedly, causing everyone to make for the windows and the door to see what was happening. I had no idea what it might be but one or two had been there before so in all probability had an inkling of what might be about to happen. I managed to get to a window, easing my head in by someone's shoulder, and strained my eyes toward the LMS track at a point far beyond the rear of our train—there it was! This dark smokey-looking object, which was quickly catching up on us, was gradually taking on the shape of an LMS engine. I could soon make out small wisps of steam on one side near the cylinder cocks, the swiftly-turning wheels with the reciprocating coupling rods now just discernible. On it came, everything becoming more distinguishable as each second passed. Steam with rather a lot of smoke, which instead of coming out of the stack in small puffs, seemed to flow evenly like smoke from a chimney fire in a woodman's hut. What a sight it was! The train drew nearer and nearer, and was at this point obviously overhauling us, with just one carriage and the mail van down.

Gaining very quickly now, the locomotive swayed and rattled its way towards our mail van. I believe the driver and fireman had seen us shortly after leaving Stonehouse, so the driver had opened his engine out and the fireman had made his fire up heavily in order to be able to act out the scene that was about to follow. As the engine drew level with us the fireman perched on his seat, looking sometimes ahead, sometimes at the interior of the cab, but mainly at our train and the engine he was about to overtake. A nonchalant expression which said to me, 'Well, what did you expect?' The little jets of steam I had been aware of were coming from somewhere near one of the cylinders, probably some gland leaking. It was very close. I could hear a very rapid pit, pit, pit, pit sound and I remember thinking that they were appearing much too fast to reach my ears as hisses, the normal sound of escaping steam. There was, of course, a much more dominant sound that almost drowned the little jets of steam--it was a combination of all other rattles and noises produced by the engine. The noise coming from the coupling rods, the pistons and valves along with muffled sounding exhaust, came to me in time with the jets of steam as very rapid rump, rump, rump, rump, rump, rumps as it slowly drew ahead. In retrospect, I remember being quite excited at what was taking place. I certainly didn't really appreciate that here was a spectacle that comparatively few people were ever likely to hear of, much less witness. Two long passenger trains, every seat and every foot of space occupied, either by a person or an item of kit or luggage, this, of course, included corridors. Between them they were carrying several hundred passengers, who were mainly service personnel, as many as possible of whom were crowding to windows and doors on each train.

Imagine scores of delighted, excited faces as they passed us, laughing, shouting, waving and quite a few V signs!

I have seen the Castles inside and out from every angle, with the exception of a view from the inside of the firebox. I never did clamber into any firebox.

Obviously I have worked quite a few trains and seen them passing at various speeds, working heavily uphill, coasting down, but I have never seen the spectacle the passengers on that LMS train saw that day. Imagine this beautiful GWR Castle, still carrying her GWR lettering and insignia. Although rather grimy through not having been cleaned for perhaps two or three years, her colours were nevertheless still visible. The green tender with the lettering, red and black stripe top and bottom, the cab with its brass engine number plate, the green boiler skin and splash guard with more lead lining, the name plate with brass letters. Below, the black wheels,

This is a view east of Tuffley Junction where the Races began or finished! To the left are the Midland lines curving down towards Eastgate station whilst a Castle 4-6-0 loco works an "up" Cheltenham-Paddington express on the western route.   *(Author's Collection)*

135

six feet eight-and-a-half inches in diameter, were turning rapidly, covering about seven yards at each rotation with the light steel connecting rods contrasting with the black-looking counter balances as they chased one another round and round. Brilliant reflections of the sun came and went in a flash, in time with the rotation of the wheels as the outside piston rod appeared and disappeared, its highly polished surface kept in a perfect state of brilliance by scalding steam and oil.

Towards the front the blast pipes and smoke box were black, buffer shanks and plates red and to complete the picture, a brass safety valve surround and a copper band on the smoke stack. The sound coming from the smoke stack was something too, as she strove to get her fourteen loaded carriages up to running speed. If only colour video film had been available in those days to film one from each train, the pictures would be unique—I can't imagine a situation anywhere else except Australia where it would be possible to travel several miles at speed, to be only a few feet away from engines like these two.

These trains were not very far apart at this time, the four sets of tracks ran very close together, two GWR and two LMS. The cheering and shouting was increasing as more people in the other train looked out and found themselves creeping past another on an adjacent track. I found myself glad to be hidden in this mail van as the cheering, jeering, faces passed.

One of the drivers said 'I can't see Tommy putting up with much of this'. He had no sooner spoken than it was as though a sudden unexpected total eclipse of the sun had occurred. The LMS train was almost momentarily hidden from our view, as black smoke belched from the Castle, sweeping back and downwards, appearing to hang at carriage height, partially carried along between the two trains. Before the smoke could clear there came another cloud, and yet another, as the fireman broke the unwritten rule of firing his engine on its last lap. The loud crisp barking sound from the Castle suddenly came to our ears, then we knew we were in for a ride.The driver had picked up the gauntlet. He must have wound his cut off out, judging from the terrific blast. It wasn't the normal way to work an engine, of course, he would have had little steam, water, or fire on a long run, but this was different.

I only knew two express drivers called Tommy—one was my great uncle Tommy Norton and I knew he was on the Cardiff run that day, so I felt sure it had to be Tommy Mustoe. The Castle was treated to four or five more shovels full of fairly slack coal, which, on being spread around in a white hot firebox, was instantly incinerated. Having served to produce urgently needed steam it would be non-evident on reaching the shed.

As the last cloud of smoke cleared, it was evident that the LMS was no longer overtaking us, but was being held. Then gradually we started to inch forward, and then we began overtaking them.

136

As the cheering broke out on our train, it abruptly ceased on the other and the scores of quickly changing expressions on the LMS train became a study in mass dejection. As we passed, the airman at the front of the first carriage (who was the first one to give us the V sign), had a face which was a picture of miserable embarrassment—I thought his cheers were about to turn to tears. I had no sympathy with him after his performance, I thought 'Yes uncle, if I had a long kidney bean stick I would dislodge your forage cap for good measure'. I suppose there was always an element of danger in these situations, but luckily the tracks separated again after very few miles.

Our train was still pulling away to the loud cheering which could be plainly heard, even at what was by now a pretty high speed considering the short distance there had been in which to pick up speed. In what seemed to be a very short time, the tracks divided and the engines were soon shut down. I reckoned we were doing somewhere around the eighties. The brakes were applied lightly on our train as the Chequers Bridge came in sight. They were still dragging as we clattered down over Horton Road Crossing, slowing us right down as we swung hard through the scissors, into the down platform.

The train always pulled right down the full length of the platform. Passengers walked from the front of the train, back towards the platform exit and forward from the rear of the train. Somehow it made more sense to drop passengers in the shelter of the station roof as opposed to having to walk two or three hundred yards in all weathers, humping their luggage as best they could, with no one to assist them. The recent experience was mentioned as we made our way back up to the shed to clock off, but it was soon forgotten—I suppose we all had so many other things demanding our attention. I believe incidents such as these were very isolated. No doubt it had been witnessed by railway management and others who would soon be originating some 'please explain' notes. Obviously, wartime or not, no two passenger trains would be deliberately booked to travel over that particular stretch of track at the same time.

One train would need to be a little early, or perhaps a little late; one minute either way would be sufficient to bring about a race. It was something I will never forget.

The Chalford Car

One day, finding ourselves stuck at Stonehouse with a train for Swindon, Ron had an idea. He said 'Hey Jockey, we have been on eight and a half hours now, why don't we nip up to the box, ring the supervisor and see if he will send relief up on the Chalford car? We can catch it on the way back down.' I was halfway down the steps

137

of the engine by the time he had finished the sentence.

For once the supervisor agreed and a set of men, including a guard, were sent up on the car to relieve us as suggested--we could hardly believe it. We left the engine and walked along to the platform in good time to catch the car on its way back down. I thought as I had never had a ride on one of the little 0-4-2 tanks, I would see if I could cadge a ride on the footplate back to Gloucester. The driver said that it was agreeable to him, but it was up to his mate to say yes or no. I knew he would agree and soon I was in this very small cab as the fireman slammed the little door shut.

This little engine was propelling one coach, or car, as they were known, at an amazingly high rate of acceleration. In what seemed no time at all we were joining the LMS track again. I watched the fireman go through his routine, working the controls that concerned him and sometimes those that hardly concerned him at all. He was like the proverbial 'cat on hot bricks' I began to wonder if he was putting on a show for my benefit but I later learned that it is one thing to watch someone do a job and something quite different to have a go yourself.

The driver and fireman were regular mates. The fireman was quite experienced and I concluded that there was an understanding that the fireman would drive as well as fire, the driver just sitting in the driving cab, or vestibule, of the coach where he was not only supposed to be, but where he could use the brake in an emergency.

We passed Haresfield going quite fast, still picking up speed until eventually the engine seemed to settle at what appeared to be its usual top cruising speed. I had no idea what speed the auto train was doing; it seemed very fast for a small local stopping train. The coach we were propelling seemed to have quite a sway on it, it seemed more noticeable than when a coach is being drawn. The little engine was rocking about a lot too and I was quite thankful for the doors. The fireman didn't relax for an instant; he would attend to the fire, look out of the cab for signals, check the water, then the exhaust injector had to be adjusted, a quick look out again, back to the fire, over to the oil sight feed and so on.

This ride was yet another experience for me. I learned quite a few things in the few minutes it took to travel from Stonehouse. These tips stood me in good stead.

I looked at the roster list while booking off one afternoon about three weeks later and was surprised to see I was booked on the Chalford car, as an emergency measure. The driver was Fred Eales (I am not sure if I have spelt his name correctly) and I knew him well by sight, but had never worked with him before; like most of the drivers, he was 'all right'.

After joining him next day he asked me if I had been on the cars before. I replied that I hadn't. He said 'Well, there's not much to it, just keep your eye on her'. Later I was to think to myself 'how many eyes does he think I've got?'.

There seemed to be less room in the cab than before, that was probably because

I was having to turn round with shovels full of coal, and work generally, whereas the first time I was standing in the corner out of the fireman's way. I was still not quite steady on my feet at speed, though the daylight made things easier with the very limited area of footplate and the safety doors. I could not fall far and I was thankful to find not a lot of coal was needed. All the time I was constantly aware of a very uneasy feeling about travelling back on my own on the engine. What if I fell out of the cab? Who would know until the train arrived at Gloucester or came to a standstill, having stopped at some signal and there was no one to blow the brakes off? I dismissed this fear when I looked at the firmly closed doors. If the worst happened I could just sit on my seat, close my eyes, hang on and hope everything lasted out until we arrived at Gloucester. As the time drew nearer for our departure on the return journey I became more apprehensive, with butterflies in my stomach. These felt more like blackbirds as Fred, with no more ado, climbed down from the engine saying, 'I'll get on down front then mate'.

I had no real problem, I knew everything necessary to fire and drive the engine, it was just that I didn't quite know what Fred expected of me. I wanted to assist him but without crossing any lines. I recall trying the remember what the fireman had done when I was riding with him recently and decided I would do the same, hoping for the best. After all, I had had no instructions as such, because the rule book says that the driver and fireman must come to a clear understanding before setting off. Drivers were so used to youngsters working all sorts of trains that they took it for granted that we would manage. I made up the fire, almost overdoing it. It went through my head that we would soon get rid of that once we were underway.

The signal was already off and as the engine was going to run in reverse to Gloucester I blew up the vacuum brakes with the ejector. I gently wound off the hand brake hoping she would stand motionless. The instant we got the right a way Fred gave me the whistle. I pulled down the ejector handle again, to top up the vacuum; it sometimes had a habit of dropping—I suppose it was like some motorists constantly checking that their hand brake is off—there was the green flag, then a blast on the whistle. I answered with the customary one whistle and we were ready. I heard a little noise by my left ear and looking round had the weird experience of seeing the regulator handle moving upwards in small jerks, with no one holding it, as we moved off at a fair pace along the platform. We sped off clear of the station and I turned my attention to shifting the reversing lever into a cut off position. It was only guess work but the engine went on gathering speed, sounding about right.

There were one or two short stops before we arrived at Stonehouse, then I banked plenty of coal into the little firebox, hurriedly topping up the boiler.

We got away from Stonehouse smartly. I soon had the lever pushed as far as I could without going into neutral, she still sounded to be running pretty evenly.

139

I was conscious of the regulator jerking up and down, I grabbed the lever and pushed it right open, there being no further movement. Fred must have been happy. The problem was most likely the number of linkages or joints between the driver at the nose end, and the regulator on the engine. Although the driver may open the regulator fully, some of it was lost en route.

I had not turned on the exhaust steam injector. I hurried to pull the water handle open, then turned the exhaust steam on, taking a swift look over the side of the door. I adjusted the flow of water until the steam and water ceased to splutter from the

Small 0-4-2 tank No. 1424 stands in Gloucester station awaiting the right away with the all stations push-pull auto-train to Chalford. When pushing, the driver was in a small cab in the leading carriage, operating the regulator and brake by means of remote control rods. It was quite an experience to be the fireman for the first time on one of these engines propelling downhill towards Gloucester! (B.J. Ashworth)

A classic study of the Chalford auto-train on the move. (Author's Collection)

waste pipe. In one stride I was peering closely at the oil sight feed, it seemed to take a long time for those blobs of oil to appear each in its own glass tube of water, where it rapidly rose up and out of sight. I stepped across to operate the water gauge handle, and heard yet another spluttering noise as the scalding water shot down the pipe and away. When the handle was returned to its normal position I had the satisfaction of seeing water near the top of the gauge glass. As I straightened up there came the sound of a loud clattering bell from the automatic train control as we passed a distant signal at go—I'd missed that one.

Grasping the firebox door handle, I steadied myself in readiness to try and put four shovels full of coal on. The firing was a bit ragged but I managed to get it all in without spillage. For the first time since leaving Stonehouse I managed to look out. The coach was waltzing and swaying along at fairly high speed, I could hear the rhythm of the last four wheels as they spanned the rail joints, occasionally speeding up dramatically as we came to a section of short rails, then back to long once again. I turned back to the fire again and threw on another two or three shovels full. The fire needed keeping up because there would be another trip back to Chalford later.

The boiler was pretty full. I shut off the exhaust injector because if we were checked or stopped approaching Gloucester I wanted to be free to do whatever would be necessary, not having to worry about a spluttering, or water gushing injector on the far side of the engine. A passing thought at this stage was that I must be as ready as anyone had ever been to eat their words or thoughts, when I said the fireman I had ridden with previously was like 'a cat on hot bricks'.

We sped down through Tuffley and as we neared Chequers Bridge I was about to put my head out when there was a piercing noise from the siren on the ATC. The distant signal was against us. I quickly pushed the little control catch up, this stopped the siren, replenishing the vacuum we had just lost. Once again I was ready to look out, but at that instant I saw the regulator close. I quickly adjusted the cut off on the reversing lever to where I had seen drivers position it while coasting. The stop signal was against us, and Fred was braking fairly hard as we approached it. I was somewhat surprised at that moment by this little engine blowing off so operated the live steam injector—I wasn't used to engines steaming like this.

Just as we were coming to a standstill, the signal dropped. I quickly blew up the vacuum brake but the hands seemed slow in rising and the brakes were still dragging as the regulator jerked open. With the brakes now free, I wound the lever in full reverse and we were pulling away hard as we approached the North box and Tramways, from where we had a clear run right in to the platform at Gloucester. I was on this run another couple of days before being taken off and going back to Ron. I was pleased to have had that experience; it would have been quite a few years before I would have been drafted into that link, 'light passenger' permanently.

141

The Tiddley Dike

Occasionally we were allocated a job over a piece of road which no longer exists. It was jokingly referred to as 'The Alps' or 'The Tiddley Dike'. It is now so long ago that apart from Andoversford, Cirencester and Swindon Old Town, not many more place names remain with me, but somehow words like Fosse, Cricklade, Withington and South Cerney seem to mean something. I am, of course, referring to the old single track that ran from Cheltenham to Swindon, or rather, it was single leaving Andoversford for Southampton, or in the other direction for Kingham--the former Midland and Southern Western Junction Railway.

We would set off for Cheltenham, branching off right at Hatherley Junction up to Andoversford, then on to Swindon Old Town. When relieved at Swindon we were sometimes lucky enough to get a ride in a truck laid on by the railway. Usually we had a long walk in the darkness, and it always seemed to be raining. I never got that job in daylight--the complete journeys were done in the darkness. It was for the main part heavy work and being a single line we were sometimes running through narrow cuttings, clattering under bridges, hemmed in by trees and hedges. With these conditions the journeys always seemed to consist of continuous work--the firelight flashed on banks, trees and walls, the noise of the exhaust beats and coupling rods increased and decreased as conditions so rapidly changed. I have often wondered what some of those trips must have been like in peacetime with a booked train. In all probability almost always in daylight with little, or no overtime. Some of these bygone single tracks ran through beautiful countryside but in four and a half years I never saw this one once.

Whenever the supervisor came in to get an engine crew things usually went a little quiet, each man hoping to be skipped so that he could go home for once on eight hours--that was a very rare occurrence. You couldn't help hearing the destination or route of any train given to the two men he was addressing and if there was ever one destination guaranteed to bring sighs of relief at having missed it, sharp intakes of breath through pursed lips, wicked grins that said 'blast your horrible luck' as you left the cabin, it was Swindon Old Town.

It came to pass that we found ourselves given such a train one murky winter's night. To the echoes of chuckles and wisecracks we unwillingly left the cabin, slowly making our way along the platform. We heard a train coming up over the bank and I asked Ron what he thought we had got here? I said 'I don't think it's a Western engine—perhaps it's a Yank?' 'I've no idea', said Ron.

The train came over the London Road bridge; the locomotive shut off to begin a slow approach to the platform. It hissed and clanked its way down through the

142

darkened station to where we were now waiting at the far end of the platform. As the engine drew nearer Ron recognised it first and said, with a grin, 'It's one of your favourites Jockey. We're going to have some fun tonight over the Tiddley Dike'. I could now see it was an LMS so I said, 'Yes, but as it's starting to drizzle a bit you will soon change your tune if we get any holdups'. 'That isn't very likely is it? You know we always get a good run at it'.

The engine ground to a halt near the starter signal by which we were standing and we clambered up on to the footplate. 'You gotta good un yer mate', said the fireman I was relieving. The odd thing about it was they were all 'good uns', no matter what condition they happened to be in. I often wondered why they bothered, it was as though they were afraid I might leap back on the platform and leave them to it.

I think the best one was, 'I couldn't keep her quiet mate, she is blowing off most of the time'. On these occasions I was very suspicious and usually with very good reason. Sometimes, when I looked into the firebox as I was being given this valuable piece of information I felt like saying 'Well, you can hardly be blamed for the engine not keeping quiet mate, you've obviously done your best—I can see the fire is nearly out'. I wouldn't like to give the impression that I was in the habit of running down LMS engines—I didn't know enough about them—it was just that I found them a bit awkward from the fireman's point of view compared with the Western engines.

My main problem with them was the fact that the driver was on what I was used to calling my side of the cab, so he was constantly getting in my way as I was standing on the left side, shovelling to the left. On more than one occasion I have been standing too near my mate when actually stoking; I would load the shovel, then stooping as I swung it towards the fire hole door, my backside would make sudden violent contact with his thigh or knee, whereupon I was projected across the cab, dropping the shovel to save myself, the coal going into the far corner. In the short, sharp ensuing shouting match, Ron would say how awkward I was, that I had nearly broken his leg, while I would blame him for taking up too much room. After all, he only had to stand there!

At this time, some years before nationalisation, there was still great rivalry between the four companies. It was to be expected that we were all likely to be a bit biased when discussing engines of another company, though of course they all had good, as well as not so good, points. Most weren't getting the regular maintenance due to them. I imagine much the same conditions would have been prevalent in all the engine sheds of whatever company, so it would follow that similar points or tasks could be overlooked or left undone.

I know, for instance, that if I was preparing an engine on a blustery pouring wet night, I would work the sanding handle, then hurriedly take a quick look down on the rails to see if the sand was indeed working. If it had managed to remain dry, I would not risk getting it or myself wet trying to top up the boxes; better to have a small amount trickling dry down on to the rails, than half a hundred-weight or more of damp sand jammed in the pipes. Apart from the rights or wrongs, it was no fun carrying a bucket full of sand maybe a few yards, maybe eighty yards, in the blackout having to avoid engine pits and all the possible obstacles I've mentioned earlier. Then, after climbing the wet slippery steps one-handed up to footplate level, the idea was to work your way along the side of the boiler in the darkness while the buckets of sand threatened to dislocate your knee joint each time it swung sideways against it. Even with my shortcomings alone, it can be seen that it was always possible to find yourself on an engine with no sand.

The reason for my retort to Ron when I saw an LMS engine we were intending to take to Swindon Old Town was that it was starting to drizzle. Should we be stopped or checked at some point up the bank, we may well have trouble with no sand—of course he understood this. In my experience we had enough problems with our engines. The LMS had steam-assisted sand of all things; I didn't work on many of them but of the few I did encounter I never once managed to get the sand to work, even when stationary in some siding. I couldn't see any and concluded that if sand was available, the steam had swept it away.

Back on the platform the signal was already off for once. I reckoned we were the only train going that way for some hours so there wouldn't be anything to hold us back once we got off the main Gloucester-Birmingham line at Cheltenham. The fireman I relieved had had the injector working as the engine coasted down through the station, so the boiler was now full. With a full head of steam we pulled away from the station, slowly making our way up over Horton Road.

I wasn't used to these engines and I wasn't happy. The engine was pulling well but as I wasn't hearing that sharp staccato barking exhaust I was used to and I felt something was lacking. After a few minutes these feelings began to fade. We were now gathering a bit of momentum and as I gave a thought to the bank up to Andoversford I hoped we would do a lot better.

We ran through Churchdown at a fair running speed; as this was a 'Government Stock' train for Southampton it was almost certain to be destined for the continent.

I had been trying to work this fire up a bit in readiness for the climb to Andoversford so it came as no surprise to me that when the distant signal for Hatherley Junction came into view, I happened to be banging coal into the firebox. We had no ATC (Automatic Train Control) so the first thing I knew of it coming up was Ron shouting 'Why the hell don't you keep your trap shut, Jockey?' 'What's up now?' I asked—something was obviously wrong. I looked ahead and in the same instant Ron slammed the regulator shut. 'I don't believe it, we've been up here a few times and this is the first time I've seen any of these signals on!' 'That's as

144

maybe, but the damned things are on now' said Ron.

We neared the signal, losing speed now on the very slight incline. The stop signals were still on and Ron was reluctantly forced to start braking. It was a heavy train with no vacuum coupled brakes, as usual it was up to just the engine with perhaps the guard's van to stop it. He had already given three blasts of the whistle, now gave three more, paused, then yet another three. By this time we were swearing at the signalman--even though he couldn't hear us it relieved the tension a little. Why on earth had he accepted us into his section if he couldn't give us the road up this perishing hill?

As we neared the final stop signal that would take us right across the four main tracks on to the branch line, it turned green. We were not quite at a standstill, so Ron released the brakesand opened the regulator up a little to take up the slack in readiness to give her the lot when we got the next signal.

This signal remained red as we approached the signal box at a slow walking pace, at about half throttle; this was now worse than ever, we were going to stop right on this steep incline and the rails were wet with heavy drizzle. Just as Ron was about to close the regulator we got the signal, but it was too late. Ron opened up again but the engine slipped, and slipped, two rotations of the wheels and she slipped again. Ron shouted 'Try that bloody sand Jockey, don't stand there with your mouth open'. Didn't he know I had been working like a pack mule and that I was gasping, not gaping? I tried to apply some sand, thinking 'you'll be lucky'. The word 'hijack' was not in my vocabulary in those days, after all I didn't know very much about America. I was hardly likely to be familiar with American slang; should this event have taken place in more recent times, what happened next on that night would have convinced me that we were, in fact, being 'highjacked'.

As this huge locomotive vibrated and rocked, slipping one moment, finding traction the next, we were both startled to see a figure come climbing up out of the steamy darkness on to the footplate. He was followed by yet another and we were wondering when it was all likely to end. As we recognised them in the firelight, Ron asked 'What the hell is going on—where have you two come from?' The figures were both laughing, looking very pleased with themselves, like the 'cat that got the cream'. The two culprits were Gordon (Mushy) Hatton from Newnham-on-Severn, and Bill (Ginger) Ellis from the Tredworth area of Gloucester. Apparently they had recently been involved in something similar. Although the exact details are a bit obscure after 47 years, the following is a rough idea of what happened that night.

One of these two lads was working on an iron ore train, waiting to come down the bank from Andoversford, the other was on a banking engine. I never worked one of those banker jobs; they were very much in demand for Kingham and Knotgrove areas, where there was apparently some very heavy working. No one ever seemed

145

to know what was causing the hold up when we were sometimes stuck for hours in some siding but once we were moving we sometimes ran the rest of the journey non stop. It all became bewildering.

On this particular evening, the sound of an approaching train had caught their attention and the crew noticed it was 'doubleheaded' (drawn by two engines). They were LNER engines hauling a long American ambulance train and they were, quite naturally, all eyes. I was told later that the ambulance train was fitted with the 'Westinghouse brake system'. It was necessary for these LNER engines to take the American coaches the whole journey, and, of course, to be piloted by a GWR driver who knew the road. This train was like a self-contained field hospital complete with kitchens, a full medical staff, and all facilities. The patients were all stretcher cases who had been brought by sea and unloaded at Southampton. As the home signal was against the train it was obliged to stop at the far end of the platform. Either the LNER driver was guilty of very careless handling of the brake, or the GWR driver was using a brake he was unfamiliar with but for whatever reason—there was a terrific snatch, resulting in the coupling being broken and people on their feet were thrown in all directions—not to mention the patients who were badly shaken.

Wondering what damage had been done, Gordon and Bill left their drivers to go across to the station to see if help was needed. The engine crews in turn walked back to the broken coupling where they were joined by American orderlies and medical staff, all shaken and wondering what had happened. As the train firemen were still with their engines, this left Gordon and Bill who were the two youngest railwaymen present--one was in his teens, the other in his early twenties. They volunteered to crawl underneath the buffers to use the spare coupling to link the train up once more. This was a dirty job, usually done by passenger train shunters wearing strong gloves and overalls against the dirt and grease. What was worse, it was now almost dark. When it was done, the Americans, knowing nothing about the couplings, thought they had performed a near miracle, praising them almost to the point of embarrassment.

The signal was off for the train, but the drivers said that they would have to wait as both engines needed water. The crews gingerly moved the train forward to a position where the leading engine could take water. Gordon and Bill were walking back towards their engine as the leading ambulance train's coaches slowly overtook them. As the train halted an American doctor shouted from an open window, 'Say, would you two guys like a tomato juice or something?' Naturally our two boys said they would, and approached the carriage door from where the doctor had called. The door swung open and someone said 'OK jump in', to which the two replied that there wasn't time, but they would like a tomato juice where they stood. The Yank was very persuasive, however, and insisted they jump in, as he put it, and in the end they

146

decided to accept his offer and proceeded to climb up, rather than try to jump, having been assured there was all the time in the world. I'm not sure what they were offered but tomato juice was only one thing; there were chicken portions (still a luxury in those days) in addition to chocolate, biscuits, cigarettes and something stronger than tomato juice which in a very few minutes produced almost a party atmosphere, with Gordon and Bill gorging as fast as they could, after all, these goodies had been unobtainable for some years. Both were aware of a movement as the train moved about sixty feet in order to bring the lid of the water tank on the second engine in line with the water column. There was a lot of talking going on now, and our two heroes were still gorging everything that was placed within their reach. Here was yet one more stiff drink for the road. I can only think that the boys were mistaking the next movement that came as pulling for a second engine, which had already taken place—both must have forgotten that the first engine didn't need to pull forward, having stopped right the first time.

As it was now almost complete darkness, the first thing that brought them back to reality was the faint glimmer of light from the signal box as they passed it--they were being taken for a ride! Then they rushed to the window on the far side of the carriage and as they passed their mates, still sitting in their respective engines, yelled their loudest to attract their attention. Luckily for all concerned they were heard. One of the drivers had to leave his engine, breaking all the rules, to run to the signal box. The signalman was astonished to say the least, and diving at his levers, threw the advanced starter to danger, in an effort to stop the train. The engines had just passed and soon there was only the tail light on the guard's van visible. It crossed his mind to give the guard a red light and slide his detonators on to the rail but although serious, it was not a matter of life or death and he wasn't risking another calamity should the guard overdo it with the brake.

The two men stood looking at each other in disbelief for a few seconds, then the signalman did the obvious—he rang the signalman at Hatherley Junction, who stopped the train so that the two stowaways could get off. I don't know what the Yanks must have thought after their train breaking in two, now these two being taken away from their engines, they were probably wondering what would happen next.

Gordon and Bill made their way as quickly as possible up into the signal box where both hurriedly explained to the signalman what had taken place and enquired if there was any way he could think of getting them back to Andoversford. He told them that as far as he knew there was unlikely to be any train for Southampton that night, so they had better start walking! The 'bobby' was joking, of course. Weighing up the situation, both began to wonder if that was so far out of the question. Gordon's iron ore train was stuck at Andoversford, Bill's banker engine would be needed

147

further up the line, so what were they to do?

One of the drivers had made an anxious phone call after they had been gone about half an hour; he was at his wit's end when told that the two were still at Hatherley and had visions of reports flying all ways for some days to come. In the end the driver decided to take a chance and bring the train down the bank without a fireman, but the signalman insisted that he had had enough happen in his section today to last for the duration, so he wasn't about to give the road to a heavy iron ore train down that bank with only the driver on the engine.

The drivers were quite capable of bringing the train down, and doing the fireman's job as well, but if the driver had been taken ill, then there could have been real trouble, like about 800 tons of flying iron ore, steel hoppers and the locomotive. Had this got away, and had it kept on the rails as far as Hatherley, the signalman— provided he knew what was happening—would want to prevent them reaching the main line, so imagine the calamity if this engine, twenty four iron ore wagons and the guard's van had to be stopped with a catch, or throw off point.

Everyone settled down to wait, no one really knowing what to do for the best, each with his own thoughts, but everyone was sure this was going to mean trouble for somebody. There were plenty of trains passing over the four main tracks, goods and passenger, GWR and LMS, but as they rumbled past so did the minutes, and Gordon and Bill fell silent after a while, they were now resigned to whatever may happen to them.

The bells in the signal box were seldom silent for more than a minute or so, as signalmen above and below Hatherley asked for the road for various trains, which were either accepted or refused entry into the section depending on what was ahead of each train. I doubt if either of the lads understood the code and at that moment they would probably not have been concentrating anyway.

The signalman was on his feet most of the time. As codes rang out, he would use his key to tap out his reply, which was, of course, ringing out the code in which ever box he was in contact with. It was during one busy spell, as he received and sent, occasionally pulling levers that required two hands and most of his weight, that he said, 'Hey, you are in luck, I've got a 'government stock' coming up for Southampton'. Gordon and Bill roused themselves, stretched, then moved towards the door. There was plenty of time, the train wasn't in the section as yet. The signalman said 'I'll tell you one thing, rather you face them than me, they will be trying to get a run at the bank. I don't like stopping them here but there's no alternative'. Gordon and Bill weren't very concerned as long as the train stopped. As the train approached the distant signal, and Ron repeatedly asked for the road with the three blasts on the whistle, the signalman became a bit uncomfortable. Here was a responsible conscientious man having to ignore our whistle when he had the road for us. The only justification for not pulling off the signals was the two nuisances, who had suddenly descended upon him, making life more wearying than usual.

'You had better get down there, but for God's sake mind where you are putting your feet or you will be under a wheel, I can't stop him completely', he said, but as far as we were concerned he already had.

He peered through his peephole that had been scratched out in the blackout paint, and watched them positioning themselves about twenty yards apart in readiness to effect their quite dangerous boarding feat.

As the engine got within about forty yards of the box he hurriedly turned from the window and grabbed the starter signal lever. Then, throwing his complete weight backwards, pulled it down with a resounding clatter. He next pulled the 'advanced starter' off, then tapped out his train on line' code to the next box ahead. Moving quickly to his peephole, he was just in time to see the head and shoulders of the second figure silhouetted against the fire hole door as he appeared above the level of the footplate. He heaved a sigh of relief as he caught sight of the first one reflected in the same firelight—thank goodness they were gone!

As expected, the sounds of the wagon wheels passing his box were intermittently drowned by the sounds of the big engine slipping violently as it sought traction on the greasy rails. He stood listening now, with anxious thoughts running through his head. Hopefully this long train would keep going somehow, because it had to be clear of the four main line tracks it was crossing. Gradually the train slipped its way up into the dark drizzly night, and the 'bobby' slumped on his chair till roused by the bells again.

'Have another go at that sand, Jockey'. Ron's voice came over the noise of the engine. I tried again and kept trying for some minutes, but things weren't getting any better with no proof that there was any sand available. I sweated and swore at the sand lever, Ginger Ellis started firing saying, 'OK Jockey, I'll have her up here for you as it was our fault you had to stop'. Well, I wasn't going to argue; he was a very strong thickset lad in his twenties, moreover he was right, the two of them had caused this situation, so why shouldn't I have a free ride up this killer of a bank?

There were the four of us on the footplate. It would have made no difference, other than space, if there had been twenty four. The engine just would not get reasonable traction, so it continued, gripping one moment, slipping the next. It was beginning to get us tensed up. Each time she managed to get some grip, I found myself waiting for the next bout of slipping, like a starting pistol. It wasn't whether, but when? It was now obvious that we had no sand available, as we gradually climbed the bank towards the worst part, approaching the tunnel above Charlton Kings.

We passed the spring 'catch point' so positioned to throw off anything running back down the bank. As we crept nearer the mouth of the tunnel she slipped and slipped. The next thing that we were aware of was that we were stationary. Ron applied the brakes and we just stood for a few seconds, looking from one to the other in silence. There was no hope of us starting off again; in most circumstances it would be possible to set back a few yards, closing some of the front buffers, then make a snatch start. But the catch point prevented us doing so. It would only require us to runback a few feet, when whichever wagon was nearest the points would be off the rails. Ron said, 'I knew this would happen when I saw the distant signal at Hatherley—you two are a bloody nuisance!' I said to Ron, while at the same time keeping my distance, 'You know how I felt when I saw this engine in Gloucester station, with the possibility of no sand working, and it starting to rain'.

Ron either hadn't heard me, or pretended he hadn't. He was rummaging through his box for his pad of green 'wrong line order form B', which when found, began filling in. When it was completed, Ron said that one of them would have to walk up to Andoversford to bring an engine to assist us up through the tunnel. Both may as well go, taking the green 'wrong line order' to the signalman. It would have fallen my lot had they not been with us, then I would have had to ride back with the

Andoversford tunnel has found a new lease of life, but not one involving railways!   *(D. A. Trigg)*

relieving engine to tell them exactly where our engine was. As it was, which ever fireman came to relieve us would know where we were so there was no point in me going. I was glad to get out of that; it would have been bad enough with three of us equipped with a small flickering paraffin lamp but it could be very unpleasant in a tunnel on your own. In the pitch black dark, so far in, a very cold stream of air travelling down hill, monstrous drops falling and with your own shadow and eerie echoing footsteps it was not a journey to hanker after. Taking our gauge lamp, they set off at a fast pace; both were getting a bit worried now. The iron ore train was still waiting for a fireman in order to go down the bank, the banker had no fireman. Now a longer delay was on the cards as we waited for them to walk to Andoversford to arrange for an engine to come down to assist us. We could do little but wait. I took the opportunity to top up the boiler, pull some coal forward and fill up the hole. Ron, who looked all in as he sat on his seat gazing at the fire, smoked a cigarette, saying nothing. He had had a busy few miles.

After nearly half an hour we eventually saw a lamp approaching, slowing down from the tunnel mouth. It was Ginger and his mate with the banker engine. As they reached us they came against our buffers. Ginger climbed down to bring back our gauge lamp, saying that the two drivers had been going mad with anxiety, but had cooled down a bit now. Ginger would couple the engines up, and needless to say, I stayed where I was.

We heard him shout to his mate, Ease up', then felt a big tank engine compressing the buffers, enabling him to drop the heavy screw coupling over the hook on our engine. When he had tightened the coupling and connected the vacuum brake pipe, he shouted 'OK' to us and clambered aboard the engine. A short whistle from each engine and we were away once more, soon experiencing the thundering clatter as the two engines entered the tunnel, blasting away at the steep hill which eventually evened off, before the drop down into Andoversford station. Whilst Ginger was uncoupling, Ron went forward to have a few words with the driver on the banker, obviously both had a story to relate. Filled with annoyance and anxiety, finally they had to agree there was a funny side to it, especially as the banker driver recalled Ginger's face as he shouted, almost in a panic, as the ambulance train sailed out of the station. When the banker finally moved off the main line, we set off once more towards Swindon Old Town. The rest of the journey turned out to be pretty uneventful, but, as was to be expected, it was raining steadily.

On being relieved at Swindon Old Town we went to enquire about transport to the main station. We may as well have saved the effort and set out walking in the first place. When we arrived at Swindon we strolled onto the platform to find a trolley on which we sat waiting for a ride home. We had no intention of working home, we made that plain to the supervisor when we were relieved. We managed to get a comfortable spot on the train that was due in Gloucester about 5 o' clock in the morning and I was no sooner in the train than asleep. The next thing I knew was a slight jolt as we came to a standstill in Gloucester.

If only I could have slept as easily in the daytime at home, I would have had no problem. I may easily have been on the job today, though I don't think I would have taken too kindly to diesels, so perhaps it's as well I left when I did.

I walked towards the shed, half asleep, picking my way sometimes alongside Ron, sometimes behind. I could hardly believe where we had been. what had happened in the last few hours; it was almost like a dream as we walked out of the time office in the darkness.

Groping my way along the wall, my eyes not yet accustomed to the dark, I found my motor bike and removed my bit of canvas from the saddle. I was thankful the bike started easily, then throwing my leg over the saddle I sank back, let in the clutch and rode away. I now find it difficult to believe that some of those rides home on the motor bike ever really happened—quite a few times I must have been in a kind of daze. I remember nothing between Westgate bridge and home. It's amazing now the amount of traffic that is travelling the South Wales road, compared to the 1940s.

After the last buses ran at night, eleven o'clock at the very latest, there was unlikely to be any traffic at all until the factory buses began next morning. If the conditions were reasonable when I crossed Westgate bridge, I would set my throttle at about 35mph, then stuff my hands in my pockets all the way home, using the centre of the road, or right hand side if necessary. I shall never know why I didn't go to sleep completely!

I was about half way home early one morning, luckily well on my side of the road, when suddenly out of the darkness came a huge car of some sort, travelling very fast in the opposite direction, with no lights at all. I can hardly believe it happened, but I know it did. It roused me like a bucket full of cold water.

152

Victory in Europe

VE Day found the railways still under great pressure. With lack of rolling stock, locomotives and staff, there was still no hope of me leaving the job to find something that would enable me to get a few nights' regular sleep. Had I tried to stick it out for another two or three years, things would no doubt have improved. At this stage I was all for leaving the job as soon as possible.

VE night, with all the ensuing celebrations which included the inevitable bonfires, found me as usual where I always seemed to be—on duty.

At 10.30 that night there was a large crowd at Gloucester Cross, similar to those gatherings on New Year's Eve nowadays. Sadly, there the similarity ends. It was a happy singing and dancing atmosphere, not a clenched fist in sight. Everyone had had enough of all that, and of course knives were utensils with which you buttered, or rather margarined, your bread.

Imagine someone on a motor cycle inadvertently riding into a New Year crowd and hoping to get through it in one piece—well this happened to me on VE night. I managed to get away somehow, with my dinner bag firmly crossed over my head, cap under my arm and right hand gripping the throttle. I was nearly off once or twice as I revved my engine, footing my way along. The crunch came when some wild woman climbed on to the pillion, put her arms round my neck, and pulled my head back until I lost all sense of balance, apparently in an effort to kiss me. We went flat on the road, the bike trapping us by the left leg. I hadn't expected a crowd like this or I would have avoided it for sure. Regaining my footing, I climbed back on the bike and tore off along Eastgate Street, over California crossing.

When I arrived at the engine shed I still had difficulty in believing what had happened. I stopped my bike engine, covered it up and hurried along the rear of the offices and stores, conscious of a terrific racket going on around me.

Rounding the corner of the foreman's office on my way to the time office, the noise became worse. Nearly every engine on the shed in steam had a heavy bar hung on the whistle chain. As each GWR engine had two whistles, one shrill light note, and one low, more like a fog horn, it was a terrific din! The blackout was almost non-existent, as cleaners (young firemen on shed duties) ran around wildly with hand and flare lamps, from one engine to another, refixing the bars each time the foreman and charge hands took them off. It was a sight and sound I'll never ever forget as figures appeared out of the darkness on one side of the footplate, and then after hurried movements that were reflected in the engine firelight, were chased off by the foreman or chargehand cleaner. I don't know how long this had been going on when I arrived. It seemed to go on for a long time after. Yes, I did get involved.

As Ron and I walked towards the station, I hurriedly climbed on to two engines that were down near the coal stage, well away from the main action. I set their whistles going and quickly left. I don't know how long it was before they were discovered—I didn't care, Ron kept walking as though he was not with me.

As we moved further away from the shed, we became aware that it was not just the Western shed that was making the noise, it was coming from the LMS shed as well. A lot of noise was being made at the two stations by trains pulling away holding down their whistles. The station pilot crew did a lot more whistle blowing than could be justified while carrying out their shunting duties.

The engines at North box and the Docks branch were all helping to swell the din, as did odd vehicle horns, whistles and church bells. The latter, one of the signals of an invasion that hadn't been heard for years rang from every belfry in the land. What an experience it must have been for those who witnessed the celebration in a place such as London, with all the Thames traffic joining in with the many locomotive depots. The war in Europe was over but anyone who thought they could wake up next morning to a changed world was in for a shock.

The blackout was eventually lifted, a supplementary petrol ration was allowed, but food was to stay on ration for several years. I recall that sweets were the very last things to come off ration. I was in Cirencester on the day it came about, working for the Post Office Engineering Department, later to become British Telecom. That was about seven years after the VE Celebrations, but things were back to normal quicker in countries that had been occupied, even in Germany.

By this time I had acquired a fairly good Ariel Red Hunter motor cycle; experience in repairing and improvising generally had been thrust upon me. I became more interested in motor cycles as time went by. So, with my petrol allowance came some freedom—imagine being able to choose where I went! I ioined the Cotswold Motor Cycle Club and found myself taking part in team trials and grass track racing. There was an amusing picture of myself with two other competitors on a hill, all facing different directions as each of us manoeuvred to a position that would give us a chance to ascend the hill. This picture was in the February 1946 issue of *Motor Cycle*, and the caption read as follows: 'I know where I'm going, believe it or not all three competitors are tackling the same section in the recent Stroud team trials'.

I bought a grass track bike for £18—that was approximately five weeks wages. It was a 500cc OK Supreme, with a JAP engine which I ran on meths. It was adapted and tuned for racing, having a high compression piston with tulip valves fitted. The three speed hand gear box was converted to a two speed foot change; with knobbly tyres it would really wind itself up in top gear. I had a lot of enjoyment from racing this bike, with quite a bit of success during the short time I used it. The problem was

154

transporting the bike about—my first ever race was at Colway in the Forest of Dean. On this occasion I was driven by a friend of mine, Harry Baker, whose father Frank farmed at Gamage Court, Ley. Harry said he would drive me with the car and trailer but, as he put it 'I had better ask the Gaffer'. Well, I met the Gaffer in the drive and as usual when asked a question, which was usually a request for some favour or other by one of us lads, his eyes began sweeping various parts of the sky with a frown, as though he was expecting a clap of thunder at any second. His pipe had by this time dropped into bottom gear, and began exuding vast volumes of smoke—looking back I still find this amusing. His answer was typical, 'I don't know about that, it would cost you a fair bit of money'. Which meant that it would be OK!

Quite a few people from the lower end of Minsterworth came to see the races. I liked to think to give me a bit of moral support at the same time. One incident that happened after the races finished will be remembered for the rest of their lives by the people who witnessed it. It happened to the late Tom Greening, who was one of the local lads. He seemed to have got behind, as all the Minsterworth people hurried for the bus. The bus was approaching and, having been called to hurry up, he had taken a short cut through some trees, sprinting as he was well capable of. The next thing anyone knew, he was on his back clutching his throat. Tom had run into a clothes line and it was several minutes before the crowd managed to get him back on his feet and on to the bus.

I had a couple of wins, along with several places, and as I said, it was the first time out so I was very pleased. My most amusing incident was less painful than Tom Greenings. It happened as, with about six helpers who gained free entrance, I was making my way through the main access to the field. I was anxious about the time and on entering the field decided that if I was going to get a bit of a warm up, I had better start the bike quickly and move down to the pits.

There were a lot of spectators, I should think about six deep round the track; after all, entertainment of any sort had been a bit scarce in the last six years. This probably accounted for the large turn out.

Several bikes were practising starts, several more having a bit of a scorch round the track, and the heads of the crowd were turning this way and that as though watching a slow tennis match. My bike had a rather loud straight-through exhaust. All agreed it revved and crackled like fried bread. It came about that as we ran the bike as fast as we could, I jumped on side saddle, and the engine burst into life. All heads swung 180 degrees, no doubt wondering what was coming at them from behind.

Other places where I attended races were Littledean, Tibberton, and Gloucester Park, to name a few. It was good fun but as in many cases, all good things come to an end. The cause? National Service!

Summer Time

The summer following the VE Day celebrations was the best for several years, good weather not being the only reason. Everyone felt better, happier, expectant, with visions of the end of rationing and all war time restrictions. The strange thing was that these hardships and restrictions had come so rapidly that as each occurred it would help us forget the previous ones, at least for a while.

I was now gaining more experience, beginning to be more confident in the way I did what was expected of me as a fireman. Maybe it was just because it was summertime, as previously mentioned double summer time in midsummer could mean it not getting dark until about 11.30pm. I seemed to be working in more daylight hours than in the previous four years. This meant that when we managed to finish work without overtime, I could go to bed in darkness and sleep.

I remember running back up through Severn Tunnel Junction on hot evenings, passing through Newnham-on-Severn, Westbury, Grange Court and Oakle Street. Oakle Street was where I would blow my code on the whistle to let the family know at home that I was at least going uphill towards Gloucester.

One of the best days I recall was a hot August day; we clocked on about 11am, collecting a train for Severn Tunnel at about 2.30pm. The engine steamed well, it looked like being a good trip. In spite of being held up at Grange Court for about two hours, we decided to have our food; for once I could see what I was eating, spam sandwiches, a homemade faggot, a few radishes and some very young shallots taken from the garden at great peril to myself—very enjoyable! I moved off the engine, taking my feast and mug of tea to sit on a pile of sleepers near Hoddle's plum orchard. The plums were practically finished, and harvest was in full swing. It was a very hot day and everywhere I looked, especially towards the railway line, a heat haze hung low and shimmering. Everything worked out perfectly. Having finished my food I was just about to find somewhere to stretch out, when clatter went the signal and we were off once more. After being sent down the loop line again at Bullo, we came to a standstill, while the examiner and his mate came out of their cabin, proceeding to examine the wagon axles, up one side and back down the other. Soon after the examination had been completed we were given the road again, this time we ran right through to Severn Tunnel where we were relieved promptly, as usual. We reported to the supervisor, who told us that he already had a job lined up for us--the train was approaching the yard now. With the thought of having our noses pointing towards home, we walked towards the station without further ado.

It was a heavy coal train for Stoke Gifford, hauled by a 2800 2-8-0 class; judging by its clean appearance it looked fresh out of the workshops. This engine was a dream to fire after some of the ones I had worked on. I had a good idea of what the job must have been like in peace time.

We pulled smartly away from Severn Tunnel, the 2800 seemed to make light work of the load. In what seemed no time we were creeping over Chepstow Bridge at five miles an hour, then opening up to pull away up the incline. The old Castle looked cool and serene in the evening sunshine; glancing down toward the river bed, which seemed pretty low, it appeared an even longer drop to the water than usual. Incidently, on bright moonlight nights it was rather an eerie experience as we rumbled slowly over the bridge, with grotesque shadows all around as well as beneath, then the Castle would take on a different aspect. This evening was different though, we could even see where the track ran beneath the cliffs, between the old Severn Bridge and Awre.

On moonlit nights there was sometimes a shadow cast by cliffs which ended in the water at high tide, so the water was shining in the moonlight. We were running just inside the shadow under the cliffs, not being able to see the tracks. For my part, during hot weather, it was a case of hurriedly slinging a few shovels full of coal in, then hanging head and shoulders over the side to cool off. In this way the heat was tolerable, it was when we stopped that things became a bit overwhelming. The whole cab was like a warm oven; if I climbed off the engine the stone ballast was very hot, and the sleepers gave off a strong smell of creosote and the rails would shine through the haze. Sometimes there would be a shadow cast by a high van, or something similar, and it was possible to stand in that shade for a few minutes but it wouldn't do much to cool me off. Sometimes, while on the run, I could see shady oaks or ash trees and longed to be able to go and lie under one, in a cool breeze. Sometimes there would be a sparkling brook, the water running between small boulders. A few yards away from the line the banks of the brook would be worn away where cattle had trampled up and down over the years. Several cows stood in the water, others lying close by. I would think how lucky they were on such a day!

I was aware of all these things as we ran back on this particular evening. Here and there people of all ages were working in the harvest fields, corn was being hauled in mainly by horse-drawn vehicles. By this time there was also the odd tractor to be seen. Usually the little basic Fordson was most commonly used--what it lacked in refinements, it made up for with power.

Corn stooks could be seen drying for a couple of weeks, with luck they would see no rain. In another field the old horsedrawn reaping machine was on the last small patch in the centre of the field. A ring of people with sticks, some with guns, plus, of course, the inevitable dogs were ready to pounce on each unfortunate rabbit or fox as it emerged from the ever-diminishing patch of corn. The corn stubble was too high for rabbits to run over with any sort of speed and once they lost their regular runs they hadn't much chance—they were, of course, a welcome source of food.

Passing through Oakle Street, I blew up as usual, hoping that for once I may get home in time to eat whatever my mother had saved for me before it was ruined. Passing the black bridge at Churcham where it joined Farmer Dennis's land that lay either side of the railway, I could see the huts recently vacated by the army. These were now being used for people, mostly teenage girls from Manchester, who would be spending their holidays at this working harvest camp. Tonight was one of their frequent dance nights and the locals were made welcome at the dances which became a source of much interest to us lads. Even though it was only 6.30pm we were getting close to Gloucester but it was still almost too much to expect to be home in time to get to the dance. If past experience was anything to go on I had no chance when I thought of the football games I had missed through excessive overtime.

The worst example was one week when, booking on at midnight, I told the local team members I would be able to play on the following Saturday, thinking that at the worst I should be home by midday. On the Friday night we collected a train for Stratford-on-Avon about 4am, we then had a slow return trip working back to Gloucester. All the morning I had been hoping we would get a move on, but matters became worse. As the game started at 2.45 we were just creeping down over Horton Road crossing. I had very little faith or optimism concerning anything after that.

Optimism was again in short supply as the distant signal was against us at Over—turning into the up loop, the question was, how long would we be held here? We pulled on up slowly to the Gloucester end and I set about filling in the hole for my relief. I didn't appear to have used much coal coming back from Severn Tunnel, if only all trips had been this pleasant and easy! I propped the shovel level in order to fill it with water for washing our hands, then the footplate was swilled off, the coal dampened with the pep pipe. It was then the turn of the shovel, and we washed our hands. As we discussed what would have happened to the glass of beer, should one have been available, we both agreed that for once we may get one later. Ron sat down and lit a cigarette. I was perched on my seat, still drying my hands and when we got the road I remarked to Ron, 'I just can't believe it, we'll have to pay for this'. He said, 'Take the handbrake off, don't worry about tomorrow, that's another day'.

I don't know what caused the engine to occasionally produce smoke rings—this engine made one as Ron opened her up a bit hard to get moving out of the loop. Suddenly it was there, a silver ring rising into the still air. When I first spotted it it was about 40ft. high and had increased to about the size of a child's paddling pool, becoming larger as it rose higher and higher. I have heard it described as perfect exhaust. If that is true, then there must have been many billions of imperfect ones!

As it emerged from the chimney, it spun within itself, that is coming up on the outside, before turning down into the centre. This appears to continue as it climbs higher and higher, becoming larger and less dense, until finally it fades away. We pulled out of the loop, under the road bridge, then on to the incline towards the station, the 2800 was still making light work of this very heavy train. We dropped slowly down into the station; and could see our relief walking along the platform. We overtook them, stopping at the starter signal to wait. In spite of my previous comments about firemen who insisted on singing the praises of every engine, no matter how bad it steamed, I felt justified in dropping into this category just for once, as I was handing over such a beautiful engine, so I stood waiting for him to climb up before I said my piece. The driver came first, struggling up through the narrow gap between the engine and the tender—he pushed his box in front of him, sliding it a couple of feet across the footplate to make room for his feet. Up came the fireman, only he, like most younger ones including myself, had not yet bought himself a proper engineman's box; as I opened my mouth to say my piece he quickly commented, 'I reckon you gotta goodun yer mate'.

Later, as I shot down through Westgate Street on my motor bike, there was little traffic apart from a couple of parked buses. I was thankful for the cool air. When I crossed Over bridge, I knew I was heading in the right direction. The sun was lower now, sinking towards the west, but still quite hot as I sped through Highnam towards Minsterworth and home. It was about this point of my journey that I was suddenly conscious of that particular sweetscented country air that is only present at harvest time on an evening such as this, when the heat of the day has passed its peak. There were one or two good things about the existence of the harvest camp, one was that Oakle Street Hotel, now called The Silent Whistle, received an extra ration of beer in order to accommodate the campers' thirsts. It did no end of good for ours as well, at every opportunity! The other exciting thing was these strange girls, when as a rule there was only about four in the whole village! After resorting to trying to get us tipsy, and twisting our arms beyond endurance, the girls managed to persuade us to walk them back to the camp by Churcham church to attend the dance. For me, at least, it finished off a near perfect day. As I, with my two companions who shall remain nameless, (sadly no longer with us) set off down through the golden field of corn stooks, now bathed in bright moonlight, Churcham clock struck a quarter to three. This was a short cut across the black bridge, over the railway line that I had so recently travelled along, up through the fields to Minsterworth village hall, then out on to the main road. It was only about three quarters of a mile to walk then, and this didn't take long as we hurried alongside the Severn, now a wide silver ribbon of moonlight, each trying to outdo the other two as we related our evening's activities.

I fell into a deep sleep once I got into bed and not even the noisy milkman woke me as he rattled and whistled his way from house to house. My mother woke me at half past nine. I realised it was work again but if every day had been like yesterday I would have looked forward to it.

Emergency Banker

One dark evening during the winter following VE Day, we set off for Swindon once again. We had a heavy 2-8-0 goods engine, a 3800; as far as I was aware, the only difference between one of these and a 2800 was the number.

These were very powerful engines with quite small wheels, making them low geared but they would amble on a bit if it became necessary. They were not put on the parcel trains or the fast vacuum coupled trains where they would need to run; they were essentially very good work horses and we were always pleased to see them.

We left Gloucester on this winter evening, climbing up over Horton Road crossing and were doing very well in every respect. Passing the North box towards India Road Bridge I could tell the locomotive was going to be OK. Steam was well up, the water was only just showing in the top of the gauge glass, while the fire was bright and clean. It had obviously recently been having the works treatment on shed, somewhere in Wales.

Whenever we went to Swindon we usually had a pretty good run, never seeming to become held up as much as Stratford, Severn Tunnel or Bristol. After running from Gloucester to Stonehouse on this trip, it came as quite a surprise to have to go into the sidings. We couldn't be accepted higher up so decided that we may as well boil our can and have our food. Ron remarked that he would take a stroll up to the signal box to see what the bobby had to say.

I made the fire up a bit, thinking that we may be away any moment, but Ron came back with no hope of us moving for some time yet. I then filled the hole in, building it up quite high in the front; should I not use it all there would be less to shovel forward at Swindon. We had been settled on our seats for some time, Ron halfway through his second cigarette, my feet on the dampers handles as usual, when I heard a whistle and looking out saw a light shining out from the box. I informed Ron, then climbed down on to the track to pick my way carefully towards the box.

As I entered I said that I assumed he had a message for us to take the engine back to Gloucester, leaving the train where it was. He gave me an old fashioned look and said, 'You'll be lucky too'. He told me there was an emergency that had only just developed. He was to ask us if we were prepared to help out. He told me that one of the two bankers at Brimscombe had just had its fire cleaned and was pretty low in fire and steam and wouldn't be ready to bank a train for at least an hour. The second engine, having just banked a train up through Sapperton Tunnel, had returned a few minutes ago but the driver was asking for another banker to be sent from Gloucester. He could then go to shed with a serious brake malfunction. The immediate problem was that the London mail train was due in about twenty minutes; its load was too much for the bank as it stood, and ours was the only engine within miles which could do anything to help.

He asked me to go back to consult Ron as to what he thought about it—after all, we were already on a train. It crossed my mind that somewhere down in the siding sat, or lay, a guard in his van. If he suddenly realised we were gone he might have a fit, believing we had broken away to leave him while he slept.

I went back to the engine and told Ron what the signalman had said. Ron replied that we might as well do what they wanted—in any case we weren't likely to go until the mail had gone through. The problem now was the suitability of the engine--the question of power didn't arise as it was capable of taking the train and the engine up the bank on its own. It was the wheel size; officially they weren't large enough in diameter to double-head an express train. Ron said that he was willing to try it as it was an emergency. He added that it was up to me as it would mean working the bank and tunnel twice. I had already thought about this, deciding that there would be no point in refusing if Ron was willing to do it.

Having agreed to their request, I set off once more to the box to let him know what was happening. He seemed relieved, saying he would inform control as the train had already left Gloucester and I had better get a move on. I arrived back at the engine,

Prairie tank number 4100 banks a goods train into Sapperton tunnel. The crew would experience a choking cloud of smoke all the way through. *(N. E. Preedy)*

161

shouting to Ron that the mail had left Gloucester and that I was uncoupling. Having uncoupled the engine from the train, I altered the headlamps in readiness, then climbed back up on to the footplate, opened the dampers wide and topped up the boiler before banking the fire up. I was now ready. There would not be enough time to inform the guard—let him sleep in peace!

Now the stage was set for more drama, which proved to be potentially dangerous, proving that in most accidents, be they land, sea or air, it is wise not to rule out the human element. In fact, in my book the human element is always chief suspect. The mail approached in great haste, giving long single blasts on the whistle, finally coming to a standstill about ten yards behind us on the main line at the home signal. The following train of events will show how easy it can be to have a disaster on your hands by a moment's lack of concentration. We received the signal to pull forward out on to the main line in order to be able to set back on to the mail engine to couple up. The points controlling the siding joined the main track very close to the end of the platform. In order to be sure of clearing them properly in the darkness, Ron had moved some yards along the platform. He stopped, ready to set back. I walked to the points with the gauge lamp in order that I could see when the signalman had put them right for Ron to run back over. The points swung across with a solid slam and I waved my lamp to Ron to come back towards the mail. In the meantime the engine crew on the mail had no idea what was going on; all they knew was that they were being held up at Stonehouse. The engine couldn't have been steaming too well. I could hear the blower was on about half a turn. There was a brilliant light flashing from the fire as it reflected on the left hand tool box and hand rail. It was plainly obvious that the fireman was taking advantage of every second to build up his steam and water. It wasn't possible to see beyond the confines of the cab as he swung back and forth with the shovel. The driver was on the right hand side of the engine, all there was to see from his side was a small red signal light, beyond that, pitch darkness, made worse by the contrasting firelight reflections.

Ron began to reverse our engine, coming back at about ten miles per hour; the signalman pulled off the main line signal for the mail, and the driver saw it as it turned green. He had used his ejector once or twice while standing, to keep his vacuum up ready to be off. When he saw the signal he presumably said, 'Right mate'. The mail was now late, the train would be stopping again at Brimscombe for the banker, and so he opened the regulator wide. The Castle set about wakening the residents of Stonehouse for the driver was certainly starting off as though he meant it. I frantically waved the red side of my gauge lamp to Ron, shouting at the same time, but no one was likely to hear me. Ron could hear the Castle behind him now; the two engines were only about 40 or 50 feet apart, and the mail was already doing a steady running pace so Ron did the only thing possible to avoid severe damage. Instead of braking, he had the good sense to slam the reversing lever into forward gear, opening the regulator right out.

The heavy 3800 was still sliding backwards, with the driving wheels spinning forward furiously, when the Castle, still pulling away very hard with the regulator open about three quarters, struck it. The momentum supplied by the mail engine, plus the already spinning wheels, caused the 3800 to take off along the platform like a dragster car before Ron could regain his balance to apply the brakes. The fireman, along with the poor old driver, came clambering down off the engine, their eyes not yet used to the darkness; both were unable to see anything for a while. What a shock they received to find a big locomotive in front of them! For the next few minutes it was pandemonium as the driver was shouting and swearing at everyone until he realised it was all the result of a moment's lack of concentration on the part of the signalman. Nearly every window was open, with people trying to find a vacant spot to stick their head out in order to see what was going on. It was a good thing that the blackout was no longer important as lights shone out on to the track.

While the fireman held a light for me, I stooped, and, picking my feet up to clear the rails, clambered and grunted my way in between the two sets of buffers to get at the coupling. After four years it was still not a position in which I liked to find myself, being very dark, apart from a little flickering flame in the gauge lamp. I was now in between these two huge black masses of steel, where almost everything was covered in grease, oil or thick dust. Although I knew Ron wouldn't move the engine until I shouted, and the last time I had seen the mail train driver, he was on his way up the signal box steps, in view of the events which had just taken place I couldn't get the vacuum pipe disconnected quickly enough. Being careful so as to avoid cracking my head on something or other, I stretched down across to free the end of the screw coupling on our engine from its hook, then, when it was hanging loose, I used the captivated bar like the handle of a vice to slacken the adjustment well out. I wanted to get the next bit right first time.

There was a fair amount of noise coming from the Castle's chimney. The blower was still on and this had the effect of making me feel more tense than I already was, being aware of all this noise, with potential dangers, as I worked away feverishly at the couplings, ever conscious of the pair of experienced eyes watching me. Then the Castle blew off—I was instantly reduced to a bag of nerves!

The passenger shunters were used to this job, they were in and out of this situation many times a day. We didn't often have to touch the couplings, it was exceptional for me to have to do this particular job. I was naturally not as at home as the said shunters. While the buffers were just in contact, there was room enough between the two engine to move about with care, everything was steel and didn't give much if you banged your elbow or some other part, but, as can be imagined, when the coupling was

163

completed the distance between the set of buffers of each engine was halved. Standing in one of these small spaces, the end link held firmly in two hands, being careful to keep fingers well out of danger, you shout loudly, 'Ease up'. I shouted, and the buffers began to disappear into the spring housing, compressing the heavy springs. The space in which I was standing was becoming smaller and smaller and I was relieved when the buffers reached the limit of travel. I heaved the coupling up, just past the horizontal, then dropped the robust link over the hook, when I was able to give a sigh of relief—the next part was easier.

I shouted 'Ease off' after first connecting our vacuum pipe to the train engine. As he opened his ejector, so easing the brakes off, the pressure on the two pairs of buffers was enough to push our engine forward a little. The buffers were once more fully extended, just a couple of inches apart. Then using the small bar-come-handle, I screwed the adjustment on the coupling up tight to ensure that the buffers were making contact again. I then quickly scrambled out. The other fireman ran to his engine steps and climbed quickly to inject water into his boiler rather than let all the steam blow away. The blower was very good for raising the steam quickly, also for dispersing excess smoke while standing. When used indiscriminately it could effect the fire condition, like the effect of excessive drugs on a human being. With the particular engine travelling all the way to London, I believe the fireman had only to turn it on temporarily.

The mail train driver, along with the signalman, must have cooled down and settled their argument, for the driver came down the steps of the box and had a hurried word with Ron. Then we were ready. I don't believe the incident was ever reported. I know Ron didn't report it—whether this was the right decision or not, I've no idea. An action of that sort could cause disaster!

We set off at last, full of apprehension, me trying to imagine what this 3800, with its small wheels, would ride like in front of this train, which was not supposed to loiter. My fire was right up before I did the coupling up, a few more shovels full would put me right for a while—after all we wouldn't be pulling very hard, just getting a move on. Ron told the driver that if he would like to conserve steam and water a little he could ease off once we were moving, then perhaps help us through the tunnel, which he agreed to do. We made a fine start with a lot of noise and before I knew what was happening I was becoming aware that it was necessary to support myself quite a bit, as once or twice the old 3800 rocked or kicked. With it being dark, I couldn't seem to anticipate when this was most likely to happen. The mail train driver had wound the cut off reversing lever back and closed the regulator down. I could tell that from the moderate, slightly uneven, exhaust noise, while ours was so fast the beats all sounded exactly the same. Those small wheels did convey the message through the main framework of the engine that they were revolving very quickly. I couldn't hear the

164

Castle's blower any more because she started blowing off—that doesn't usually happen up a steep bank but of course our 3800 locomotive was doing the work.

Up beyond Chalford we started to come right against it, although Ron didn't drop the lever out at all. He did find it necessary to open the regulator wide because we were now slowing down a little. It was at this point that the mail train driver opened up the Castle and what a sound—it nearly caught me unawares. It was only a few feet away, just the length of the tender. The smoke box and chimney seemed to loom in an overwhelming manner, but that must have been about the best position to hear the blast from an engine while on the run.

This occasion was now developing into something special for me, once again I experienced this feeling of elation, of great power, as these two huge locomotives now began in earnest to blast their way up towards the tunnel. As we had slowed down somewhat, I could now hear our own exhausts more clearly, by listening over the side I could get equal volume from both chimneys. This was the most complicated sound I had ever encountered from steam engines; as the Castle's wheels were roughly a

It was quite an event to get a gleaming clean locomotive fresh from overhaul. Even so a banker would still usually be needed for Sapperton. Grange class 4-6-0 number 6820 "Kingstone Grange' toils up the incline with rear end assistance. *(Author's Collection)*

165

third larger than ours, there was a certain amount of off-beat. Every now and again the two exhausts would synchronise for an instant, then separate again in staggered beats; it is not easy to describe—this sound can be heard on records, it's a sound once heard never to be forgotten. One sound that I've never heard since was the one these two engines made as we entered Sapperton Tunnel

On this occasion the tunnel and the hill above was just a dark mass looming in front, then above, as we approached. In daytime, apart from the heavy working, it was quite a pleasant ride up through the valley to the point where the line curved to the right between the grassy banks on either side, and above, where trees and bushes were dotted about. As we passed the highest point in the tunnel and levelled off, we were picking up speed quickly, the next thing I knew we were out of the tunnel and braking hard, as we approached the signal box.

We stopped to uncouple and as I stepped down again between the buffers, I was aware, once again, of the close proximity of these two black-looking monsters and once more the Castle blew off, threatening to deafen me. I was just becoming used to

The Chalford end of Sapperton tunnel, pleasant to observe from the lineside but not a pretty sight if you were about to enter it when it was full of smoke. *(D. A. Trigg)*

this noise when I suddenly became aware of a vibration, which was increasing rapidly, followed by a rumbling noise which engulfed the noise from the Castle's safety valve. I was just fixing the vacuum pipe on our engine when the commotion burst in on me through the narrow gap between the two engines; it was a freight train going in the opposite direction, pulling hard up towards the mouth of the tunnel.

First, the noise of the engine blasted its way into the gap as this engine passed only about 8ft. from me. It was standing a good deal higher than me, the train being upon the rails, me in a semi-stooping position. As I prepared to climb back out from under the buffers, I received the full volume of everything that was going. When the engine was well past me I could hear the mostly regular banging from the wagon wheels on the rail joint just a few feet away; the rhythm of these wheels was very different to that of carriage wheels spanning joints. The more common sound of carriage wheels, which give four bangs, then a longer space between that and the next four, contrast considerably with the noise from the standard wagon wheels. The distance between the axles seems about equal to the distance from the axle of one truck, to the axle of

Huge brick-lined, vertical smoke vents were required in steam days to try and ventilate the tunnel. This is one of Sapperton's.   *(D. A. Trigg)*

the next, so causing a fairly regular beat.

I climbed back up on to our engine after putting a white light on the tender, a red one on the front, ready to go tender first back to Stonehouse and our train, only to face this bank and tunnel again, but this time with a different load—and a very slow climb.

We pulled out of the way of the mail, which set off once more for London, happier, I thought, than when it had arrived at Stonehouse—then it was obviously doing rough. Now it had a full head of steam, a full boiler, a downhill start and with a blast on the whistle, it hammered its way off into the night. For the last few minutes I had been spraying the footplate, the tender and boxes, but mostly the coal; it was never funny travelling tender first. We had put our coats on, turning up the collars, ready for the horrible cold blasts that would gust over the tender and swirl around us as we travelled down through the tunnel, where we would be splashed continually by dirty great blobs of condensation not to mention the cold draught, the noises, the water, and in spite of the drenching I had given the coal, occasional black dust blowing into our faces. Everything was pitch black apart from a slight flicker of light from the fire hole doors, which I had to keep shut because we were coasting and consequently having no draught on the fire. We got a fair amount of smoke trying to seep out through the doors, so once again the blower came into its own.

I pushed back into my corner by the window against the boiler casing and thought that if only it were hotter this could easily be the road to hell. As these thoughts were running through my head, there came the last straw—we met another goods train which had now overtaken us on the road to Swindon. It's one thing to pass a train in a tunnel running normal way round where there is a chance that your own slip stream may retain some air in your cab but going tender first into all the smoke and steam laid down by a labouring goods train defies description. We were soon out of the tunnel, drifting down through the valley quite quickly, through Chalford and Stroud to Stonehouse, where I was hoping our train had somehow disappeared but no such luck! As we backed on to our train I coupled up, and while replacing the headlights I suddenly once again had the feeling that I had been there before. Incidentally there was still no sign of the guard; later, at Swindon, he had no idea what we were talking about when we mentioned the mail train, so he had been asleep!

We reported back to the control to be told that we were required to work back home, this didn't always happen—we usually got a ride home on a passenger. When Ron came from the supervisor's office with the news that we had to work back I wasn't very pleased to say the least. The time was about 8.30am, we had boooked on around teatime the day before, so we were now on about fifteen or sixteen hours. We had worked our heavy freight from Gloucester, plus the delay, and extra work banking the mail, now I was expected to work back home with no food or drink of any kind, except water. I didn't even know where I might find a tap so I forgot it. I asked Ron when he

168

reckoned we might get back to Gloucester, I thought about lunchtime if we were lucky, adding that I was too tired to work home anyway. He answered, 'We should be home pretty soon, this job was guaranteed to keep me awake'. I said, 'What the hell is it then, a travelling steam fair?' 'No', he said, 'It's a special for Birmingham, we'll get relief up above the North box yard'. This was where the road ran to the right towards Cheltenham, forming part of the triangle. I said, 'Well, they will give us the road and I can't see us getting home any quicker by any other means. I don't understand why we are getting a special, the men are usually booked and told before-hand'. He said that it was probably because this was empty stock, or empty carriages. As most passenger specials were troop trains, this was then known to some of us as an 'Empty Trooper'.

We made our way to the point where we would take over the train—it was almost due. Ron remarked that we had best not try to get a cup of tea in the station canteen because the train would be sure to appear before we would be able to drink it. I replied that I didn't even know there was a canteen.

Right on time our train arrived, (oddly enough, even in wartime, trains had a habit of doing this) and with obvious haste pulled up to the water column where the fireman jumped up into the tender. By the time we climbed up into the cab the bag had been inserted and the water was running full. I went to the water column to relieve the driver so that he could hand over the engine to Ron, telling him of any known faults. When the tank was full and the bag swung out over the side, the fireman closed the lid, then, jumping quickly down on to the coal, he began furiously filling the hole, where I joined him as soon as I was able to climb back on to the footplate.

The engine was a 2900 Saint class 4-6-0, similar in appearance to a Star. Everything appeared fine, a good clean fire, well made up, so well that there appeared little room left in the firebox. I knew this wouldn't last long once we got underway. We had nine empty coaches so the load was better than it might have been—anyway the old Saint didn't seem to complain when Ron gave her some stick as we got underway. These day turns were the ones to be on, even through eyes that were hardly open, everything looked different.

The watery wintry sun broke through for a while; the countryside looked good in daylight when I could strain my eyes open long enough to see it. We were travelling at a different speed now to when we were on our way up. We soon passed Purton, speeding on towards Minety, where we were checked by the distant signal, almost squealing to a halt before the stop signal was pulled off, then we received the road right through to Kemble.

This was to be my last fast run. I couldn't help thinking how different this was proving to be from my first semi-fast with the tanks nearly four years earlier. Hundreds of tons of coal had gone through the fire hole door since that eventful morning, incidentally I do mean through the door—not over the driver's feet! The fire was right up, so was the steam and water. I was steady on my feet, apart from the few occasions when this old Saint gave the odd kick. When this happened I was obliged to either grab the hand rail or pause, one hand on the fire door handle, the other holding on to the shovel as it was wedged under the coal.

We came belting up the slope towards Sapperton Tunnel; for once I had no fear of the smoke catching up on me as, with a piercing blast on the whistle, we entered the blackness. Ron closed the regulator, so I was obliged to shut off my exhaust injector and turn on the live steam injector—at that instant the old Saint started to blow off. The steam billowing back over the tender illuminated by the brilliant firelight, for the fire doors were wide open; this was a sight I had seldom witnessed.

I don't know how fast we were travelling as we approached the end of the tunnel. I heard the rush of air as Ron dropped the brake into her, and I was able to feel the brakes taking effect as we shot out of the tunnel mouth once more into the winter sunlight.

The engine lurched as we emerged from the tunnel into a fairly sharp left hand bend--the remaining curves weren't too bad and our speed had now dropped considerably as we passed down through Chalford, Brimscombe and Stroud. We had picked up speed a little through Stroud, roaring away from Stonehouse faster still; just after joining the LMS track we were really moving on. I said, 'Hey up Ron, here comes a Midland catching us up, give her some stick'. He looked back and then said, 'You bloody liar Jockey'. Open her up he did, causing me to hang on in a couple of places. I don't know how accurate the speedometer was, but just beyond Haresfield I walked (or staggered) over to have a look—it read 82mph—that was pretty fast considering the short distance in which we had picked up speed.

Somewhere down past Tuffley Ron closed the regulator and wound the lever out a bit and we coasted on down towards the town. Once again the Saint started to blow off and I used the injector for a final top up. I did this realising that I had been so excited about the run from Stonehouse that I had forgotten to use the exhaust injector. The distant signal was against us, then we were stopped briefly, as a GWR train pulled up past us towards Stonehouse. While this was happening and while we were pulling down to where our relief was waiting, I was up on the tender, scrabbling and shovelling coal into the hole as fast as I could. After the relief had taken over we then had quite a long walk down past the Tramway Junction to the engine shed to book off. I turned the corner of the foreman's office, setting off to find my motor bike. Ron went off on his bike shouting, Cheerio Jockey, I'll see you when you're twelve hours older'. I thought, 'I don't know about that but I do know I'll feel older'.

Bygone Branch Lines

Now that the local branches have gone, I am sorry that I never had to work over the Ledbury or Hereford branch; these were two more jobs that were generally nice day turns, worked by the men of the top goods and light passenger link. No doubt I would have had a turn, filling in for someone, had I stayed on the job. As it was, I was never at the right place at the right time.

The Ledbury branch turned off at Over Junction; the branch ran beneath the main road, continuing on between the Dog Inn and the Isolation Hospital, as it was then. Skirting to the right of Highnam, appearing under the main road at Barber's Bridge, then half way between Barbers Bridge and Newent it came towards the road from the left, travelling towards Newent, where the road bridge can still be seen just on the Newent side of Rymes farm on the right; the line then continued on to Newent.

The Hereford line started at Grange Court Junction, making its way through

Working tender first was always a draughty experience but on a cold wet night it could be a nightmare! This ex-Great Western 0-6-0 engine, unable to turn at Ledbury, is working back to Gloucester tender first with the branch pick up goods. *(B. J. Ashworth)*

Blaisdon, Longhope and Mitcheldean. There was not a lot of traffic on the single lines, perhaps a couple of passenger trains each way daily, plus the 'pick up' goods train; this would be another easy going little job.

Most of these little stations were busy in their own quiet way though there was sometimes provision for loading cattle of any kind, with strong corrals on a ramp. Quite often a local coal merchant would have a truck or two of house coal left, while he worked to unload them in order to gain a quick turn round on the wagon—this saved paying demurrage.

There was, of course, seasonal freight like fruit, sugar beet, potatoes, etc, so the little old engine would shunt one off wagon here, then pick up one or two at the next station. I believe these were the easy going jobs we sometimes read about, where there was time to get to know of any produce that may be going, which was very valuable in the war years.

There must have been time during the afternoons—when there wasn't much doing—to have a cup of tea with the signalman, as they sought the whereabouts of

A disused railway soon becomes overgrown with only a few clues as to where the trackbed once was. The bridge illustrated is near Rymes Farm, Newent, on the former Gloucester-Ledbury branch line.

(D. A. Trigg)

172

A study at Grange Court Junction with a lone figure watching the train from the footbridge. One of Hawksworth's new coaches is prominent behind the large prairie 2-6-2 tank locomotive. This train is at the Hereford platform and will soon pull away onto the single line branch, with Blaisdon Halt the next stop.   *(Westrail Enterprises)*

The cattle dock at Blaisdon Halt, photographed looking towards Gloucester, obviously had not been used for years when this photograph was taken. The rake of wagons are ready to be picked up from the siding by the branch goods train.   *(Author's Collection)*

any eggs, rabbits, fruit, plants, or even home cured bacon. It was there if you were in the know, or had enough cheek. These two tracks ran right through the heart of the countryside as I imagine many others all over the country did. There is still ballast under foot in places, some remains of the once-robust fence, a few odd bridges, and I know of the shell of a lengthman's hut that would have been good for years with its well-preserved timbers but vandals had to have a go at it, as with so many other places and things to do with the steam era. It's sad to see it all gradually fading, leaving only a double line of rough trees here and there to mark its one-time pleasant passage. Soon these will no doubt fall victims of a chain saw and greed, thus leaving nothing to remind us of where the trains once drifted in and out of little stations and halts, passing undisturbed rabbits and pheasants.

During May, local birds of every kind nested near the track, taking no notice of these little trains, while in winter the trains often made their way through deep snow only to find themselves surrounded by floods a few weeks later.

I had one day working on the little Cinderford branch; this left the main line at Bullo. I don't remember much about it, it was certain to have been quite uneventful, except for the tunnel. What I do remember was that it was a beautiful autumn day, with the whole forest in resplendent autumn colours.

Blaisdon Halt again, with all the track lifted after closure, looking towards Ross-on-Wye/Hereford. Nature soon takes over to reclaim its former territory. (D. A. Trigg)

I believe we did a bit of shunting at Bullo, before making our way up to the colliery siding, leaving empties and picking up full trucks of coal. This train of coal was brought carefully down from Cinderford, then taken up to Gloucester, where it was left at Over sidings. It later formed part of the Stoke Gifford train. I remember we had a very small tank engine, which made very slow hard work of the climb up into the forest.

It was while travelling up through the forest scenery that I encountered a tunnel which I believe was at Soudley, though I can't be certain. Of all the many times I have worked through tunnels of various lengths, under various conditions, this one was to provide me with my worst experience. Had I been aware of what to expect, I would at least have inhaled deeply, as it was I was completely unprepared for the conditions I encountered. I was doing my best to keep the little tank going; the footplate was a little cramped for heavy working and I was having my work cut out to maintain steam and water. Suddenly we were in this tunnel, I didn't even know it was there until everything went dark and the noise increased. This single line tunnel was much smaller than I ever imagined and as we were travelling so slowly the steam and smoke were in the cab with us all the way through. It could not have been far, but it seemed a very long way to me, as I began coughing and choking, searching for a bit of air.

I didn't know how the driver was fairing at that time, I wasn't interested. He probably set off with a deep breath which helped him most of the way. As for me, I was, as I said, caught unawares; the fact that I was breathing heavily to begin with meant that I started off through the tunnel with my lungs partially filled with smoke.

Once again, as on other occasions, I held my handkerchief over my mouth, trying to breath through it, taking very quick small breaths in and out. I was certainly losing the battle and with my handkerchief covered in saliva, I thought my time had come.

As this little engine laboriously crept on up through the tunnel, I began to think how ridiculous it was for me to feel as though I was going to lose consciousness, after all people were doing the same thing daily. I thought that perhaps I was having another bad dream, when suddenly there was daylight and—more important—air! The day ended with us bringing down full coal trucks to Bullo.

These branch line trips must have been lovely runs during all fours seasons of the year for the regulars who knew where they were and what to expect. That forest track has now gone, though there are probably still one or two bridges and perhaps the tunnel is still intact, providing shade or shelter for forest sheep. For the main part, practically all that remains of the line from Bullo will be a dent or a slight gulley here and there in the landscape to show the course it once took.

My Last Relief

It was soon after the trip from Swindon that I developed another of my throats, followed by yellow jaundice. I was off work for three weeks and I didn't feel right when I went back to work. Life went on much the same as it had done for the last four years, with the long hours and very little food, although the war in Europe had ceased. The war in the Pacific was, unbeknown to us, nearing a conclusion. I was getting worse with my sleeping, if that was at all possible, and was feeling completely exhausted so decided to visit the doctor once again. He agreed that I wouldn't be able to carry on without sleeping, saying that he would write to the Ministry of Labour to that effect, to recommend that I be released from the job. His letter did the trick. In spite of everyone assuring me that I wouldn't be allowed to leave, I was indeed permitted to do so. Ron said that although he would be sorry to see me go there was one consolation; he thought he couldn't get anyone worse than me for a mate. I answered with the only word of two syllables that his facetious remark deserved!

That had been nearly a month ago. It had seemed more like a year, but here, finally, was the last time I would say 'right away' to Ron, and release my hand brake, stick my head out, as I had done hundreds of times before. There came the familiar rattle; I knew what it was before I looked out, and for once I said, 'Here we go then', winding my handbrake off slowly as Ron opened the, engaging full forward gear. The 2800 had to really dig her toes in to get started up the incline; she had the full weight for every inch she travelled, as all the couplings were tight as they were when we had come to a standstill on the bank. This was the last time I would feel this source of seemingly irresistible power under my feet, vibrating through my whole body as I rested my arms on the side of the cab. Every move I made from now until I left Gloucester would be for the last time.

The recollection of all this is proving to be a little nostalgic for me, even after 47 years, but at that time I wasn't at all sad, it was all going to be so wonderful to be able to go out with my mates and go to bed at night. Later I was to experience some mixed emotions as I heard trains rattle all the way up or down, past Oakle Street— we could hear them quite loudly over about three miles between the Downs bridge and Grange Court.

If I was at Oakle Street Hotel, either inside or crossing the bridge in either direction and a train ran through the station, I would find myself wondering who might be on the engine, where they were going, and how they were doing for steam. Sometimes at night in the crowded bar I would hear an engine blowing up for the road, then later as it started off, I could tell I was the only one present who even realised it was there. I could visualise what was happening on the footplate and I must admit there were times when I had misgivings about having left the job, until my thoughts went back to how I felt through lack of sleep, then I realised I had done the only sensible thing possible.

Back on the train we reached the highest point, to begin slowly dropping down past the signal box, then on to the platform road and into the station, passing two men who were, in all probability, our relief. I wound on the handbrake for the last time. The old 2800 blew off; it sounded so good down through the station, after coming down so many times in the past with the blower full on. I worked the injector for the last time and before the fireman could say a word, I was determined to say, in the dialect I knew this chap would appreciate, 'You gotta goodun yer mate'.

As I stepped off the footplate for the last time I should have felt just a bit sad, but I couldn't stop feeling as though I was walking on air as we made out way to the shed to book off for the last time. As Ron and I said our final goodbyes, I must admit I did find this a bit emotional—rather tending to spoil the moment I had longed for, for so long. We had been many miles, shared some rough trips together as well as good, over the last three years. Although we had obviously had our differences I like to think we parted good mates.

I heaved a great sigh of relief as I crossed Over Bridge and felt as though a weight had been taken off my shoulders, it was almost unbelievable that my whole life had been affected just by lack of sleep. There was a goods train pulling into the sidings, travelling downhill, another in the siding facing uphill; that one was probably there behind us as we were stopped on the bank, and I thought, 'Damn your horrible luck mate'.

I took a steady ride home, and when I arrived the old paraffin lamp was still burning downstairs, so I knew someone was up. My mother had waited for a while keeping the fire going; as it was my last night she intended going to bed if I was not home by twelve, but she had dropped off to sleep. The kettle was still hot so we made a pot of tea and I singed myself a piece of toast by the embers.

Taking a candle and the remains of the hot water in the kettle, I went out to the back kitchen to wash, this was indeed a luxury—I usually had to draw cold water straight from the pump in the yard, whatever the weather.

Mother had now gone to bed and after my wash I sat by the fire for a warm before creeping up to bed. The time was now well after one in the morning, everything was quiet and I was sinking into the longest sleep I managed to get for years. The last thing I remember hearing was the distant rattle of the down one o'clock, the London to Cardiff mail.

The Whistle Blows

A few days after leaving the railway I thought I was in heaven, just to be able to get to bed at night and sleep soundly. It had been worth waiting for.

I set about finding a job because, as ever, money was short. All my mates seemed to have money in their pockets and doing very few hours for it. I wasn't sure what I wanted but I was willing to take anything until the right job turned up. Strange to say, I am still waiting.

There was a motor cycle repair shop on the point of opening in Barton Street, a short distance from the baths towards the Cross. I called in and saw the owners, who immediately jumped at the chance of someone who, by this time, knew a little about motor bikes. I think at that time I could have had any number of jobs. Everywhere I went there seemed to be vacancies galore.

The reason was that everyone was either in the forces, down the mines, on the land, or working in war factories, while I was a free agent. I was not, however, to be allowed to remain in these happy circumstances for long. One morning, after I had been at my new job for about five weeks, an envelope arrived marked 'OHMS'—inside were my calling up papers.

I was called up for the Royal Engineers. I could see myself in uniform, back on a little shunting engine day and night, at some place perhaps like Long Marsden. We had often seen these operations while running past and I could see the clouds beginning to come into my life once more.

The Personnel Selection Officer told me what I had been called up for, and asked me if there was any comment I would like to make, so I told him of the circumstances leading up to my leaving the railway.

He said 'Can you ride a motor cycle?' When I said that I could and was quite keen on motor cycles, he said, 'Good, we need trained Royal Signals despatch riders urgently. It's easy to get plenty of motor cycle orderlies, but for the work we have in mind they must be fully trained signalmen.'

They needed DRs and Special DRs to augment the Royal Signals lines of communication, forming a chain, some in Italy, some in Scandinavia, connecting places like Flensburg, Kiel and Hamburg in Schleswig Holstein, down to Southern Germany. Here the motor bikes were swapped for specially-covered Jeeps, and carrying armed escorts, resulting in some more exciting trips.

Of course, all that is another long story, but I will just add that in the first months of training I experienced quite a few rides behind some of the LMS engines, up and down to York. I still usually ended up standing in the corridor as there was no sign of any let up in the pressure on the railways.

About six years later I had long since finished with the army and was on about my fourth job since leaving work in the motor cycle shop in Gloucester. I had now been married about two years and we were living in one of two cottages in Churcham which were situated in the third field from the main road, and about 500 yards from the railway line.

This was closer to the railway than I had been for some time; we were conscious of the trains running past but they weren't close enough to disturb conversation or be in any way obtrusive.

Although these cottages were sometimes very difficult to reach during a bad winter, in spring the setting was perfect. Autumn has always been my favourite time of year, but while I was living in this cottage I had to admit that spring was wonderful. There, beside oak trees and hedges shooting their green leaves, were elms which are now practically all gone. Rooks calling, swooping and haggling over the nesting materials in the elms about the end of February was a sure sign that winter was going. A little later we saw flocks of lapwings, or as we call them, peewits, swooping about, calling loudly above their well-concealed nests in the young green wheat, while at any time from early morning to late evening, the curlews could be heard giving vent to their wonderful high-pitched warbling cries.

We soon became aware that when we were in bed, we could more or less tell the weather by the sound of passing trains, as the window opened on to the field through which the line ran. In clear weather, either frosty or sunny, the exhausts of the up goods trains could be heard distinctly, until the train passed Downs Bridge—down hill, when not pulling so hard, we heard a sort of quiet cling, clang, cling clang noise from the coupling rods gradually fading for several minutes until the noise finally ceased beyond Grange Court. Rain didn't seem to alter the sound a lot. Of course the wind did, depending on its strength. Snow was different; we could always be sure when it was snowing and to some degree when it had stopped, having left a decent layer on the ground. We would suddenly become aware that the sounds of passing trains were changing, they were becoming more and more indistinct, until all we could hear was a sort of deep muffled rumbling.

One very cold night we had unchained our dog, so that she might have a final run round, giving her the usual dish of hot tea. It was obvious that it could snow at any minute. When the alarm clock wakened us at 6.30am the following day, we had a quick cup of tea in bed and as the odd few trains passed we knew it was still snowing, having, in fact, produced about three inches during the night. The next night, as we went to bed, it had begun to snow again and the trains were rumbling. I was just about to doze off when I was aware of yet another train coming down hill. Suddenly I was wide awake; there was this whistle—I had never heard a train whistle on that stretch of line before—there was nothing to blow at, so I was puzzled. The train rumbled

179

nearer and nearer, through the falling snow and there was this whistle again, I couldn't think what the driver had wrong. It came yet again, loud and shrill through the snow and I was out of bed feeling for the light switch—this time it was quite distinct, a dot, a long dash, followed by two more dots. Just before the engine passed from view I could make out the figures on the footplate as they opened the firebox doors. It was, of course, my old mate who had seen my father at Over Junction while stopped in the loop. He must have told Ron where I was living.

From that night on, whenever he passed he blew up; we, depending on whether it was daylight or darkness, either flicked lights or waved a towel, or anything that came quickly to hand. This continued for the next three or four years until we moved to Mayhill. I did, however, see Ron again in Gloucester when we were both much older.

Back to Gloucester Station

When journeying back and forth to York whilst in the Army, I always travelled via the LMS station, so the last time I saw Gloucester Western Station was the night I last stepped off the 2800 class engine, on the final trip; even then it was in darkness.

This lasted about 36 years until my wife and I took one of our children to the station. Although the booking and enquiry offices were different, and the refreshment room and paper stands were different, it wasn't until I passed through on to the platform that it really hit me. I was almost stunned at what I saw; I didn't recognise it as the place where I had spent so much time and had seen so much activity in previous years.

Except in early childhood, I had never before seen the opposite platform completely deserted—there was always a crowd, in many cases four or five deep when trains were approaching, as they clambered up the steps into the carriages, dragging whatever kit they had with them. Now every doorway and entrance was bricked up; no canteen, enginemans' cabin, RTO office, or way out of the busy entrance to and from Great Western Road.

At the east end of the seemingly endless platform, the signals that I knew had all gone, together with the signal box. At the west end there was the same story; the signal box had gone, so had the once prominent and extensively-used water column, from where it stood down towards the end of the platform, between the two down tracks.

The water column, where as a lad I had so often hurriedly taken water, sometimes not waiting for a full tank so that we could get out into the countryside quickly. Filling up as searchlights swept the skies, while the heavy pulsating drone of

German bomber engines could be heard all around, sometimes drowned by the anti-aircraft guns at the top of Upton Hill as they pumped shells at any plane caught in their powerful beams.

The spot where I had witnessed the arrival and departure of quite a few mail trains, as I helped feverishly, shovelling, pulling and scraping a ton or 30 hundredweight of coal between us in about five minutes. At times it appeared as though we were racing against time in order to rid ourselves of this black-looking monstrous piece of machinery as it hissed and flashed its firelight. It seethed away for a while, then seemingly in desperation and as a final warning, blew off—we were glad to see it roar away from the station.

Over on the left side of this platform where the small bay is still more or less intact, I recalled sunny afternoons as a child, sitting in one of the carriages that were destined for Hereford, the doors all open to let in a little air. In ones and twos passengers would come panting their way along the platform, some sweating in the hot sun, as they carried their various purchases. No one was in a hurry, the engine was only just making its way slowly down past the end of the platform in order to be able to reverse on to the couple or so carriages.

I stood momentarily in a day-dream; once more hundreds of service personnel milled in all directions as a train hurried in, the huge engine finally grinding to a halt. The smell of steam and smoke as doors burst open the full length of the train, the sounds of many voices, trolleys being hauled this way and that, loaded with parcels or mail. A goods train hammered its way through the station, first the engine, then the wagon drowning all the other noises, as it topped the brow over London Road Bridge. Then the noises of the station took over again, only to be drowned yet again as the station pilot shunted carriages back and forth. The doors were slamming, there was the guard's whistle and green flag. One shrill blast on the whistle, and the big loco set the echoes once more back and forth across the station, up and over the bridge, until at last the tail of the guard's van slipped silently from view.

A movement caught my eye, bringing me back to the reality of the 1990s. It was my wife who, having realised I had doubled back from the station exit, was walking along the platform towards me. 'I was wondering where you were', she said in an enquiring way. I thought to myself, 'So was I'.

A Few Facts 1939-1943

The following details will give a slight idea of the situation on the combined British Railways at about the time I was starting on the Main Line.

All four companies are under centralisation control.

160,000 special troop trains, in addition to hundreds of thousands of trains operated for the movement of passengers, coal, foodstuffs and supplies of every kind. Estimated 140,000,000 wagon loads of traffic despatched by rail since 1939. Control responsible for distribution of 1,250,000 freight vehicles, 408,000 wagon sheets, 219,000 wagon lashing ropes, and 17,318 containers.

The largest railway wagon unit in Britain had 56 wheels and can carry a load of 150 tons.

A scheme for quadrupling a section of track was estimated to take 30 months, it was completed in 12 months.

A section which, prewar, carried little or no coal, now carries 4,000,000 tons per annum, requiring 160 trains weekly.

A special troop train is originated by central control on instruction from the War Office, giving number of troops and equipment. This train is given a number. Its course is plotted from area to area and from Company to Company, and information about halts for meals is worked out. As the details and information is passed from one section to another, great secrecy is observed; it is known only as Special number X-X.

In eight days since the evacuation from Dunkirk, 620 special trains carrying 300,000 troops were run without prior knowledge, using 2 ,000 carriages drawn from a pool formed by each of the four companies.

When the Americans arrived, by the summer of 1942, special trains for troops and supplies were running at the rate of 5,000 per month, over and above the ordinary services.

For the First Army on its way to North Africa, the movement of traffic meant the transport of 185,000 men, 20,000 vehicles, 222,000 tons of stores. This needed 440 specials for troops, 680 specials for freight, and 15,000 wagons for ordinary goods service from depots to ports, as stated, in all some 160,000 specials from the outbreak of war until February 1943.

Materials for building factories, raw materials, the work force, then the finished product, have all been carried by the railways.

Loads range from the heaviest naval guns to rifles, aircraft, petrol and fuels, ammunition, bombs, mines, shells, and foodstuffs.

In 1941 325 million journeys were made by holders of workmens' tickets; in 1942 it rose to 400 million.

Coal previously carried by sea was now carried on the railway, totalling some 4,000,000 tons weekly.

Rail was used in every case in preference to road to help save fuel and rubber.

In 1942, compared to prewar, passenger service increased by 10,000 million passenger miles and freight for another 7,000 million ton miles.

In 1938 when the LNER Pacific 'Mallard' gained the world speed record of 126 mph, more than 100 express trains were scheduled to run at more than a mile a minute for start to stop speeds.

Seventy nine London Transport underground stations were made available for 75,000 air raid shelters, or 100,000 in emergency. Eleven tons of food were provided nightly during raid periods.

20,000 steam locomotives were the mainstay in moving wartime traffic, with electric and diesels also in service.

LMS heavy freight engines handled increased loads exceeding 1,400 tons. LNER hauled 1,700 tons of iron ore. GWR 2-8-0 type hauled 1,490 tons. GWR freight engines recorded were 1,500 miles between Monday and Friday. Some locomotives were attaining 100,000 miles between general repairs. 143 powerful freight engines, specially equipped for service overseas, plus all their spares, were shipped abroad.

1,600 steel-framed 12 ton wagons were specially built in double-quick time by working night and day. They were turned out one every 37 minutes.

There were 544,715 railwaymen, 105,703 railwaywomen, 102,984 in the forces, 90,000 are trained as Home Guards, 170,000 trained in Civil Defence.

Track repairs have been generally completed within 12 hours of the air raid, 3,000 signal wires in one week, 600 electric cables in eight days.

Railway lineside allotments, 82,588 covering 4,282 acres.

A vacuum-braked express train with thirteen coaches travelling at 60mph could stop in approximately 360 yards. The railways owned 10,000 horses and 53 hotels. Longest prewar nonstop run was LNER 'Flying Scotsman, 392.5 miles on 1st May 1928. World's longest nonstop run in wartime was 234.75 miles by LMS, Glasgow-Crewe. World's busiest junction, Clapham Junction SR handles 2,500 trains in 24 hours. Number of sleepers to one mile of track, 2112. Sleeper dimensions 8ft.6in. x 10in. x 5in. Weight 17 to the ton. Standard length of Bull Head rail 60ft., weighing 95lbs. per yard. Ballast used annually, 1,700,000 cubic yards. Total mileage of single track including sidings, 50,958 miles. Total route mileage, 19,272 miles. Railways owned and operate 35,000 horse and motor vehicles. Total number of railway wagons in service, 1,250,000. There were 10,300 signal boxes. Longest tunnel, Severn Tunnel, 4 miles 628 yards. There were 400 snow ploughs in service.

There were 141 water troughs on British Railways. First streamlined locomotive was LNER 'Silver Jubilee' which commenced operation on 30th September 1935.

During the Second World War some locomotives were converted to burn oil instead of coal, and could always be recognised by the rectangular tank on the tender. This must have made the fireman's life much easier. Only after vast sums of money had later been spent on setting up storage facilities and converting locomotives did the government of the day suddenly realise it could not afford to import the oil—the balance of payments would not allow it! (Author's Collection)